PETER JACKSON
From Gore to Mordor

PETER JACKSON
From Gore to Mordor

EDITED BY PAUL A. WOODS

Plexus, London

All rights reserved including the right of
reproduction in whole or in part in any form
Copyright © 2005 by Plexus Publishing Limited
Published by Plexus Publishing Limited
55a Clapham Common Southside
London SW4 9BX
www.plexusbooks.com
First Printing

British Library Cataloguing in Publication Data

Peter Jackson : from gore to Mordor. – (Ultra screen series)
   1.Jackson, Peter, 1961- – Criticism and interpretation
   I. Woods, Paul A.
   791.4'3'0233'092

   ISBN 0 85965 356 0

Printed in Great Britain by Biddles Limited
Cover and book design by Rebecca Martin

CONTENTS

FORGOTTEN SILVER

THE FRIGHTENERS

THE LORD OF THE RINGS

KONG COMETH!

INTRODUCTION
by Paul A. Woods

'. . . If you were entrusting $270 million to someone making three movies, you wouldn't choose me.'

There is much truth in Peter Jackson's modest self-deprecation. How many would entrust a provincial writer/director of splatter movies, with one arthouse hit to his name, with a hugely expensive movie franchise based on a literary masterpiece that had previously proved unfilmable?

Not only that, but he hailed from the former Antipodean colony of New Zealand – a place so remote and sparsely populated that when, in 2004, Jackson took the podium to receive several Academy Awards, he was described in the New York press as a 'bespectacled Australian'.

But Jackson has built a perplexing and remarkable career as a genre moviemaker with a distinct sense of locale. Born on Halloween 1961, in Pukerua Bay, outside the capital city of Wellington, the popular culture that sucked him in as a young boy transcended national boundaries. Expect no apologies for the amount of times you will hear about little Peter's early infatuation with the original *King Kong*, or the 'Dynamation' monsters of Ray Harryhausen in movies like *Jason and the Argonauts*.

With the exception of the *Living Dead* trilogy of gore pioneer George A. Romero, Jackson has always been in thrall to commercial pop culture. In the traditional gothic horror stakes, England's Hammer Films were favourites, as were Roger Corman's adaptations of Poe's short stories. As he told one of this book's central contributors, Lawrence French, 'whenever there would be double bills of the Hammer horror films, I would try to get in by looking as much like sixteen as I could. In fact, one of the very first movies I made was done in Super 8, *Curse of the Gravewalker*. It was a film about vampires, although I never finished it. It was set in Transylvania, and it had a Van Helsing-like vampire hunter in it, all very much influenced and done in the style of the Hammer vampire films. Then when I cast Christopher Lee in *The Lord of the Rings*, I thought, "I should get Christopher to do a little cameo as Dracula, in case I ever go back and finish my little Super 8 vampire movie." But I never asked him to do it.'

Another early hero included Buster Keaton – the poker-faced silent comedian who maintained sphinx-like impassivity as the world fell down around his ears. It was the combination of bloodshed, pathos and knockabout humour that would ground Jackson in what was later called 'splatstick' – gory horror movies more comical than they were dark or transgressive. As he recalls of the period spanning the late 1970s through to the mid-1980s, 'there was a real excitement about splatter movies – *The Evil Dead* and *Dawn of the Dead* and *Re-Animator*, all those balls-to-the-wall horror films.' Despite some genre writers including Jackson among a coterie of moviemakers with a 'punk' attitude, however, the laidback, hirsute figure has always been an ardent fan of the Beatles rather than any dark-hued gothic or industrial music. Similarly, blood and gore were, to him, just cinematic effects intended to entertain, rather than shock and nauseate.

Movies aside, the quiet, imaginative only child was fascinated by the cheapskate fantasy of TV. The young Peter grew up with shows such as Gerry Anderson's *Thunderbirds*, the puppet sci-fi series, the 1960s *Batman*, and its campy, self-mocking take on the superhero genre, and, not least, *Monty Python's Flying Circus*, the BBC's long-running surrealist comedy show, which span off into (occasionally gore-drenched) feature films.

The sensibility of Jackson's early films bespoke an obsession with horror, science fiction, fantasy and comedy transplanted to a uniquely downhome setting. In this sense, he is surely one of the most 'authentic' Kiwi filmmakers that Pakeha (white European) New Zealand will ever see. Initially subsidised by his supportive parents Bill and Joan, the financially better-equipped New Zealand Film Commission would later take up the baton on their behalf. For the best part of a decade, Jackson would be a government-assisted filmmaker, known only by genre aficionados, until the advent of his first Hollywood movie (*The Frighteners*, 1996), filmed with the suburbs of Wellington standing in for smalltown California. As a major director, Jackson has broken the Hollywood mold in many ways – not least by having been a state-subsidised independent filmmaker until shortly before his world-conquering breakthrough.

But Peter Jackson would never have been the subject of a critical anthology if he hadn't progressed beyond his debut, *Bad Taste* (1988). The film is fun, in a lowbrow sixpack style (though lay off the pizza for those vomit-eating and brain-exploding scenes), but exists primarily as a amateurish document of 1980s gore-mania, and a group of Kiwi guys messing around at weekends. However, as *Variety*'s review of the time said, 'What the film certainly does . . . is serve notice that Jackson's next picture will be one to look out for.'

The gleeful offensiveness was honed to a finer point with his 'Muppet' movie, *Meet the Feebles* (1990). Combining off-colour gags about Aids (around the time that the virus was killing a huge number of gay men and starting to decimate Africa) with vicious showbiz satire and the type of lavatorial humour that's heard any time boozed-up young guys get together, its cruel black humour was born not out of world-rejecting misanthropy, but from a mild-mannered New Zealander who liked to have a couple of beers and make up sick jokes with his mates. (Jackson tells of a Hollywood screening of *Meet the Feebles* for Lisa Henson, daughter of the late Muppet creator Jim: 'She was quite shocked when she saw Kermit nailed on a cross!') It's emblematic of a young man's need to make light of subjects which disturb or distress him, light years away from the nihilistic fuck-you subculture of a young John Waters (whose early films were banned in New Zealand, during Jackson's formative years in the 1970s and '80s).

In his early days, it was only ever horror genre journalists who praised, or indeed noticed, Peter Jackson's films. Read Philip Nutman and Giuseppe Salza's 1989 piece 'Peter Jackson: Master of *Bad Taste*', and see how keenly the young director responds to the suggestion he could become 'New Zealand's answer to Lucio Fulci' – doubtless without witnessing that Italian horror filmmaker's nastiest excesses, or his brutal misogyny, due to NZ film censorship of the time.

More aptly, Jackson in the early days was compared with the more *outré* American gore-humourists, like Sam Raimi – director of the wonderfully effective *The Evil Dead* – who, much like Jackson, left exploitation movies behind with the big-budget *Spider-Man* franchise, and Frank Henenlotter – creator of the hysterical *Basket Case* and *Brain Damage*

– who never made it out of the gore ghetto. Like Raimi, Jackson is possessed of a dexterity and ingenuity which has served him both in low-budget splatter movies, and, later, in multi-tasking on the set of a Hollywood blockbuster with state-of-the-art CGI effects.

But still, there was little in Jackson's early CV that indicated he would be anything other than a splatter moviemaker, with a small but avid fan cult. In a gap between movies in the early 1990s, he and his screenwriting collaborator Danny Mulheron even wrote an unproduced *Nightmare on Elm Street* screenplay, in which the teens of the Middle American town of Springwood use barbiturates to enter the dreamworld of the murderous Freddy Krueger. Perversely, Jackson has claimed in recent years that he was never a big fan of the horror genre anyway – at least not *straight* horror. 'Give them a few good scares and some good laughs, and no one takes it too seriously,' is how he defends his school of severed tongue-in-cheek.

Constant throughout his career has been Jackson's refusal to analyse his body of work. This may be a wise aversion, given the hapless hero's absorption into his zombie mother's womb in *Braindead* (1992). ('Peter Jackson doesn't need psychoanalysis to help him with his Oedipus complex,' commented the *Sydney Morning Herald*. 'He definitely must have worked it through with *Braindead* . . .') His inspiration comes, he stresses, not from any degree of intellectualising, but from cinematic ideas that arrive almost fully formed in his brain.

This explanation seems less adequate in terms of Jackson's critical breakthrough film, the enchantingly disturbing *Heavenly Creatures* (1994) – a treatment of New Zealand's infamous Parker-Hulme matricide case of 1954, which received an award at the 1994 Venice Film Festival from a jury headed by David Lynch. It presented a breathtakingly subjective view of two emotionally unstable young girls' inner fantasy worlds. One of the film's debutante female leads, Kate Winslet, observed of her director, 'He can be quiet, but he's an emotional man . . . I'm telling you, when *we* wept, *he* wept.'

Despite brief scenes of 'real' or imagined violence, *Heavenly Creatures* seemed to be Jackson's farewell to blood-and-guts for the hell of it – and, in its magical evocation of the imaginary kingdom of Borovnia, gave sign that he had both the imaginative and technical ability to realise a world of fantasy on a much grander scale. Its subject matter was suggested by Jackson's very significant other, Frances Walsh, with whom he has lived since they worked on *Meet the Feebles* together, and with whom he has two children, Billy and Katie. (Ms Walsh was initially with Stephen Sinclair, one of Jackson's co-screenwriters, who maintained his creative relationship with the couple up to the *Lord of the Rings* films.)

An integral part of the Jackson filmmaking team, she would later prove her mettle as co-screenwriter (along with Philippa Boyens and Sinclair) and uncredited co-director of the *Rings* trilogy – though she shuns the spotlight more than her unassuming partner, uncomfortable with the media attention that has descended on him. 'Everybody says to me, "Oh, don't you wish you could clone yourself and do two things at once?"' Jackson has remarked. 'In a way, I regard Fran as someone I trust as much as a clone of myself.'

It also became notable from the mid-1990s onwards that Jackson, far from being just some gore-obsessed fanboy, was a highly cine-literate film geek with an almost scholarly approach. Seen from outside New Zealand, what's most remarkable about Jackson and Costa Botes's celebrated TV mockumentary, *Forgotten Silver* (1995), is not its status as a grand hoax on the NZ public (covered here extensively, including before-and-after pieces from the complicit *New Zealand Listener*), but its close approximation of early cinema aesthetics; not only in the aging techniques that make the supposedly rediscovered films of Colin Mackenzie look grainy and antique, but in the convincing film within a film, the mock-D. W. Griffith epic *Salome*, and the pre-Sennett/Chaplin/Keystone Kops silent slapstick of the fictional 'Stan the Man'.

But Jackson was also prescient in adopting the techno-aesthetic of the modern commercial cinema. Beginning with *Heavenly Creatures*, and continuing with *The Frighteners* (1996), the emergence of Jackson's digital FX company, Weta Digital, owed as much to his collaborators Richard Taylor and George Port as it did to the director himself. *The Frighteners* is a darker spin-off of that school of comic horror that runs from Tim Burton's *Beetlejuice* to the remake of *House on Haunted Hill*. Apart from its mild black humour and sophisticated CGI effects, its main point of interest is that Jackson claims to have witnessed an actual ghostly presence several years before the film was made: 'the bedroom door was open, and suddenly this woman just kind of drifted into the bedroom . . . . [She] looked scary because she had this kind of fixed scream on her face – her mouth was wide open . . . . She was kind of transparent, like a photographic negative of an image. She drifted past the end of the bed . . . and then she disappeared through the far wall.'

But the special effects techniques of *The Frighteners* were also the catalyst that determined the rest of Jackson's career. If he'd not been willing and able to swim with the commercial creative current, then none of the *Lord of the Rings* films (or the forthcoming *King Kong* remake) would have been possible. As Christopher Lee – Jackson's veteran Hammer horror hero, who later played the dark sorceror Saruman – noted, live action films of Tolkien's trilogy became possible because of 'a man like Peter Jackson, who has the talent as an artist, the love and understanding of the material and the technical skill; and the computer technology which the cinematic world hasn't had at its disposal until fairly recently.'

Of course, if the appeal of the *Rings* trilogy had been solely reliant on special effects, it wouldn't have risen so quickly to its prominent position in the commercial cinema canon. The long-term ambition (noted in these pages) to film a screenplay entitled *Blubberhead*, pitched somewhere between *The Lord of the Rings* and Terry Gilliam's *Brazil*, was eventually supplanted by the real thing. As Jackson admits, however, 'We weren't prepared for the denseness and enormousness of the backstory. It's not just a book, but a whole mythic philosophy.' And so he would be forced to commit nearly seven full years of his life to the project, from screenwriting and preproduction to filming the special effects and inserts for the final film, almost half of his professional filmmaking career up to that point. As he said at the time, 'The trick is to take the essence of events that Tolkien wrote,' without following the books' basically uncinematic structure too slavishly.

That New Line Cinema's gamble paid off in spades is now taken as read, measured by the audiences who crammed theatres over Christmases 2001-3, the 100,000 people who filled the streets of Wellington for the December 2003 premiere of *The Return of the King*, sales of tie-in merchandising and the compellingly completist 'special edition' DVDs, the almost unprecedented number of Academy Awards showered on the former gorehound director and his collaborators, ostensibly for *The Return of the King* – and, not least, in the commercial success of three epic films that each run to a duration of three hours or more.

The trilogy also consolidated the former gorehound and cheap gagmeister as a great favourite of his actors – with a cast ranging from relative newcomers like Elijah Wood and Liv Tyler to Sir Ian McKellen – and as a genius of minutiae, whose multi-compartmentalised brain simultaneously handles soundstages, location shooting, a cast of thousands (many of them computer-generated, in these labour-saving days), vastly elaborate battle scenes and special effects.

It's with *The Fellowship of the Ring* (2001), *The Two Towers* (2002) and *The Return of the King* (2003), their synthesis of pre-Christian myths and earthy adventure stories, that Jackson has enjoyed his great commercial triumph. As Andrew O'Hehir observes in his review of *The Fellowship*, any expectations of an effete fairy tale are overturned by 'a sense of human terror and danger and grit under . . . nails'. As Jackson himself said, 'the style of the shooting and the performances and the design is to make Middle-earth feel real and lived-in'.

(Author/philosopher Colin Wilson, during interviews with this writer, was dismissive to find I'd come to *The Lord of the Rings*, one of his favourite books of the twentieth century, via the films. But it took Jackson, with his passion for making dreams and fantasy *real*, to overcome any prejudice felt by former sceptics like myself. He brilliantly translated what Wilson sees as the essence of Tolkien's trilogy – melancholic defiance in the face of annihilation, the necessity of keeping on, even if it's only based on a fool's hope.)

As the moviegoing public awaits Jackson's life and career coming full circle with his remake tribute to *King Kong* (2005), the film he first tried to re-make in his mid-teens 'with a rubber gorilla and stop motion . . . [and] the top of the Empire State Building made out of cardboard', it's hoped by this writer that the sense of Kong as an unleashed 'monster of the Id' that haunted my own childhood dreams – towering disproportionately over the city skyline, as in the classic re-release poster – is realised by Jackson in his interpretation.

For Peter Jackson is no longer an independent filmmaker, or a gore movie maker, or even just the award-winning director of *LOTR*. He is, in the breadth of his tastes and the richness of his vision, all that is hopeful about modern commercial cinema. Speaking of the *LOTR* production process, he notes, 'at the weekends I'd actually put some films on that I admired and were directed with some particularly stylish flourish . . . I used *GoodFellas* and *Casino* a lot because their directorial flourishes are fantastic, and *Saving Private Ryan* because I liked the visceral quality.'

But he is also a cinematic dreamer, a compulsive fantasist. As he says, 'I do what I do because I have these visions and I have to bring them to life.' Through his eyes, everything is transformed into what the French call *le fantastique*. Even the sad familial homicide of *Heavenly Creatures* became a fantasy not so far removed from the epic textures of *The Lord of the Rings*, a feat of the imagination that may, we can hope, be repeated with the mooted Jackson-Walsh adaptation of the wistfully melancholic novel *The Lovely Bones*, about the spirit of a murdered young girl.

Jaded cynics may feel (or effect) boredom at his seemingly limitless, childlike imagination; armchair nihilists may bemoan the lack of genuine nastiness or misanthropy in his bloodbath horror movies. But that's all beside the point. To dismiss the films of Peter Jackson is to deny that modern cinema holds any appeal at all. His best films (*Heavenly Creatures*, the *Rings* trilogy, even *Braindead*) have achieved a visual richness and vital electricity equal to – or often surpassing – anything else currently seen on the screen.

BAD TASTE

TALENT FORCE
by Jeremy Clarke

The personal film is often regarded with scepticism by the international film community. Orson Welles' *Othello* was shot over four years in bits and pieces whenever he had some money to finance it. The odds were impossible – every time the back of an actor's head is seen, it's a stand in (and there are a lot) because of the four year shooting schedule. A recent New Zealand film, *Bad Taste*, is both equally personal and represents a similar degree of human endeavour in the face of seemingly insurmountable obstacles.

At the start of *Bad Taste*, a tacky looking machine with a vertical row of lights by a vertical list of names light up beside the name 'the boys'. The boys – Barry, Derek, Frank and Ozzie – work together as the Alien Investigation and Defence Service; it is their allotted task to investigate any reports of extraterrestrial visitors. The Kiwi meaning of the word 'investigate' means that the lads go in like a down under version of the SAS, guns at the ready, to a quiet seaside town. They search for survivors, but the local population have already been dismembered and packed away in cardboard boxes by the aliens – an unsavoury bunch led by Lord Crumb who needs fresh meat for his intergalactic fast food chain.

As *film qua film*, *Bad Taste* is a remarkable achievement. It comprises 2,302 shots (*Othello* had just under 2,000) – too many for the National Film Unit's laboratory grading computer to handle. Like Welles' film, much of the interest lies in the *mise-en-scene* – racing steadicam shots, edge-of-the-seat clifftop flight sequences, extras playing numerous different roles. But a second facet of the film is that of the amateur film maker cum technical whiz kid, the sort of movement that brings together huge armies of enthusiasts, spawns numerous magazines in the States, and gave us directors like Spielberg or Brian De Palma. The latter's *Dressed to Kill* has an exemplary character who uses a Super 8 time lapse camera concealed in the back of a motorbike to record details of a murder suspect's comings and goings. The wizardry of *Bad Taste* is even more evident when one learns that producer/director/writer/actor/cinematographer Peter Jackson was not only responsible for all his own special effects, but also built his own camera crane and steadicam for virtually no money!

Yet *Bad Taste* is neither European nor American in feel – it's very definitely Kiwi. Where else would a sheep make a fleeting appearance to bleat at camera to inspire our sympathy in one shot before being blown to pieces a few seconds later? As one critic commented: 'This is more than a New Zealand film, more than a regional film, it's a Pukerua Bay film.' It's also very funny – 'a laugh with every drop of blood,' as Peter himself puts it.

Peter Jackson has a long history as an amateur film maker (*Bad Taste* is actually his twelfth film, albeit the first to reach full feature length or even completion) which began when his parents – credited on *Bad Taste* as 'Special Assistants to the Producer (Mum and Dad)' – were given a Super 8 movie camera one Christmas. Says his mother, Joan

'Whenever I watch a gore movie, it makes me laugh . . .' The young Peter Jackson impales himself through the throat, all in the name of art.

Jackson: 'We used to film people walking towards us, things like that, but Peter had other ideas. He'd have them swinging round and all sorts of things.' Her son, sporting a Rupert Bear T-shirt, recalls the arrival of the Super 8 at the Jackson home. 'I immediately grabbed it and got a load of my mates in the garden. We got a lot of World War II uniforms and ran around acting out something out of a war comic, full of action and high drama.' This short, *The Dwarf Patrol* (1971), also featured his debut in terms of special effects. Prop guns would be made at next to no cost from home-drilled aluminium tubing, cardboard and Flymo modelling material, the actors would shake them to give the impression of recoil from firing, and white flashes would be optically burned into the film.

Other early work included an homage to stop-frame animator Ray Harryhausen, *The Valley* (1971), in which a youthful Peter hurls a spear at a giant animated model beast dangling a sailor from his hand like the Cyclops in *The Seventh Voyage of Sinbad* (1958). However, many of these early films were never completed – Peter lost interest whenever he realised he didn't have the money or expertise he needed. When he took a job as a photolithographer at the *Wellington Evening Post*, the incoming money led to a corresponding increase in production value. *The Curse of the Grave Walker* (1981) was made in 8mm Cinemascope with a specially acquired lens. The film also has a protagonist shooting a bolt into a vampire, a precursor of the more spectacular bazooka fired at the house in *Bad Taste*.

It was in 1983, with Peter's purchase of a secondhand 16mm clockwork bolex, that work began on the twenty minute project *Roast of the Day*. The projected shooting schedule was one month; the film – later titled *Bad Taste* – took over four years! Various old friends and *Evening Post* workmates were persuaded to work weekends for deferred salaries. The Jackson dining room table became the editing bench while Mum's oven was used to bake latex alien heads which were subsequently laid over fibreglass with wires to control the lips and give the appearance of speech.

The film was dogged with setbacks. One was a lack of funding, despite repeated grant applications to the New Zealand Film Commission by the young film maker – they did eventually provide some funding in late 1986. Then there was the first edit, when Peter discovered he had no ending! Yet another problem arose when actor and crew member Craig Smith (the hapless charity worker who enters the town unaware of the aliens' culinary intentions) married and had to cut back his commitment – and another ending had to be written! At this stage, three extras were promoted to star status and Peter himself took the role of Derek, leader of the assault force. In one sequence, Derek battles Robert the Alien, also played by Peter. The two characters were shot a year apart, yet such is Peter's understanding of film grammar that the illusion is completely successful. Orson Welles would have been proud of him.

THIS HAS BUGGERED YOUR PLANS FOR CONQUERING THE UNIVERSE
The Making of *Bad Taste* by Ken Hammon

I met Pete Jackson at Kapiti College in 1978 when we were both sixteen and assigned the same class (in New Zealand a college is the equivalent of a high school in America). Both being film buffs we got on well and started hanging out together. Pete had been making amateur movies for years using a super 8mm camera his parents had bought for him. His films were fairly awful, actually, but he used to write, direct, shoot, edit and stage the special effects and he learned a great deal from them. In 1978 a popular New Zealand kid's TV programme called *Spot On* announced its first ever amateur film making competition. Pete, me and some other kids (including Pete O'Herne, who grew up in the same town as Pete and appeared in several of his early shorts) went out and made a short film called *The Valley* over a bunch of weekends. The other entries in the competition ran, like, three minutes tops but *The Valley* ran twenty minutes and featured way more violence than the judges either wanted or expected. The film was heavily influenced by Pete's love of Ray Harryhausen movies and featured two stop motion special effects sequences, which Pete staged himself, building the models and performing the stop motion. The stand out sequence involved a fight to the death between me and a hulking Cyclops creature based (or stolen, if you prefer) on the one from *The Seventh Voyage of Sinbad*. Anyway, we didn't win the competition (which pisses me off to this day) but we did gain some notoriety in school when they screened clips of the film on TV.

At the end of 1978 Pete and I left school and got full time jobs. I ended up at the Housing Corporation of NZ, where I met Craig Smith, and Pete started at Wellington Newspapers Ltd in the production department where he met just about everyone else who appears in *BT*. On the weekends we shot another super 8mm short, this one based on Pete's love of James Bond. Called *Coldfinger* it basically consisted of two fights to the death between Bond (Pete doing a terrible Sean Connery impression) and me and Pete O'Herne as the ill-fated bad guys.

After doing so many short films, Pete had the idea in 1981 of making a feature on super 8mm. Called *The Curse of the Gravewalker*, it was a vampire story inspired by Pete's love of Hammer horror movies. We shot for twelve months with Pete playing Captain Eumig (named after my super 8mm projector), a fearless vampire killer, O'Herne playing the evil vampire leader Murnau (named after the director of *Nosferatu*) and me playing a motley assortment of vampires in different costumes and make-up. Pete made all the fake swords, crossbows and armour, made all the costumes and designed and applied the make-up. We then went out and charged around Wellington graveyards, filming big fight scenes to the bemusement of the general populace. After a year of this, sanity returned and we realised that shooting a feature on super 8mm bordered on lunacy. We abandoned *Gravewalker* and resolved not to film anymore until Pete had saved up enough to buy a

16mm camera and we could shoot something that would have the actual possibility of being seen somewhere.

In 1983 Pete bought a second-hand spring-wound 16mm Bolex camera and we set out to make a ten-minute short film called *Roast of the Day*. The plot was simple: Giles, a collector for famine relief, goes to Kaihoro, an isolated coastal town, for collection day. He finds the town eerily lifeless, even by New Zealand standards. On the way back to his car he is attacked and pursued by Robert, a maniac with a bayonet. He gets to his car and drives like the clappers through the countryside, until he gets to a large house (Gear House, a stately house in Porirua, north of Wellington); he stops to call the authorities but the house is occupied by cannibals related to the nutjob on the beach. They knock him on the head, cook him up and relieve their famine. The End.

On 27 October 1983 we had our first day of filming in Nakara Beach, a small seaside town that, along with Pete's hometown of Pukerua Bay, was used to portray Kaihoro. The disaster prone Craig Smith – employed at the time as a clerk for the Housing Corporation – played Giles. Pete – still at Wellington Newspapers Ltd – played Robert and I – after spending most of 1983 on the dole – was working as a store man in a pharmaceutical warehouse. The first day's filming was uneventful except for one incident. One of the first shots we did was of a signpost Pete built pointing the way to Kaihoro (the other sign on the post points to Castle Rock, which is a Stephen King reference). We stuck up the sign, shot the footage then took the sign down again and drove away. About an hour later a cop drove up and said we had been seen vandalising road signs! Luckily we were able to convince him it was our own sign and the whole thing blew over.

After the first day we fell into a style of filming that would stretch out way, way longer than any of us could ever have imagined. When Pete had scraped together enough money to buy a roll of film we would convene on a Sunday at a location and shoot until the sun went down or we ran out of film. Since the film was never scripted, there was a tendency to add details and for simple sequences to end up much more elaborate than planned. The first major addition grew out of Pete's fascination with the S.A.S. (Special Air Services), New Zealand's black clad, black hooded, armed anti-terrorist squad. Pete decided there would be a sequence where three S.A.S. men break into Gear House and ostensibly rescue Giles from the cannibals. We had a hard time figuring this into the plot but finally decided the S.A.S. men would be fake and actually turn out to be part of the cannibal family and they staged the whole rescue scene because they like to play with their food! Roped into playing the S.A.S. were Pete O'Herne – then an office worker for the Ministry of Transport – Terry Potter and Mike Minett – two colleagues of Pete's from the WNL production department. Through the winter of '84 we shot the increasingly complicated S.A.S. rescue action scenes.

About a year after filming commenced, Pete hired an editing bench from the National Film Unit and cut together the footage we had shot; it came to a whopping 50 minutes! Somehow our ten-minute short had grown like a cancer. In July 1984 *The Evil Dead* had screened at the Wellington Film Festival, and its success had convinced Pete you could make money with a 16mm semi-amateur horror movie. We resolved to keep shooting and make a full-length feature, adding a ton of gore along the way (the film at this point had no splatter effects at all). Somewhere in here I came up with the title *Bad Taste*, a title

Pete never liked but it was the best anyone could come up with (Pete preferred the title *Giles' Big Day* but we all hated it). To add to the length of the film and to get more special effects in there, Pete decided the cannibals would turn out to be aliens.

We worked out that the S.A.S. who saved Giles would unmask, showing human faces, then transform into their alien shapes. They would drag Giles back to Gear House to be killed and cooked but he would go apeshit, kill a bunch of aliens with a chainsaw and escape. There was then supposed to be an elaborate special effects scene of Giles in an alien flying car, fighting to the death with a stop motion monster called the Botha Beast of Trom. After somehow defeating the monster, Giles would stumble across the alien space ship. Getting a bazooka from the alien's weapon stockpile, he would blow it up as it took off.

We shot a lot of this storyline through '85, including the scene where O'Herne's face morphs into an alien make-up quite different from the one used in the completed film. Then disaster struck; Craig Smith had gotten married, had a nervous breakdown and become a born-again Christian, and declared he could no longer appear in such a violent and sleazy movie. Around this time, Terry Potter had also gotten married and was planning to move to Australia, and asked to be written out as well.

With some difficulty we came up with a new storyline explaining all this: the S.A.S. men would not be aliens, they would be humans working for the Alien Investigation and Defence Service of the NZ government sent to Kaihoro to investigate reports of an alien invasion. O'Herne was called Barry, Terry was Ozzy (named after his idol Ozzy Osbourne), Mike played Frank and Pete was added to the mix as the AIDS leader Derek. We finished up Craig and Terry by shooting a scene where Giles and Ozzy are found dead, then spent the rest of '85 through '86 shooting footage introducing 'the boys'.

We shot the early scenes of Barry in Kaihoro (a word that in English means 'eat greedily') where I play Whitey, the first alien to die, wearing a bad blond wig, and the scenes where Barry is chased through Kaihoro by a group of aliens (it was a joke in the film that O'Herne, the least athletic of the cast, was the one who was made to run the most). Some of these scenes were shot at O'Herne's mum's house with her garden shed and garage putting in appearances. We also shot the scenes of Derek on top of the cliff; a sequence I remember as the most gruelling of the shoot. We spent months every Sunday schlepping heavy equipment up to the top of this goddamn hill in Pukerua Bay, shooting all day over a precipitous drop (which never looked as dangerous on film as it did in real life) and then schlepping everything back down again. This sequence involved the famous scene with Pete where he, playing both Derek and Robert, has a fight with himself. We shot this with Pete first playing Robert and me doubling as Derek, then Pete had a shave and a haircut and played Derek and I put on a wig and played Robert. Somehow, it all cut together and Robert was able to push Derek off the cliff to his death. However, Pete liked Derek so much that he later decided that he wasn't, in fact, dead, and he brought him back later to complete the film.

In 1985, Pete had sent a copy of the initial 50-minute cut of *BT* to the New Zealand Film Commission to apply for funding. The Commission, and its CEO, Jim Booth, were amazed by the footage but declined funding, suggesting we keep filming and apply again later. We applied again in 1986 and this time the Commission couldn't deny the quality

On the four-year location shoot of Bad Taste *(1988),
Jackson's low-budget ingenuity made it all work. Here he
devises the film's exploding cranium shot*

of what we were doing. But the NZFC is a government agency and runs scared of public controversy. Jim Booth, who liked the movie, felt the Commission could put a little
money into the film and then play down their involvement. For the film to get a large
grant it would have had to go through the NZFC Committee for approval. Jim didn't
think the Committee would approve a film so lacking in redeeming qualities, so he
avoided the process altogether and paid us small sums of money out of the NZFC Script
Development Fund over which he had approval. Jim and Pete became friends through all
this, and Jim later quit the Commission to become a producer and worked with Pete on
Meet the Feebles, *Braindead* and *Heavenly Creatures*. With the money from the Commission,
Pete was able to quit his job at WNL and work full time on *BT*. He designed and built
the most elaborate SFX of the film, including the alien make-up, Derek's do it yourself
brain surgery and the Gear House conversion into a space ship.

Terry came back from Australia, and Craig's religious fever wore off, and they both
ended up back in the film. Finally, the last day's filming took place, the phenomenally
gory scene where Derek is born again, and *Bad Taste*'s never ending shoot actually – Free
at last, Lord, Free at last – came to an end.

One of the miracles of *BT* is that no-one was badly hurt during its production. I was
talking once to a stunt coordinator while doing extra work on *Braindead*, and he said,

'Some of that stuff looked dangerous, what kind of safety equipment did you use?' And I went, 'Safety equipment!? SAFETY EQUIPMENT!!? Why didn't we think of that!?!'

Probably the nearest thing to a bad accident involved Mike Minett, who was damn near hit in the face by a flying ten-kilogram sledgehammer during a fight scene. Pete's worse moment had him as Robert dangling upside-down over a cliff. If the rope had given way he would have kissed his arse goodbye. (Pete later spent hours hanging from the ceiling for the scene where Derek slaughters Lord Crumb, thereby setting some sort of world record for a director hanging upside-down.) Craig's most celebrated close call came when one of the explosive charges we used to simulate bullet strikes (Pete made them at home) went off with way too much vigour, nearly hitting him in the slats! Craig complained about that one for years afterwards. My own worst near disaster came when we were shooting the scene where Derek's van swerves off the road and runs over one of the aliens (played by Costa Botes, a film-maker friend of Pete's who went on to collaborate with him on a number of projects, *Forgotten Silver* most notably, and who is now filming a behind the scenes documentary on *The Lord of the Rings*). Since we couldn't afford a camera bracket, I simply sat on the hood of the van with the camera as Pete drove it at great velocity towards Costa. Unfortunately, we didn't realise there was a sodding big tree stump hidden in the long grass we had to drive through. The van hit the tree stump and came to a dead halt; I, on the other hand, went flying like a fucking lawn dart straight off the van and arse-over-elbow through the air and right towards Costa, who had to dive the hell out of the way! Somehow I, and more importantly the camera, survived. This became a rare example of a shot where it was decided, 'We ain't doin' that one again!'

My most memorable stunt performance came in the scene where, during the raid on Gear House, Frank strafes a tree with machine gun fire and a whole bunch of aliens fall out. Since Terry and I were the only ones insane enough to fall out of the tree, we played all the aliens between us. Terry and I jumped out of the tree, two other blokes took our places on the ground, we put on different hats, jumped out again, and then got up and did it one more time. Terry and I had a competition to see who could do the best fall, which I think I won with a darned impressive face-first dive smack into the dirt.

The worst actual accident I can remember involved me, naturally. We were filming a shot of Derek's van driving along by the beach in Pukerua Bay. I was standing up, filming through the sunroof of the late Phil Lamey's car, and we hit a bleeding great pothole and I was thrown like a rag doll from one side of the sunroof to the other, damn near breaking my ribs. I spent the next few weeks hobbling, with ribs that were black and blue.

The most frequently asked question when it comes to *BT* is, 'Did you really blow up a sheep?' Craig always answers, 'Hey, it was an old sheep.' Actually, it was a carpenter's workhorse covered with some old sheepskin rugs, but it was originally planned for the sheep to have a much larger part in the movie. Unfortunately, this plan resulted in a day's filming that was disastrous even by our standards. The original idea is that Barry and Giles are heading through the countryside to get help and they run into a rabid, homicidal sheep that chases them through the paddocks, until meeting an untimely death from a stray bazooka shell.

We went out to Caroline Girdlestone's farm near Waikanae and set up to film with pet sheep borrowed from some friends of Caroline's. The sheep was a perfectly clean, well maintained pet, so we had to try to scuzz it up a bit by throwing mud and pinning strag-gly bits of filthy wool to it to give it a kind of sheep-gone-punk sort of look. Pete at one point wanted it to wear an eye patch (which is a *Monty Python* reference) but that idea got dropped. We got the sheep all grungy and set up the shot. The sheep would be let loose and the crew would rush it, making it run towards O'Herne and Craig, who would run away looking terrified as though this dangerous beast was attacking them.

Pete gave O'Herne, Craig and the sheep their final instructions: O'Herne and Craig were to keep looking behind them, note where the sheep was and try to stay in front of it. Action was called and the shot commenced. O'Herne and Craig started running straight ahead; the sheep was released, and immediately started running hell for leather for the hills! The sheep set some sort of land speed record with the crew in hot pursuit; it hit the fence line, started running alongside the fence and threw itself off a cliff!

We were all gobsmacked, thinking, 'Holy shit, we've killed someone's beloved pet!', but it turned out the cliff wasn't that high, and the sheep survived its plunge. It was becoming clear that this sheep didn't have the slightest interest in show business, but, God help us all, we decided to try the shot again. We set up, this time with a crew member off to the side to block the sheep heading in that direction, and called action. O'Herne and Craig trotted off; the sheep was released and shot off to the side again! Craig followed instructions and tried to stay in front of the sheep, O'Herne just lopped off into the dis-tance, and the sheep fled like a cat on fire with the crew hot on its tail. The sheep ran straight for the cliff again, but proved itself smarter than it appeared and slammed on the brakes, and ended up teetering on the edge of the cliff. It looked at us, then at the cliff, then back at us, then back at the cliff, and gave the impression it was considering suicide rather than appear in our movie.

Anyway, we finally got the camera shy animal down from its perch and made one of the only sensible decisions in the history of the making of *Bad Taste*; we decided to scrap the fucking scene and go home.

As we loaded that goddamn sheep back into its trailer to return it to its life of obscu-rity, Caroline Girdlestone got in the last word: she said, 'Peter, if this was a real movie we would've started training the sheep weeks ago!'

When the boys get recognised in pubs, people always say, 'You guys must've had a great time making *Bad Taste*,' but actually the experience was torture and it went on for years. We always seemed to shoot in winter and were always freezing our arses off. (Craig, one bitterly cold day, announced he was wearing his wife's pantyhose. He claimed it was because of the cold but I ain't so sure.) Because rain doesn't show up clearly on 16mm film we often shot in the rain (there's one shot where you can see it's raining). Since we mainly shot on Sundays, the cast and crew (well, the cast was the crew) were usually seedy and hungover. And screw-ups, accidents and gaffes happened on a pretty much weekly basis. There was one Sunday where we all arrived at the location only to discover Pete had forgotten to bring any film (he rang his mum and she brought it out). There were a couple of days where no-one other than Pete could be stuffed turning up, and he had to turn around and go home again. There was a day when hardly anybody turned up and Pete had to get some kids on the beach to operate the camera crane, making *BT* proba-bly the only movie in motion picture history to feature a crane shot where the crane was operated by nine year olds.

Perhaps most devastating psychologically for a splatter movie, we were never able to get Derek's stinking chainsaw to go; we just dubbed in the sound of it going and used a smaller, newer saw for the shots of it actually cutting through things.

Finally, though, after years of freezing cold Sundays, nervous breakdowns (Craig wasn't the only one), wasted actors (you know who you are), cast desertions, amateur stuntwork, homemade explosives, rooted chainsaws, run-ins with the law and a sheep that took direction even worse than Terry Potter, the filming of *Bad Taste* was finally wrestled into the dirt. The film went into post-production and, like *El Mariachi* a few years later, more money was spent on post-production than was spent on production. The film's soundtrack was completely created in post; there isn't a single second of live sound in the film. *BT* was mainly shot silent, there was some live sound recording but it wasn't that great and was scrapped. *BT* looked really ragged before it was polished up, the quality of the post was such that it helped the film a great deal.

BT got its first screenings at the Cannes Film Festival in 1988, where its strong reception amazed the Film Commission. It then played sold out houses at the Wellington Film Festival with the boys in attendance. This was when being involved in the film finally became fun; seeing it at the Embassy Theatre with a shrieking, laughing, appreciative audience. And the other part of the filmmaking process I really enjoyed happened around then; we started making money from it.

Bad Taste was a unique filmmaking experience. I always say that *BT* is Pete Jackson's film, but if he had made it with a different group of people it would be a different movie. Maybe just as good, but it wouldn't be *Bad Taste*. Everyone who worked on the film, and the way it was shot, gave it a one of a kind character. I'm glad I was involved.

BAD TASTE
reviewed by Kim Newman

Kaihoro, a small town on the coast of New Zealand. Following a telephone call from a resident, the government sends in a team from the Astro Investigation and Defence Service to deal with a suspected alien invasion. Scientist Derek and gunman Barry catch an alien in human form, but find the rest of the town strangely deserted. Barry escapes from a group of aliens, while Derek tries to torture information out of the captive, whose cries alert his comrades. During a battle, Derek falls off a cliff and is presumed dead. Frank and Ozzy, two more of the AIDs team, arrive, while Giles, a charity collector, turns up in Kaihoro and is captured by the aliens, who are headquartered in an old house on the edge of town. Giles is marinaded overnight in preparation for a celebratory feast. Lord Crumb, the alien leader, congratulates his people on efficiently capturing and slaughtering the entire population of the town. Crumb is an intergalactic fast-

Physician, heal thyself: in one of his dual roles, as alien-fighter Derek, Jackson replaces the pieces of brain that will leak from his head through the rest of the movie.

food entrepreneur, and hopes that the introduction of human dishes will help his company regain ground recently lost to competitors. The AIDS team rescues Giles, and Frank disguises himself as an alien to learn their schemes, whereupon he is forced to join a disgusting ritual involving drinking green vomit. In a pitched battle, Frank, Ozzy and Barry shoot down most of the aliens and damage the house, which is actually a spaceship. Derek, meanwhile, has recovered from his fall by shoving brain tissue back into his ruptured cranium, and has entered the house with a chainsaw. Crumb, back in his true form, sets off to take his samples of human flesh to an extraterrestrial fast-food authority. But Derek despatches the alien with the chainsaw, dressed up in Crumb's corpse, and prepares to take on the uiniverse.

'Don't forget, Oz, we're only authorised to use violence when there's a threat to the planet Earth,' states the leader of the AIDS team, whereupon his second indignantly retorts, 'and the *moon!*' The verbal humour of *Bad Taste* is almost all on this endearingly ramshackle level, frequently getting laughs because of its obviousness and shoddiness. The whole production has a makeshift feel that derives from four years of shooting, during which the project underwent radical changes. Originally, the central character was Giles – who is now marginal to the plot – but his role diminished when actor Craig Smith got married, thus cutting down on his weekend spare time, and developed an aversion to the chainsaw ending, whereupon the script was rewritten to make the AIDS team ('I wish they'd do something about those initials') the main characters. This scrappiness allowed director Peter Jackson to step in and become Derek, the most engaging character of the film, but also caused a great deal of confusion which shows up on screen in the blatant overdubbing of all Giles' dialogue, frequently with lines said through closed lips. Along the way, the title changed from *Roast of the Day* through *Giles' Big Day* to the entirely apt *Bad Taste*.

The hand-to-mouth budgeting also shows through in some variable colour quality and in the tedious repetition of the endless central shoot-out between identically clad aliens in blue jeans and shirts and the indistinguishable heroes in black balaclavas. Withal, *Bad Taste* is some kind of triumph in its horror-comic verve, settling into the genre next to the excesses of *Dawn of the Dead*, *Street Trash* and *The Evil Dead*. The opening section contains a succession of inspired sight gags involving the shooting or slaughtering of the moronic aliens, one of whom is brained with a sledge-hammer held by a comrade, and then wanders around with the hammer in his skull and a severed arm dangling from the handle. Another has the top of his head shot off, whereupon a hungry associate scoops out his brains to eat them. Brains also feature strongly when Derek's head develops a flap into which he shoves stray bits of grey matter from time to time.

The mainly ordinary gun battle, which is the film's only major dead spot, is enlivened by a borrowed joke from *The Three Musketeers* as a dozen aliens fall from a machine-gunned tree. Other throwaways include Ozzy booting a severed head neatly out of the window while delightedly exclaiming 'the old magic's still there,' and a stray rocket shell streaking harmlessly through the house to explode a placid and traditionally New Zealand sheep in a nearby field. Finally, the film confronts its repulsively rubbery monsters – whose buttocks and pot-bellies explode through their human disguises – with the vengeful Derek, who administers a spectacular *coup de chainsaw* for the finish. Diving down on to Lord Crumb from above, Derek saws through the alien's head and wriggles through his entire body, emerging bodily from the creature's crotch claiming, 'I'm born again!' While the effects are never technically as good as those in a George Romero or Sam Raimi film, they do serve well enough in their slapstick pantomime way to defuse any potential offensiveness in the horror content. Given the paucity of the resources available – and standing up to comparison with such recent expensive sf-horror extravaganzas as the remakes of *The Blob* and *Invaders from Mars* – *Bad Taste* is quite a remarkable achievement. It follows *The Quiet Earth* and *The Navigator* in establishing New Zealand as a leading source of *cinéfantastique*.

PETER JACKSON, MASTER OF *BAD TASTE*
by Philip Nutman and Giuseppe Salza

Things sure have been dry on the gore front. Sure, the spheres returned in *Phantasm II*, but the MPAA got uptight and wouldn't let Don Coscarelli do his blood spurt special. They likewise castrated *Friday the 13th Part VII: The New Blood*, as well as anything else aiming for a high red content. What's a lively gorehound to do? Rent bad direct-to-video schlock? Well, take heart, gang, New Zealand's *Bad Taste* is about to put the squish back into splatter.

Simply stated, *Bad Taste* does for brains what McDonald's did for hamburgers: spread 'em all over the place. Shot on 16mm by 26-year-old Peter Jackson, the flick has a raw creative energy somewhat similar to *The Evil Dead*. It spoofs alien invasions, cannibal movies, chainsaw massacres and anything else you care to think of. It's whacky. And gory. *Very* gory. The picture's irreverent attitude is summed up on its original poster, which features an alien with a machine gun in one hand, giving the finger to the viewer with the other. If gorelessness is a disease, this guy's the cure. Of course, this means the film can kiss an R rating goodbye.

Jackson, a serious *Fangoria/Gorezone* fan, has an almost squeaky clean appearance. As the saying goes, never judge a book by its cover. A typical movie junkie of the post-baby boom period, as a youth, he made Super-8 FX epics. 'I was nine years old,' he informs. 'Grew up watching movies, reading science fiction and horror magazines, whatever I could get my hands on. Ray Harryhausen was my biggest hero. All I wanted to be was a stop-motion animator. *Fango[ria]* basically taught me how to do make-up effects.'

How the amiable New Zealander, born and raised in Wellington, came to make a heavy duty gore flick is an amusing and atypical story. Once Jackson had left school, he started working for his local newspaper, not so much out of an interest in journalism as a way to earn enough money to buy a 16mm Bolex camera and upgrade the quality of his short films. He planned a short project called *Roast of the Day* as his first in the more expensive medium, something simple enough to allow him to master the camera. By accident rather than design, however, this little number mutated into *Bad Taste*. One year he had a homemade short; the next, a feature.

Moviemaking is a team sport, but *Bad Taste* is definitely Jackson's baby. He wrote the screenplay, produced it, directed it, was co-cinematographer and co-editor, did the FX and, when one of his leading actors wandered off to get married, acted in it. The film is the result of four years of work with a team of friends and was made for $400,000, much of which came out of his personal savings account.

The film started production on October 27th, 1983. 'I decided the movie was going to be very simple, just so I could get used to operating the camera,' he recalls. 'We came up with the idea of a young man who goes to a town in New Zealand to collect money for charity. He finds the town deserted and is then kidnapped by a bunch of extraterrestrials who have killed the entire population in order to open up the first human fast food chain. In the original outline, the charity collector gets killed off at the end, but that soon changed.'

Jackson's crew consisted of several fellow newspaper workers. Since they were working six-day weeks, they could only shoot on Sundays. 'Sometimes we couldn't even do that, since some of the actors were not available when I needed them,' he reveals. 'After about a year of doing that, I decided it was time to seriously look at what we'd shot. Although we hadn't quite completed the ending, I was restless and wanted to start cutting. As it turned out, the rough cut was almost an hour long, which surprised the hell out of me. Having that length made me rethink my ideas. It was strange to think I almost had a feature. Obviously, it would have been foolish to stop there, so I took a "got to keep going" attitude.'

With a new focus, Jackson retitled the flick *Giles' Big Day*. Since actor Craig Smith (who was playing the charity guy) got married, the director decided to take the story on a different path, introducing a government commando squad called the Alien Investigation and Defence Service as a force to fight the evil space invaders. When Jackson couldn't persuade anyone to act for free, he took on the role of Derek, a commando who turns into a chainsaw-wielding psychopath. Derek also has one of the best

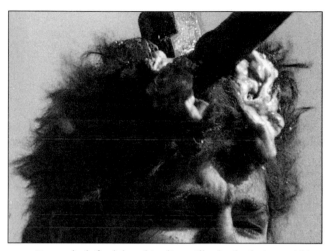

It may look fatal, but this alien will take the brain-squishing sledgehammer in his stride.

scenes in the movie: He falls off a cliff, tears open the top of his head, performs brain surgery on himself, then goes ape.

Bad Taste's lengthy production schedule was problematical, a situation compounded by the director's having to finance nearly everything out of his own pocket. 'My $12,000-a-year salary didn't go very far,' he admits. 'Sometimes I couldn't afford to pay the lab bills or buy new film. In fact, at one point we couldn't shoot for six weeks because I had no money to buy film and owed the lab $700.'

By this time, the flick had its current title and was creeping its way nearer to completion. On two occasions Jackson had approached the New Zealand Film Commission for aid but had been turned down. Fortunately, he persevered, and it was a case of third time lucky. The government-funded company has a stake in nearly every movie made in the country, including Geoff Murphy's end-of-the-world SF drama *The Quiet Earth* and David Blyth's gut-crunching splatfest, *Death Warmed Up*. The Commission allocated Jackson $50,000 to refilm a more spectacular ending and cover some other general production costs. This sum, however, was not enough to cover postproduction. At the same time, veteran editor Tony Hiles was brought in as consultant producer to guide the picture. He was, Jackson acknowledges, a key figure in shaping the film.

'I really don't know if *Death Warmed Up* actually had any real influence on the Commission's decision to put money into the film,' he comments. 'The main reason comes down to the fact they felt they could get their money back once it was distributed. They can't just give out money, they have to act like a bank.' Originally, the Commission considered releasing *Bad Taste* on video, but a screening of the rough cut convinced them to put up another $40,000 to have it blown up to 35mm for possible theatrical distribution.

The sleaze element of Bad Taste *was outdone by* Meet the Feebles, *while the splatter/zombie-movie pastiche reached its outrageous apotheosis in* Braindead.

As for the flick's gore content, Jackson decided to go over the top. He finds excessive blood funny. 'Whenever I watch a gore movie, it makes me laugh,' he admits. 'I can't take that stuff seriously. I see it all in *Monty Python* terms. That type of humour appeals to me, and I kept that at the back of my mind while I was filming. I've not seen any of Herschell Gordon Lewis' films or John Waters' – not for want of trying, mind you [they're banned in New Zealand] – so if *Bad Taste* is influenced by anything, it's the Pythons.

'It was always my intention to make it incredibly gory and funny, the main reason being I'd had some experience doing effects for my little brat movies and blood and guts are the easiest effects to do,' Jackson continues. 'I make no apology for liking spectacular gore.'

Bad Taste is no work of high art, but on the gore score it goes right off the scale, featuring everything you can imagine and then some. Jackson handled most of the grisly FX himself, assisted by Cameron Chittock, a professional makeup FX artist and close friend of the director. 'I'd never used latex before this film,' Jackson confides. 'It really was a crash course in that respect. Tom Savini's *Grande Illusions* book was my main reference source throughout. Cameron's help was invaluable during the last year, which was when he had to make all the aliens.'

It wasn't until this year's [1988] Cannes Film Festival that Peter Jackson realised that he'd made a hot property. *Bad Taste* suddenly began attracting foreign distributors in droves, and then went on to win an award at the annual Paris Horror Film Festival in June.

Although the film has not had any censorship problems in its native land, Jackson firmly believes that if it's submitted to the MPAA in the United States, it will automatically be awarded an X rating. 'That's no problem, as far as I'm concerned,' he states. 'I only hope the distributor doesn't decide to cut it to an R, because that defeats the whole purpose. I would rather not have it seen at all, if that's the case. If you cut the gore down, you're going to lose a lot of the humour. In New Zealand it was awarded a 16 rating – but then, our censorship's fine. *Evil Dead* got a 16, so did *Dawn of the Dead* and *The Texas Chainsaw Massacre*, neither of which were cut. The only movie that was banned for a number of years was the original *Mad Max*; it was felt the film would encourage gang warfare between bikers and car clubs.'

Beyond *Bad Taste* lies an ever gorier project Jackson has already written with two other friends. 'It's a totally over-the-top zombie picture, but again it'll be funny in a black comedy sense,' he discloses. 'We're aiming for 35mm and Dolby stereo. We're currently trying to raise the $1.3 million we need to do it properly. Things are looking good, so we could be in production very soon. I originally wanted to call it *Brain Dead*, but that's too close to [Frank Henenlotter's] *Brain Damage*. My alternative was *Housebound*, but that's too similar to *Hellbound* [*Hellraiser II*]. So I have no idea what to call it right now.'

There's also the possibility of a *Bad Taste 2*. 'All I can say about that at present is that it's about a mad scientist,' Jackson hedges, 'although where he fits into the story, you'll have to wait until it's completed to find out.'

On the strength of this lot, it seems Peter Jackson may become known as New Zealand's answer to Lucio Fulci. 'Hey, that's fine by me,' he laughs.

Bad Taste. If you've got it, flaunt it.

Meet the Feebles

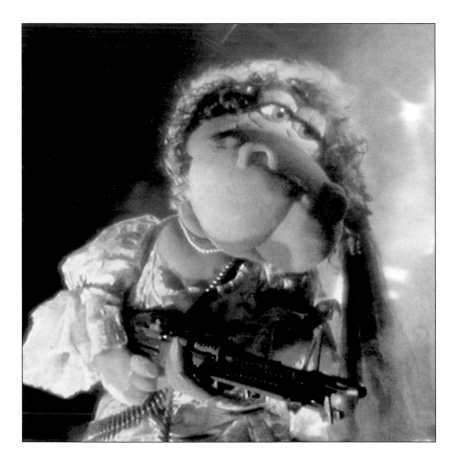

MEET YOUR CREATURE FEATURE
Foam Rubber Depravity In *Meet The Feebles*
by Ian Pryor

It's probably self-evident that concepts like reality and illusion can get more than a little disordered when you're dealing with a medium as adept at showing off as the movies. The very idea of chopping up pieces of space and time into handy little narrative units implies some fairly major distortions of the real world, but as if that were not enough, many filmmakers today seem just as concerned with using the medium to show off their mastery of cinematic trickery as they are with telling a good story.

The two functions are not mutually exclusive of course. And however much many film theorists may have hungered for 'real' (read non-fantastic) cinema in the past, it is a fact that a major part of the popular appeal of movies has derived from their ability to let us escape into other, more stimulating fictional worlds and realities. Thus over the last decade especially we have been bombarded by films brimming with creatures and situations we know do not exist; all displayed to us through dizzying camera movements which take the concept of the narrative eye to points, high and low, few dream of; and whose shots are edited together at a pace which turns reality into a pop video on a course headed for self-destruct.

From Fritz Lang to Adrian Lyne many directors have taken the cinema's capacity for exhibitionism to truly ridiculous extremes, yet others have shown there is nothing to stop a film telling a convincing story at the same time as celebrating its own visual artistry (here I would include both *Citizen Kane*, 1941 and *Blade Runner*, 1982). In theory at least there is no reason why adding strange worlds or alien creatures to this formula should change anything, but for one practical problem: a great many of those who make and finance 'fantastic' films still see their commercial appeal in terms only of hardware (gadgets, spaceships, etc.) or monsters (for teen and sub-teen appeal). In such cases, storytelling and characterisation tend to be neglected.

The question of cinematic reality versus illusion gets even more complicated when you hit upon a movie in which 'real' human characters are only minor players, or are not evident at all. And I am not referring here to animated features, movies in which the cast is often made up entirely of talking animals. Call me an escapist, but I will be avoiding traditional animated features in this article – and concentrating instead on 'creature' films in which the creatures appear to exist on the same physical plane as our own.

On-screen fantasy should be about creating an alternative reality – something fantastic yet still believable on some level. A world populated by non-humans seems an obvious potential contender. Yet there are few examples of films set in what appears to be real time and real space which are populated by non-humans, and most of those there are have cheated by using traditional techniques of frame-by-frame animation, manipulating the camera to make their inanimate creatures come to life, then often using optical process shots to integrate them with the real world.

For all the mastery of stop-motion pioneers like Czech Jiri Trnka, America's Willis

In Jackson's sleazy, scatological puppet movie, Meet the Feebles *(1990), bad taste was taken to gleeful extremes. Miss Piggy-alike Heidi the Hippo prepares to massacre her fellow puppets.*

O'Brien and later Ray Harryhausen, their very method of animation reminds us that we are witnessing illusion. On the one hand Trnka, the Russian Alexander Ptushko and New Zealand's Len Lye* would base short films around what were usually small toy dolls or articulated figures, which for all their magic were clearly inanimate objects tricked into life. On the other hand O'Brien (*The Lost World*, 1925, and *King Kong*, 1933) and Harryhausen (*The Beast from 20,000 Fathoms*, 1953, *Jason and the Argonauts*. 1963, etc.) animated primarily malevolent prehistoric dinosaurs or monsters that everyone knew were long since dead, or had never existed at all. Some of their work was dazzling, but frame-by-frame animation of unmoving objects almost inevitably resulted in a strobing effect which gave viewers a subliminal warning that what they were watching was not real.

Separating stop-motion from live-action filmmaking has become much more difficult for cinemagoers with the invention of go-motion. With the aid of precise computer control (or motion control), cameras and models can now be made to move during the actual process of shooting each frame of frame-by-frame animation. The blurring which results is more convincing to the eye. First used to bring to life the victim of Disney's flop fantasy *Dragonslayer* (1981), go-motion was also used to great effect for the forest sequences of *Return of the Jedi* (1983). Computer animation has not yet reached the point of being utilised for convincing flesh-and-blood characters, though the glass man in 1985's *Young Sherlock Holmes* is a sign of the progress being made in this area.

In the past stop-motion has been both too expensive and too time-consuming to have been used for a fully-fledged 'creature feature' in which the majority of characters are non-human. The full potential of these other advances still lies in the future.

So far then, the human element remains hard to escape. The framing of *Who Framed Roger Rabbit* (1988) thrives on the interaction of animated cartoons and human actors. Almost everything which comes to life via stop-motion in Czech animator Jan Svankmajer's dazzling *Alice* (1988) is inanimate bar Lewis Carroll's heroine. Ridley Scott's live-action fantasy *Legend* (1985) is populated by all manner of mythical creatures – but it is Tom Cruise and Mia Sara who get the plum roles.

One magic solution is missing – puppetry – and despite all its Eastern European traditions the man who has done more than anyone to make it a media moneyspinner has been the American Jim Henson. His long-running variety show *The Muppets* utilised marionettes and string, rod, glove and suit puppets to create an animal cast which has become part of television history. A couple of cinematic Muppet capers carried the proven formula of endearing puppet characters and celebrity guest stars over to the big screen.

In the 1982 fantasy *The Dark Crystal* Henson created cinema's first full-length feature to be populated only by live-action, non-human characters. Sadly, on viewing the result, the fact that Henson had developed his richly-textured alien world well before the well-worn Tolkien-style quest plot became increasingly obvious. But probably what lets the film down most are its humanoid central characters, the Gelfling. In a world 'peopled' with imaginative and convincing non-human creatures we quickly learn that our two pointy-eared heroes have the physical and emotional range of the bad Muppets that they are.

At \$US30 million *The Dark Crystal* was one of the most expensive features in cinematic history; its American returns totalled only \$23 million. Henson learnt at least part of his lesson and into the quest story of his next fantasy *Labyrinth* (1986) he injected two valuable components missing from *Crystal* – a sense of humour (courtesy of *Monty Python*'s Terry Jones, who wrote the script) and human goodies and baddies. Unfortunately one was played by a rock singer who kept wanting to sing (a villain who keeps interrupting the plot to trailer the movie's soundtrack is not going to do much for anyone's sense of wonder) and a young actor who kept wanting to learn how to act. *Labyrinth* was another American bomb – Hollywood movie executives are still puzzling at why it did so well here [in New Zealand].

All of this history shows us that our very own *Meet the Feebles* is something of a landmark in movie-making, for not only is it the first complete 'creature' film aimed at adults and one of the few not to rely on stop-motion effects, it is also the first live-action all puppet feature in the history of movies you can really believe in.

The second film from newly-crowned kiwi bad taste king, Peter Jackson, is New Zealand's most potent example yet of how cinematic illusion can create a bizarre reality. With a budget of only $650,000, *Meet the Feebles* is a backstage theatrical satire which celebrates its own artifice at the same time as its foam-rubber characters have us caught up in some inexplicable kind of warped spell. There is a prima donna hippopotamus singer with bust measurements to match her snout; a fly-on-the-wall journalist whose home is the toilet; a drug-addicted knife-throwing frog with nightmares of 'Nam; a whole clutch of dirty rats; and towering over all, their philandering boss Bletch (a walrus), with some nasty habits of his own.

Their backstage world is one of grimy liftshafts and decaying corridors; of prop-stuffed baskets, hanging stage-ropes and empty beer bottles. Production designer Mike Kane has done such a miraculous job that on set it was hard to tell where movie-making reality and offstage fantasy converged.

Yet the best thing about *Meet the Feebles* is the non-human cast. As the title implies, this film is their showcase. They vary in personality and personal style as widely as any group of animalised stereotypes ever would. They display all the varied insecurities of being undiscovered, unloved, drug-addicted, over-sexed and on their last paws.

That their inspiration remains the Muppets – without so many painful goodie-goodie types of course – is most graphically illustrated by the film's first few minutes. The fascination of that opening glitzy yet stilted production number is not the infantile lyrics – 'Meet the Feebles . . . we're not your average ordinary people' – but the old Muppet-watching matter of noting how almost all the puppets are mounted on a slowly-circling platform with just enough room beneath for all the required puppeteers.

The song ends abruptly with a cut to a handheld tracking shot towards the slimy Trevor the Rat, who sits smoking on the side of the stage. His first line: 'All right you fat slag, move your ass.'

Watching the Muppets I used to get sick of seeing all those shots of Kermit the Frog's upper torso; on *Meet the Feebles* there is never the chance. In fact it is amazing how quickly most viewers unconsciously start accepting the Feebles as 'real' characters. Clever framing and editing are the final important touch to the work of talented and long-suffering puppet designer/maker Cameron Chittock and a gifted team of voice artists and puppeteers.

(Says Jackson: 'I had a phone call recently from a couple of people in Los Angeles who had seen the film the night before and they were talking about the fly: "We were just assuming it was some really nice blue-screen work and motion control," and I said, "No, we just dragged

Wynyard the junkie frog flashes back to Vietnam, in a scene that pastiches The Deer Hunter.

it on the end of a piece of string."')

Jackson and his crew have used all the tricks in the book to bring these inanimate hunks of glued rubber and wool to some kind of life. Yet the Feebles have achieved some extra, unexplainable vitality, divorced from script and clever special effects. They just are.

As for the comic aspects of this very black comedy the fly perhaps puts it best when he tells the new arrival, Robert the Hedgehog, that he is always 'interested in little stories . . . anything spicy . . . or even smutty.'

Perhaps Jackson should have been a journalist himself. *Feebles* has its share of satirical barbs and silly moments – Robert having motivational problems while playing a pennant-bearer during a big musical number, for example, and the most hilarious *Deer Hunter* take-off I've yet seen – but its forte is bad taste.

It seems unfair to reveal too much from *Meet the Feebles'* catalogue of sicko moments; cult movie fans are likely to be savouring or slobbering over them for some time to come. However I asked Jackson how he justified probably the film's most stomach-turning scene, where the journalist-fly is seen in close-up eating excrement (really mince) in the toilet. 'When we wrote the script we were having a lot of fun with bringing metaphors to life. The scene came into being so we could have a journalist who was hanging round the place. We thought perfect – we can have a fly on the wall. Someone, I think it was Danny [Mulheron], came up with the saying "shit-eating journalist". The way I try to deflate that scene with humour is that he's eating the shit with a nice silver spoon and he has this really funny line of dialogue. 99 per cent of people won't hear that line because they'll be far too busy freaking out.'

They certainly will be. But then depending on your sense of humour one is likely to find it innately laughable or innately sickening to be watching foam rubber creatures engaging in acts of urination, regurgitation and (nasal) ejaculation. Perhaps what *Feebles* has that offends viewers most is the perversity of showing puppets indulging in on-screen activities which are still largely taboo in mainstream cinema.

Does Jackson think there are too many bodily secretions in the film? He shrugs. 'The film is a celebration of bodily secretions. That was the whole point of doing it – otherwise you'd just end up with *The Muppet Show*. The entire movie was made so we could be as disgusting as possible with puppets. There was absolutely no reason to make it unless we could make a terribly depraved and gross puppet movie, and we tried our very hardest to make that. We were terribly worried when we wrote it that the puppet "gimmick" would run out even after ten minutes, so we really piled on the depravity to make sure we weren't left with too many scenes of straight soap opera. I think it's hilariously funny for a puppet to break open and be full of tiny organs and guts. That's the basis of the movie – they look like they're made of foam rubber, they act like they're made of foam rubber, but they secrete out of every orifice imaginable . . . which just makes me laugh. I find it funny.'

Jackson's obvious joy in the destruction of his characters has a detrimental effect on the film as a whole. While he gleefully makes sure we get to witness all their dilemmas, diseases and depravity, the film's biggest weakness is its lack of a strong central narrative to tie all the heartbreak together. The fact that they are all Feebles is a rather weak link. Bletch and Heidi the hippo's deteriorating relationship comes closest to being the core one in the film, but it is never really allowed to dominate; *Meet the Feebles* betrays its small-screen origins through its multitude of characters and plotlines.

When *Meet the Feebles* first went before the cameras last April [1989] on the top floor of a house in Wellington it was intended as a 30-minute short for a proposed anthology TV series called *Uncle Herman's Bedtime Whoppers*. After a seven-minute trailer of completed *Feebles* footage caught the eye of a Japanese distribution company Jackson and his co-writing team of Stephen Sinclair (*Ladies' Night*), Fran Walsh (*Shark in the Park*) and Danny Mulheron (*The Sex Fiend*) suddenly found themselves with complete artistic freedom and three weeks to write a feature-length script before cameras rolled, courtesy of a Japanese pre-sale and a loan from the Film Commission. To the Film Commission's dismay they were to go four weeks over schedule.

With this spirit of haste in mind it is perhaps no surprise that *Meet the Feebles* is bursting with comic ideas yet lacks a cohesive narrative, a problem which grows more pronounced as the film progresses. The much-needed tension over whether the Feebles will get the chance to perform live on television near the end is milked for only a fraction of its dramatic potential, while for all its impressive model work the wharfside B-movie tribute is both messy and simply not in keeping with the Feebles universe built up so convincingly over the preceding hour. (Just as it can be argued that watching Bletch and his cohorts doing deals on the golf course serves less to 'aerate the film' – Jackson's words – than to remind us that these creatures are most convincing in their own world.)

Heidi, rejected by Bletch, suffering delusions that the cast hate her, ultimately wins our sympathy. Yet what she does next is likely to satisfy only Sam Peckinpah fans. The massacre would be funny were it not for the fact that in some perverse way we have grudgingly come to feel something for these detestable Feebles. By movie's end it seems we are the only ones that really care. The 'happy-ever-after' closing subtitles look as tacked-on as they are.

As the mystical Indian rubber man illustrates for both Peter Jackson and his intended viewer, things are funniest when your head is up your rectum. The director, then, becomes the movie magician for whom bad taste and cinematic overkill are states of nirvana. 'The movie is what it is,' says Jackson. 'It makes me laugh. I don't analyse it.' *Meet the Feebles*, whatever its faults, undeniably makes for a raw and unsettling brew. Perhaps the ultimate tribute to its power is that the film forces audiences to care for a host of characters they would rather never have met, let alone have been conned by.

---

* Lye of course also experimented with normal hand-drawn animation, while his films painted directly onto celluloid take the concept of frame-by-frame animation to its logical extreme.

Ian Pryor is the author of Peter Jackson – From Prince of Splatter to Lord of the Rings *(NZ, Random House; US, St Martin's Press)*

MEET THE FEEBLES
reviewed by Philip Kemp

Twelve hours before their first live TV show, the Feebles, a puppet troupe, are busy rehearsing under their director, Sebastian the Fox. The MC, Harry the Hare, introduces the lead singer Heidi, a hippo with a weight problem. Her lover, the show's producer Bletch the Walrus, has dropped her in favour of Samantha, a sexy cat from the chorus. Robert, a naïve young hedgehog, joins the troupe and falls for Lucille, a pretty seal who has also attracted the lecherous attention of Bletch's assistant, Trevor the Rat. Meanwhile, the knife-thrower Wynyard the Frog, a hopeless junkie with a Vietnam trauma, vainly begs Trevor for drugs, and Sid the depressive elephant is served with a paternity order by his ex-lover, Sandy the Chicken.

Bletch, accompanied by Trevor and the thuggish Barry the Bulldog, meets Cedric the Boar on the golf course to fix a drugs deal with Cedric's boss, Mr. Big the Whale. Trevor, shooting a porno movie on the side, hits problems when Daisy the Cow accidentally asphyxiates her partner, Wally the Cockroach. The prurient office boy, Denis the Anteater, is roped in as replacement. Harry, who has broken out in a rash, learns from Dr. Quack he has The Big One – information overheard by the Fly, a gutter-press journalist.

Rehearsing her big number, Heidi is shaken by gargantuan belches that bring down the set. Rushing to Bletch for comfort, she finds him being fellated by Samantha, and locks herself in her dressing-room. Trevor, having drugged Lucille's champagne, is about to rape her when Robert appears. Outraged, the hedgehog storms off before Lucille can explain. Mr. Big's heroin arrives, but proves to be borax. Bletch and his minions confront the whale at the docks. Both Barry and Cedric are killed, but Bletch and Trevor escape down Mr. Big's gullet and out his anus.

Thanks to the Fly, Harry's terminal illness is headlines. But when the show starts he indomitably goes on, only to vomit all over the audience. Sid, pushed on to fill in, is confronted by Sandy with their love-child. The stoned Wynyard skewers himself with his own knife. Heidi, after attempting suicide, finds one of Bletch's machine-guns and guns down Samantha, and then Harry (who has just discovered he doesn't have myxomatosis after all). Erupting on stage, she massacres most of the troupe, ending with Bletch. Trevor wounds her, but she kills him. The only survivors besides Heidi are Robert (who nobly saves Lucille), Sebastian, stage manager Arfur the Worm, and Sid and his baby. End titles tell us what became of them.

In high-concept terms, *Meet the Feebles* is easily defined: it's *The Muppets Go Sleazebag*. Aiming to do for the perky world of puppets what *Fritz the Cat* did for animation – i.e., overwhelm it with filth, sex and drugs – Peter Jackson's film sets out to be relentlessly, gratuitously offensive. Most of the time, fortunately, it succeeds.

Jackson's previous movie, the live-action *Bad Taste*, was a ramshackle SF/horror splatter comedy, blithely tossing in gags and parodies from whatever source came to hand.

Feebles is better organised but almost equally eclectic: we get a black-and-white moody torchsong flashback, a 'Nam movie flashback (complete with Russian roulette), and – in the intercutting between Heidi's backstage slaughter and Sebastian's big production number – a parody of the baptism/bloodletting sequence from *The Godfather*.

The massacre rounds off a film in which no excuse for spurting bodily secretions – blood, pus, vomit or whatever – is passed up. Not all the humour, though, is quite so grossly visceral, and Sebastian, the effete (and, of course, English-accented) director gets several of the best lines. 'You mean it's not part of your act?' he asks testily when an Indian contortionist gets his head stuck up his arse. 'Pity – we could call it *Passage to India*.'

Meet The Feebles
reviewed by Spencer Hickman

The best way to describe this film would be, 'Heck, it's just a PORNOGRAPHIC MUPPET MOVIE!' Yep, 'Bad Taste' is back in the form of Peter Jackson's adult puppet tale; it concerns the Feebles, the biggest TV sensation of the year; we've got Heidi the Hippo (the overweight star of the show), Arthur the Worm (stage manager), Trevor the Rat (who sells drugs to the rest of the cast) and loads of other wild characters. Robert the Hedgehog (complete with speech impediment) joins the show and falls in love with Lucy the Poodle (I told you it was wild), Heidi's husband Bletch (a big fat bastard walrus who owns the show) is having an affair with a young cat and is also a drug baron, a chicken accuses an elephant of being the father of her baby, Trevor is making porno movies with Daisy the Cow in the basement which have titles like *Daisy Does Denis* and *Anal Antics*, Harry the Hare sleeps with anything that moves, the cleaners go on a 'Minge Binge', sniffing the girls' undies, and the knife throwing frog is a heroin addict who frequently kills his assistants!

Harry gets told by the doctor that he has Aids. Meanwhile, during a show, the contortionist gets his head stuck up his ass and can't get it out, and Heidi walks in on Bletch getting a blowjob from his bit on the side. The frog goes on stage smacked out of his head, throws his knives all over the place, and the elephant pisses over the chorus line! Heidi freaks out and kills the pussycat, Harry finds out that the doctor made a mistake and he only has bunnypox, while, jumping for joy, he gets shot to pieces by Heidi and her machine gun! A fox goes on stage and sings about the joys of *sodomy* while Heidi kills the entire cast and crew, just like some kind of fuckin' female Rambo! She then sings 'Garden of Love', gets put away for ten years, gets out and works as a checkout girl!? This movie has it all, even tortured Vietnam war flashbacks; it's a total one-of-a-kind movie and you gotta see it, believe me, it's crazy.

BRAINDEAD

I WALKED AS A ZOMBIE
by Michael Helms

A little over a year ago, at the invitation of director Peter Jackson, I found myself wandering into the arrival lounge at Wellington International Airport, magnetically drawn towards a smiling woman (Sue Rogers) clutching a copy of the press notes for Braindead, *or* Brain Dead *as it was known then. Although I had my suspicions, little did I realise then that I was in for some serious fun. From the early morning huddle around the nearest cofee urn to post-dusk screenings of rushes and the excitement of mixed showers for zombie extras, I was made to feel completely at home during the five days I spent hanging around the set of this crazed splattoon. That is, except for the night I turned out to be the only Australian at a party held at the same time as an International Rugby final between New Zealand and Oz, when the cultural differences of two English-speaking countries began to loom too large for this little black duck. The following collection of interviews took place at various locations, from the spooky, gothic set and the production's offices (based inside a semi-obsolescent TV studio complex on the outskirts of town) to several lounge rooms – including the one dominated by a huge model of Thunderbird One that Peter Jackson claims as his own, where he kindly consented to spend a large part of his only day off for that week with a more-than-slightly-hungover Australian zine publisher. But that's indicative of the whole* Braindead *operation, which was staffed by folks as intent on creating a most salubrious working atmosphere as they were on making the best possible final product. From my perspective* Braindead *was one happy film set. These interviews should reflect that fact, and at this point I'd like to thank Sue Rogers, Jim Booth, all the cast and crew who I spoke with, and of course Peter Jackson.*

PETER JACKSON

FOREIGN TERRITORIES: It's not that I'm not interested in how the films perform in foreign territories like France or Germany, it's just that, once the film is finished, I have my personal feelings on it, whether good or bad, and I have a video tape copy of it that I can watch and reappraise at any time. I guess that sums up my whole attitude to filmmaking, in that I really make them for myself, and when they're done they sit on my shelf for me to enjoy. That others like them is just a bonus. How the films go in other parts of the world doesn't really interest me though, as you could work yourself up into terrible knots over how they go.

MAKING *BRAINDEAD*: *Braindead*'s definitely been the easiest. *Bad Taste* was sort of an incredible endurance test that stretched out over four years, and was very, very difficult just in terms of the length of time I had to think about it. *The Feebles* was made dirt cheap and was physically very taxing, what with puppet wrangling and the fact that I was operating the camera for most of the time. Budget and schedule were constant problems. Comparatively, *Braindead*'s gone very smoothly. Basically, I just walk around and tell everyone what to do and they do it [laughs]. For me it's not too strenuous, although the constant requirement of my concentration is very tiring. Also, I guess, with it being my third film I'm beginning to figure out how it all works [more laughs]. Preparation and planning is the key. We storyboarded the whole film, which we use as a general guide but have

His bloody ribcage exposed, a juvenile delinquent joins the flesh-eating zombies.
Braindead *(1992) is a delirious cartoon synthesis of horror and action sub-genres.*

never really faithfully stuck to. While things were changed for various reasons, storyboards are very handy though. I came up with lots of gags that weren't in the script, mainly visual things. I gave myself a month of intensive thought specifically to design as many visual gags as possible. You can't really do stuff like that once you're on the set and shooting. This allowed the time for Richard [Taylor] to get the effects together and tested.

GENESIS OF *BRAINDEAD*: We were going to make it in 1989 on the first draft of the script. Now we're on the ninth, so it's gone through enormous improvements structurally and character-wise. It's been polished and tightened up so much that I'm really glad we never shot the original. It would've been an entirely different movie. The one thing that hasn't altered greatly has been the effects. The only real major alterations involved the drama.

SPECIAL EFFECTS: I have no fear of them or problems with them. Richard Taylor, *Braindead*'s special effects designer, and I have a very good working relationship. He feels he works the same as me. Sculpting, casting, rods and wires. Where we work well together is that he trusts me. If something he's made looks a bit dodgy in real life, he'll accept my word for it that it will be effective enough to film and let it go. I know exactly how I'm going to shoot it and he trusts my judgement. A lot of FX guys spend too much time making stuff look really fantastic when it's not completely necessary. There are only so many parts to the human body and they've all just about been used in films before. The way you use them and the situations you place them is how you achieve some originality. It's what the entrail does is where the entertainment comes from. It all comes down to the story, and entrails and guts can be characters just as much as anybody or anything else.

THE *BRAINDEAD* ZOMBIE LOOK: For the leads, I wanted to steer clear of the weathered skeleton type of zombie and go for a more greasy, welted, slimy, bloated look. The vague plan was to get them looking like they'd been underwater for about three weeks.

SETTING A ZOMBIE FILM IN THE FIFTIES: The idea of setting the film in the fifties came about at a very late stage, about two months before we started pre-production. One of the dilemmas I've always had about the film was convincing the audience that this 25-year-old guy lives with his mother who treats him really badly, and yet he still hangs in there. There is a real problem there if your leading man gets laughed off the screen in the first half hour. The film would then be virtually over. The concept of setting the film in the fifties came to me when I was going through the SPFX with Richard. We were doing the embalming room stuff and I was saying it should look really old, like something out of the fifties. Suddenly it all made sense, and the whole mother/son relationship problem became believable, at least to me. Today, no one would put up with the sort of stuff Mum pulls, but there is some sort of credence having it going on in the fifties. Also, the period setting helps the overall mood and tone of the film. It gives it a freshness too, because the fifties we're depicting here is not an American *Happy Days*/Fonzie-type fifties, but a more austere post-war British sort of world, which is exactly what New Zealand was like then. I think the whole idea of setting a horror/zombie/splatter film in this period is something new anyway. It should set the film apart, even if you do confuse the title with all the rest of the *Dead* films. As far as recreating the fifties with any degree of historical accuracy is concerned, there's actually not that many exteriors in the film. There's a trip to the zoo and the shop that the girlfriend Paquita's parents own, but we've mainly relied on the costuming.

MAKING FILMS WITHOUT SPFX: Right now I can't really envisage myself making a film without SPFX. From about the age of eight through to twenty or 22, all I ever wanted to be was a SPFX guy, which is what I did in all my spare time over all those years. My earliest heroes were Ray Harryhausen and Jim Danforth. Perhaps my only regret with *Braindead* is that I haven't got my hands dirty with the FX. On *The Feebles* I made puppets, quite a few actually. I also did most of the *Bad Taste* stuff as well.

SELLING YOUR FILM: I tell you what, Jim [Booth)] and I spent about two weeks earlier this year ['91] in Los Angeles, along with previous attempts at various film markets to get American pre-sales. There were lots of companies vaguely interested, but no one really latched on to it or wanted to do a deal. So, in the end, when we got the financing together from within New Zealand via the Film Commission and Avalon Studios, I realised, well, if we haven't got any American companies on our backs, why the hell do I have to worry about their marketplace? If we'd had an American deal they would've been in the position to dictate the content. I thought, we don't have to suck up to Americans so why impose restrictions on ourselves? After all, we're making a New Zealand zombie movie and it'll screen here as an R16. It'll be a very difficult film to cut for an MPAA 'R' rating. If the Americans can't handle it, well, too bad. They're just going to have to accept it on the comedy level and say, well, it really is funny despite and because of those gruesome effects.

THE EFFECT OF FX: If any ratings/censorship board judge it solely as a horror movie, they'll have enormous problems cutting it because of the integral part that the effects play within the story. The gut puppet, for instance, is a legitimate character. Cutting *Bad Taste* was ludicrous because films like it are totally harmless, one of the reasons being that, as gore movies, they are meant to go completely over the top. I mean, some people just hate the idea of gore movies and hate to look at *Bad Taste*, and yet, if a censor comes along and reduces the gore, taking out the odd shot here and there, what they're doing is removing all the over-the-top stuff and bringing it back to being a much more intense horror movie. What's implied is always worse than what you ever show, so I show an enormous amount which actually takes the edge off it. It takes the violence out of it in a way. It does make it more comic book or cartoon-like. Someone coming in behind me and snipping all those shots out just brings the film down to a more dangerous level. As far as I'm concerned, it's stupid, and it's just like them shooting themselves in the foot, trying vainly to protect the public.

WHERE COMEDY MEETS HORROR: The mistake lots of people make is that they try and make excuses for the horror by saying, 'Well, it's first and foremost a comedy,' and that really they don't want to make horror movies. I think both aspects of film and storytelling go hand in hand without demeaning each other. It's a fine balance though. I think horror comedies have fallen into disrepute due to becoming a favourite genre of the studio executive. They think in terms of, 'Yeah, there's money to be made in horror films, but we don't want to be seen to be making them so let's add comedy.' I treat comedy as I have with all my films, totally straight. I mean, comedy is a serious thing. None of the actors in this film are playing for laughs. When each actor comes in, I always give them a little pep talk along the lines of the film being a serious drama and I don't want them to be funny. Everything that is happening to their particular character is a life and death situation. Big things are at stake. I'll do the comedy, you guys just give me a dramatic performance. That's the way I've approached *Braindead*. Once you load a comedy/horror film with comedic performances is when they begin to break down badly. Comedy and drama are very closely related. There's

A technician works on the model of the Sumatran rat-monkey (inset), seen chittering from his cage (above).

not very much of a gap between them at all. If you get too carried away with the drama it can unintentionally become comedy. I want people to laugh but I don't want them to relax or get complacent. I want to induce a sense of unease and create a situation where you really don't quite know what's going to happen next. For one thing, *Braindead* has a very fast pace.

AVALON STUDIOS: I found it endlessly humourous. The only two shows now shot at Avalon, which used to be a veritable hive of TV production, are *Sale of the Century* and *Wheel of Fortune*. The fact that we're shooting there, with blood-soaked sets and embalming machines being built next to all these little game-show wheels and things, I find really perverse. I also love it when they have all their contestants and audiences in the cafeteria and we wander in with all our hideously scarred zombies. I don't really know whether the management realise they've got one of the goriest films ever made shooting under their roof. Some novelties never wear off, and one example certainly is having lunch in the cafeteria with all the zombies.

HOPES FOR *BRAINDEAD*: What would please me more than anything would be for people to rank *Braindead* right up there with *Dawn of the Dead* and the *Evil Dead*s, films I've enjoyed the heck out of myself. Those films were my inspiration. In some respect I hope that fans of this sort of stuff from across the world can enjoy it now, in this climate that is not necessarily conducive to making films like this. I really hope it fills a gap and hits the spot. I'm operating completely independently here in New Zealand and can do whatever I like. It may take a while for me to get the money, but once I do I'm a free agent and have no restrictions put on me by anybody. The net result of this freedom is that *Braindead* will be a pure example of something where I've been allowed to simply let her rip and go for it.

RICHARD TAYLOR (Special FX Designer)

BECOMING *BRAINDEAD*: I've had my mind on this job for quite a long time because of the fact that we started it over three years ago. Even though it folded back then, I hoped from the bottom of my heart that it would get going again. Consequently, it never really left my mind. In a way, both Peter and I had always been thinking about the effects, so when we finally came back to it after *The Feebles* we were that much more prepared for the organisation of it. In hindsight, it was actually a godsend to spend all those nights sitting at Peter's computer writing up the effects, because if we hadn't we just couldn't have pulled it off for this money. We tried to nut out every possible thing – how to do them as simply as we could and get them looking as good as we could.

MAKING FX: We've got a nine-person FX crew. In New Zealand, special effects means anything that has to be manufactured, like a puppet or a creature or even pyrotechnics, basically anything that does a whizz or a bang or looks funny. Anyway, we set up a workshop from scratch. I knew we'd need a huge number of body parts for the carnage scenes, and what I wanted to do, because most of the guys working on it were quite young and didn't have that much experience, was to start them off on something that was simple but which they could really get their teeth into. So we got Tania [SPFX Administrator]'s sister and did a full algenate cast of all of her body parts, and began mass producing limbs. For three weeks or so I had people just making arms, legs, heads and torsos. Then, as each actor was cast, we then got to do our own casting of them and their heads and started reproducing them as puppets. I was a little apprehensive about that, seeing as very few actors from New Zealand have had experience with full face casting, which can be a freaky experience for the uninitiated. But they were all pretty relaxed. My rule for head casting is the more people the merrier. So, I was working with four people at a time. The method is you get in there and go incredibly fast and get them out as quick as possible. One bloke did panic but Tania, as always, holds their hands. The worst thing we found was that if the room goes quiet they begin to think something is wrong. So we just babble on, and make sure we keep a constant stream of chatter going.

THE INPUT OF BOB McCARRON (Prosthetics Designer – based in Sydney): We met Bob when the film first went ahead. He's very much from the Dick Smith school of prosthetics. He's a wizened old hand who at no stage wasn't ever less than ready, willing or able to offer advice. At any turn or difficulty he was there. The scariest thing for me was the management of the whole unit, and working out how to keep everything ticking over, at the same time maintaining the quality of the work. Bob looked after all the prosthetics, which was too much of a job for us. There's simply not the people here in NZ to produce the sort of work in such a short time span. The amount of prosthetics required by *Braindead* is huge.

MOST AMBITIOUS EFFECT: Baby Selwyn is definitely the trickiest piece of effects work. We've had to keep him simple because we haven't had the money to build some sort of intricate animatronic puppet, but he's got to do a variety of things and, in fact, have as much presence as any of the secondary actors. He's got a role as strong as Nurse McTavish or Father McGruder. I spent a very long time sculpting Baby Selwyn. I had to develop a design for Baby Selwyn that gives him the ability to kick, punch and bite people, virtually moments after his birth, and not look farcical. Trying to build a hand puppet that small was incredibly difficult, and completely tested me. I built it all around Tania's hand.

ALL THE FX: On one level the FX in this movie are completely low-tech. They're not likely to set the FX world on fire, mainly because we're using ideas and stuff that's come straight from the pages of *Fangoria* – I mean hey, why and try to reinvent the wheel? We're not making something with a huge budget, but we're doing something with a huge amount of FX. What we've got here is a film on the lines of, say, a Frank Henenlotter project, or something that is built on energy, enthusiasm and number eight fencing wire. At the very least, our love for this project should shine right through.

THE FX SHOP – A QUICK GUIDED TOUR: Slush-molded latex with a wire armature inside for when Mum pulls Uncle Les's head and backbone out of his back. Articulated skulls. A spring-loaded statue arm that pierced up through the chest, effectively de-gutting him at the same time. Assorted ripped-off arms, legs and heads. Rita ripped in half, hands punching out her ears. Leg splitting. A stop-animation rat monkey for a 23-second burst of screen time. A cat-dog experiment by a Nazi vet who also has a swastika armband-wearing cat. From amidst this carnage, presided over by the mother monster, Taylor promised that, with the exception of the two leads, no one gets off lightly. The rest of the cast are all seriously maimed, torn apart or chopped into bits.

STEPHEN SINCLAIR & FRAN WALSH (screenplay)
NZ FILM COMMISSION: We ourselves are sometimes mystified by their involvement in this exploitation picture, which contains a high graphic violence content that is sure to offend many people and bring flack to the Commission. But, apparently, they're much happier in their involvement with *Braindead* as opposed to *Meet the Feebles*, because of the use of real actors.
THE FLICK: This film has zombie sex with instantaneous pregnancy and birth. *Braindead* is a satire of the family not necessarily *for* the whole family. Whatever you do, don't see it while under the influence of angel dust.
THE FUTURE: Of course, we're looking forward to the release of *Braindead* in Arab countries, where we feel the severing of hands will carry a special significance, but our intention is to turn it into a splatter musical that will reach a wider audience. Absolute Grand Guignol. Pus, blood and FX live on stage, but that's another story.

*B*RAINDEAD
reviewed by Karl Quinn

It seems unlikely that Peter Jackson will ever make another splatter film. Even if we discount his claim in an interview with *Time* magazine that he is 'sick of all the blood', *Braindead* is just too complete a synthesis of the elements of the genre to make any return to it worthwhile. In fact, it is so much the definitive splatter movie that one wonders if it signals the complete redundancy of any further efforts at the genre.

Braindead is set in Wellington, New Zealand, in 1957. The specificity of the time frame is a little puzzling, given that history has, on the surface at least, no more than design significance in the film. Lionel (Timothy Balme) is a daggy young man whose feeble life is completely dominated by his mum (Elizabeth Moody), who enjoys playing monarchic matriarch from her weatherboard mansion overlooking the city. The furthest Lionel's leash extends is to the corner store at the foot of the mansion, and it is here that he meets Paquita (Diana Penalver), the Spanish shop assistant with whom he begins an extremely circumspect relationship.

Ever afraid that Mum will discover that she is not the only woman in his life and be prompted to wreak a horrible revenge, Lionel sneaks off to the zoo with Paquita for a first date full of romance, joy and screeching animals. Mum, of course, suspects that Lionel is up to something and sneaks along behind in order to spy on her little boy and the 'tart' who is leading him astray. She does so in disguise, wearing a large hat and a pair of outrageous sunglasses more than a little redolent of Dame Edna, whose persona this version of the domineering, class-conscious mum so strongly echoes.

While at the zoo, Mum stumbles against the cage of a fierce creature which we have moments before witnessed ripping the arm off a monkey in a neighbouring cage. It is the Sumatran rat monkey, the product, so a keeper tells us, of the rape of native Sumatran monkeys by marauding rats from Dutch ships. As Mother falls against the cage, the rat monkey leaps at her and tears a chunk of flesh from her arm before Mum is able to bring first her umbrella and then her heel down upon the head of the vile creature. The monkey – which is as rare and invaluable as it is vile – is reduced to a bloody pulp, while Lionel is reduced to the role of dutiful son, leaving Paquita to find her own way home as he takes care of Mum.

The bandage Lionel slaps on his mother's arm seems quite sufficient to the task of healing her wound, until it suddenly begins to squirt jets of pus around her sick-room. Alarmed, Lionel sends for Nurse McTavish (Brenda Kendall) who advises Lionel that his mother just needs to rest in bed. That she steadfastly refuses to do, as she is having Mrs. Matheson (Glenis Levestam) – the head of the Wellington Ladies' Welfare League – for lunch. But when Mum starts weeping pus and dropping ears into the custard, it becomes clear that Mrs. Matheson and her husband (Lewis Rowe) are having her for lunch.

When the rapidly decomposing but decidedly undead Mum attacks Nurse McTavish, even the dim-witted Lionel cottons on to the realisation that his mother has transformed into a zombie, and has the power to infect all those with whom she exchanges bodily fluids. Only a powerful liquid tranquilliser which Lionel purchases from an ex-Nazi chemist seems to have any efficacy in stemming Mother's thirst for blood, and Lionel uses it to knock his mother and the nurse out for long enough to lock them in the basement. Of course, Mother escapes, and comes looking for Lionel in the site of his first betrayal of her: the corner store where Paquita works. On her wicked way she is hit by a tram, and within minutes buried. But not dead.

Soon enough, Mum has burst forth from the grave and swelled the ranks of zombies by four rockers and a reverend. When Lionel's sleazy Uncle Les (Ian Watkin) arrives on the scene to blackmail Lionel into handing over his inheritance (discovering the sedated zombies in the basement, he concludes that Lionel is a serial killer), the scene is set for a rock 'n' roll showdown between the zombies and the ever-diminishing ranks of humans. Only one thing can save the day for Lionel: his trusty two-stroke lawnmower. Strapping it on to his shoulder, Lionel wades into the thick of the zombie horde (swelled by Les' party guests to several score) and lets rip in a scene of bloodletting that may set something of a record in terms of time, number of corpses and sheer volume of liquid spilt. The film might well have been called 'Wellington Lawnmower Massacre' rather than *Braindead*.

From the above it should be clear that *Braindead* is above all a comedy. It also operates very much in the terrain of parody of other people's cinema (*Psycho*, Romero's zombie films and *Arsenic and Old Lace* are just a few points of satirical reference that come to mind), as well as serving as an apparent endpoint to Jackson's own explorations of the medium to date. If *Meet the Feebles* was to some extent a departure from the territory Jackson had begun to traverse with his first feature, *Bad Taste*, *Braindead* is a return to form and format par excellence.

But while *Braindead* is an enjoyable – on occasion, hilarious – romp (or wade) through tides of blood and fields of gore, there is something quite unsettling about it at a sub-textual level. The oedipal conflict between Lionel and his grasping mother is the most apparent example of this, and perhaps the most easily dealt with; because it is so conscious, one might suggest, it must be parody. It would seem that Jackson is not simply passing around the same old fear-of-mother scenario, he is deliberately exploiting it for its innate comic potential. The finale, in which Mum appears as a giant latex zombie with womb agape ready to gobble Lionel up, is both the comic apotheosis of this theme, and the elaborate realisation of an unstated gag which has Mum as the Mother of all Zombies.

But the obvious AIDS metaphor (including the jibe at monkey-linked explanations of the origin of the virus), unrelated Nazi references and a host of other throwaway lines, like the rape joke, are less easily redeemed by notions of 'parody'. Splatter aside, *Braindead* shares much with *Les Patterson Saves the World* (George Miller, 1987), most notably an uninhibited willingness to transcend notions of political correctness and good taste when dealing with some undeniably delicate issues. Whether we are to laud or loathe Jackson and Miller for boldly going where no one has gone before remains one of the unsolved questions of the Twentieth Century.

Whatever difficulties Peter Jackson and his film might pose for an Australian critic or audience, however, are as nothing compared to the unease with which the New Zealand film community apparently views this maverick goremeister. Jackson has repeatedly been categorised as a filmmaker with little connection or relevance to his country. Still, the New Zealand Film Commission (NZFC) has refused to pay too much attention to such criticisms, providing financial support to all Jackson's features to date. Indeed, it is hard to understand why Jackson should be seen as being disinterested in New Zealand when *Bad Taste* and *Braindead* seem so indebted to a vision of the country as trapped in a 1950s time warp (whether overtly stated, as in *Braindead*, or merely implicit as in *Meet the Feebles* and *Bad Taste*), inhabited by the characters from one of those anti-New Zealand jokes that Australians enjoy so much. It may not be a vision that many New Zealanders wish to perpetrate, but it is no less a legitimate and specific vision of the country than Barry Humphries' is a legitimate and specific understanding of Australia. We can quibble with the politics of those visions, with their self-loathing and with their reductionism; but to suggest that they are unconnected with the country which supports them (which in the case of Humphries is now only marginally Australia) is ludicrous. Let's hope the NZFC continues its good sense in backing Jackson's films of bad taste and faith; and I'm sure that, with one eye firmly on the successful export of Australia's only truly famous person (in Clive James' view, at least), it will.

ANTIPODAL SPLATTERMEISTER
by Ken Miller

After the screening of *Braindead* at Nuremberg's *Weekend of Fear* festival, Ken Miller of *Film Extremes* questioned the bearded Mr. Jackson outside the cinema on a quiet German street . . .

In Braindead *there is an animated rat monkey and, in the main character's bedroom, a poster for* The Beast from 20,000 Fathoms. *Are you a fan of movie animator Ray Harryhausen?*
Oh yeah, very much so. I love *The Seventh Voyage of Sinbad* with the Cyclops.

A film project of yours that has yet to go into production, called* Blubberhead, *seems to be set to be a showcase for some model animation. Can you tell me something about the storyline?
Blubberhead is sort of an epic fantasy film that's set in a *Lord of the Rings*-type world with dwarves, hobbits and dragons. There's an Indiana Jones type of hero who takes on the tax department of a large city. The chief accountant of this city is called Rotuscus Blubberhead and it's a weird fantasy, like sort of *Monty Python*-ish, but it's got a lot of action and stop motion creatures. I talked to Jim Danforth [the animator of *When Dinosaurs Ruled the Earth*, *Jack the Giant Killer* and others] about *Blubberhead* but he reckons that he's retired.

***Who did the animation of the rat monkey in* Braindead?**
Richard Taylor and I did that.

***Are you a secret tram fetishist? I ask this as you went to the effort of filming tram models in some of the street scenes in* Braindead.**
We had to make models because we had to shoot them in streets and the real trams, in a museum, are in the countryside with no streets around. I didn't know anything about trams before I started work on *Braindead*. Because I wanted to make one I sort of got interested in them.

I thought that, maybe, you had one on your sideboard?
I do have them on my sideboard because I actually made the models. That's the only bit of FX that I did on *Braindead*.

What about the fifties-style plane at the beginning of the movie?
That was a model, but somebody else made that.

The film is crammed full of inventive splatter scenes. Do you have a favourite sequence?
My favourite gore effect, which I laugh at, is when Void, the tough guy in the leather jacket, is cut in half and the two girls rip his legs in half.

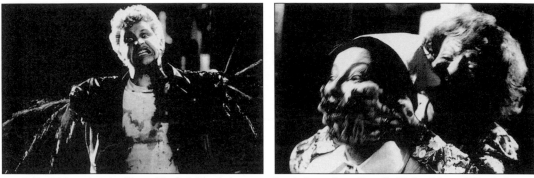

Left: This rock 'n' roll zombie (Jed Brophy) proves that he's armless after all. Right: Mum (Elizabeth Moody), in full zombie flesh-eater mode, attacks Nurse McTavish (Brenda Kendall).

How did you do the dismembered legs scene when they're shown to be walking on their own?
In some shots we had some legs that were controlled on a pole which came out of the back and into the wall behind and was in the camera's blind spot: the legs masked the pole from the camera.

Weren't you involved in the construction of the Mother-monster at the end?
I was involved in everything to the extent that I supervised it all, but I didn't actually make the monster. The monster was built while we were shooting the movie. It was the last thing that we shot at the end of twelve weeks.

Were the close-up shots of the monster's head talking animated?
No, the [full size] head was shot at twelve frames a second which is why it looks a little bit jerky but we had to try and get the lip synch working. We didn't animate it because we wanted it to interact with humans quite a lot and we hadn't got the technology to do rear screen projection.

Was the monster as large as it appears on screen?
It was as big as a person.

Did you use forced perspective to make it look so huge?
Yes we did, you're quite right.

Was the scene in which the lawnmower moves across the grass and over the camera, showing the spinning blades underneath, hard to film?
The lawn was built up on some wooden boards and we had a hole in it. We laid fake grass on top and had a cameraman in the hole and the lawnmower went straight over.

When you see a lampoon of kung fu movies in a western-made film it's not usually that good, but the graveyard fight scene in Braindead is the best such kung fu take-off ever. Have you seen any Jackie Chan movies?

I'm a Jackie Chan fan. I've been watching Jackie Chan films for years.

When the hero appears at the doorway holding the lawnmower as a weapon it was very Bruce Campbell-esque. Did you set out to out-Raimi Sam Raimi in* Braindead*?
Not consciously. People liked *Bad Taste* but I thought that it had its faults so I wanted to do another splatter movie that was a little bit slicker.

EXTREME FILM CHOICE – PETER JACKSON

Well I probably haven't seen a lot of the films that the readers of this magazine would've seen. I would have to say *Evil Dead II* is the most extreme film that I've seen. *The Texas Chainsaw Massacre* was definitely extreme ... extreme in the really psychological, violent feel it had to it. That's one of the few films where I felt extremely uneasy when I watched it.

A CRITIQUE OF THE JUDGEMENT OF BAD TASTE OR BEYOND BRAINDEAD CRITICISM: The Films of Peter Jackson by Lawrence McDonald

I
Peter Jackson is an axiom. By himself alone he constitutes an industry, and his presence in any film whatsoever suffices to create beauty. The uncontained violence expressed by the sombre phosphorescence of his direction, the rivers of blood unleashed by his narratives, the inner being divulged by his camera angles. This is what he possesses and what not even the worst script can degrade.

One can say that Peter Jackson, by his existence alone, gives a more accurate definition of cinema than films like *Vigil* or *An Angel at My Table* whose aesthetic either ignores or impugns Peter Jackson.[1]

II
'The genre of the horror film has been short-circuited – it has no duration, no depth, no points of contact. As an object of analysis, if you set aside a few coteries which fetishise it in their own way, it meets with an ignorant smile from people who don't really know why they are smiling and should perhaps begin to do a bit of thinking.' – Roger Dadoun.[2]

The *New Zealand Listener's* recommended New Zealand video slot of February 13, 1993 reads: '*Braindead*: sick, slick homegrown comedy from bad taste specialist Peter Jackson. A cascade of gore, entrails and slime.' So that's it then?, the essence of all local Jackson criticism to date, encapsulated in two brief sentences. What can one possibly add in the face of such conciseness? It seems that what you see is what you get (or is that the other way round?) and that like Wittgenstein in the front row of his local cinema . . . whereof one cannot speak one must remain silent.

However, I haven't come to give you a pile of severed adjectives in place of an absent body of criticism; just some observations on a remarkably coherent body of work.

Although Jackson's three features (particularly *Braindead*) have achieved some success with local audiences, there has been a tendency to place them outside the arena within which New Zealand film is discussed in cultural terms.[3] The most accommodating reception spaces for Jackson's films have been sub-cultural, fanzine-style magazines such as *Cinefantastique* (USA), *Fangoria* (USA) and *Fatal Visions* (Australia) whose editors, writers and readers immediately respond to the films' direct address because they share a common language and set of enthusiasms with the filmmaker. And just as they once welcomed Sam Raimi, Stuart Gordon and Brian Yuzna into the pantheon of post-Romero body-horror (splatter), so now they have welcomed Jackson.

Thus in international terms Jackson is a known commodity, a welcome addition to the higher echelons of splatter, who with *Braindead* has upped the ante in the most recent phase of the special effects driven gore movie. Yet within the much smaller context of the New Zealand film industry, Jackson is something else again. Quite simply he is the most consistent and consistently successful practitioner within a single film genre that New Zealand has ever produced. Specifically it is Jackson's no-holds-barred, total immersion, literally his *exploitation* of the possibilities inherent in comedic-splatter (post Stuart Gordon) and its attendant special effects potential (post Carpenter, post Raimi) that mark him out from the sporadic, half-hearted attempts of the few, genre-hopping New Zealand directors before him.

The only New Zealand director prior to Jackson to hint at the enormous potential open to local directors willing to court a specialised (i.e. cult) national and international audience by working out their obsessions in exploitation genres was the pioneering David Blyth. But Jackson's excursions into this area go further than Blyth's flirtations because his roots in generic filmmaking are much deeper. Not the least of the services performed by Tony Hiles's delightful documentary, *Good Taste Made Bad Taste*, for those wishing to understand the Jackson phenomena is that it lays bare Jackson's extraordinary home apprenticeship in genre film making. It's like being let in on the formative years of a local John Waters as the documentary moves between formal interviews with Jackson's parents to extracts from his fledgling 8mm films. An excerpt from *The Dwarf Patrol* (1971) looks like nothing so much as a child's version of *Revolt of the Zombies* (1936, USA, director Victor Halperin); *The Valley* (1976) is a tribute to special effects master Ray Harryhausen who effectively authored the *Sinbad/Jason and the Argonauts* films; *James Bond* (1977) features Jackson himself as 007, displaying some swish flick knife technique on the Kapiti coast; and finally, there's *The Curse of the Grave Walker* (1981), a fully-fledged homage to Roger Corman's brand of horror film making, shot in a primitive letter-box form of cinemascope!

All these childhood and spare-time, apprentice short films – the latter ones shot while Jackson worked at another apprenticeship, photo-lithography for Wellington's *Evening Post* newspaper – work up to his breakthrough, twelfth film, *Bad Taste* (1988). Initially planned as a ten-minute film, four years later, after an extraordinary production history, it emerged as a feature for its first screening at the Cannes Film Festival and went on to win a French gore award in Paris.

III

'Slapstick: literally a comic weapon, originally called a batte, comprised of a pair of lath paddles or long, flat pieces of wood fastened at one end and used by comics (especially in the commedia dell'arte and English pantomime) to create a great deal of noise with minimum danger when another person is struck. According to one story, told by Buster Keaton, Harry Houdini used this word during the time of the Keaton-Houdini circus in which Keaton's father worked with the escape artist. Keaton points to the Evans and Hoey's rough-and-tumble act that played the Columbia wheel towards the end of the nineteenth century as the first knockabout act. It is obvious that the literal slapstick was translated into a term to describe physical and broad comedy.'[4]

My basic starting point in looking at Jackson's oeuvre is that he is fundamentally a writer/director of comedy films. This may seem too obvious to need pointing out but I think it's necessary to first state it and then elaborate upon it. Over the course of his three feature films, Jackson has employed three major modes of comedy: parody, satire, and slapstick.[5] Although each of the three films uses at least two of these modes, it is arguable that in each case one is predominant. *Bad Taste* makes particular use of the parodic mode; *Meet the Feebles* (1990) is largely cast in the satiric mode; while *Braindead* (1992) eventually gives way to unremitting slapstick.

However, Jackson is not only a writer/director working within the *form* of comedy, a trait which links him with other directors going all the way back to (his hero) Buster Keaton, but also a director working at the forefront of a specific film genre; a relatively recent mutation within the older and larger generic entity of the horror film. But unlike earlier, psychologically anchored horror films, the gore/splatter film has rapidly become a 'saturated' genre with 'saturated' codes and conventions. The term comes from an important early paper on the genre by Philip Brophy[6] who provides a succinct definition of what this 'saturation' entails in a later essay: '. . . it is not the manifestation of psychological impulses which await our individual identification due to their implicitness, but rather fictitious possibilities of an unqualified textuality awaiting our individual consumption of their absurdity.'[7]

Furthermore, within the overall confines of the post-*Blood Feast* (1963) body-horror genre, Jackson has recourse to the codes and conventions of other genres such as the alien/sci-fi genre (*Bad Taste*); the Muppet film/TV show (*Meet the Feebles*); and the retro-period movie (*Braindead*).

Thus, to bring together and sum up the points in the previous paragraphs: the particular structure and flavour of Jackson's films comes about by the operation of a comic sensibility, alternately or simultaneously employing the parodic, satiric, or slapstick mode within the contemporary body-horror genre to produce filmic effects equal to or in excess of previous efforts in this area. These films then provoke the laughter of shocked recognition because they stand in a relationship of the second-degree to the sub-genre itself (i.e. they function as comments on the genre itself). What makes possible an amalgam of, say, slapstick and splatter, to produce the neo-logistic splatstick is the fortuitous fact that both derive from a physical, body-based focus, rooted in a 'low-cultural' comedic mode and a 'low-cultural' sub-genre.[8]

IV

Left: Lionel (Timothy Balme) shoots a tranquiliser up his zombie Mum's nose. Amidst all the splatter, Braindead *is perhaps the most Oedipal horror movie ever made. Right: 'Step right up you creepo bastards!' Creepo Uncle Les (Ian Watkins) goes crazy with a meat cleaver.*

'I didn't think it'd be quite so gory as what it is but then as he said:"there's a laugh with every drop of blood, Mum."' – Peter Jackson's mother in *Good Taste Made Bad Taste.*

'We don't want, do we, to dwell unduly on the "bad taste" ingredients of comedy, but they are there, and, being touchier than more innocuous aspects of our topic, require appropriately laboured discussion.' – Raymond Durgnat.[9]

There is a remarkable sequence towards the end of *Bad Taste* in which Derek (Peter Jackson himself) is driving an unusual double-deckered utility vehicle. He pulls round a bend on a forest road only to spot an alien (film critic and filmmaker Costa Botes) brandishing a machine gun in front of a tree. He veers off the road with the exclamation 'bastaaard,' and proceeds to mow down the alien whose guts splat in a heap on the ground after he has been hit and dismembered. Then there is a cut to a close-shot of wipers clearing blood from the windscreen, behind which we see the amazed and appalled gazes of first John Lennon, then Paul McCartney (in cardboard effigies of their *Sgt. Pepper* look; out of shot are Ringo and George who share the front seat with them).

After Derek walks to the back of the van, we get a close shot of his hand pressing the face of an inset pocket calculator and, presto, a bright red chainsaw is revealed. He starts it up and advances towards the severed upper torso of the helpless alien who is playing incredulously with his dangling entrails. The alien throws a pine cone which hits Derek on his wounded head; he retaliates by kicking the alien's head and then lurches off towards the road.

What is noteworthy about this sequence is the skilful way in which it manages to combine seemingly incompatible elements from quite different areas of popular culture, all within the framework of broad slapstick or, if you will, splatstick comedy. Thus the blood and entrails of a figure from genre cinema, the sci-fi alien, are literally collided against the surface of a customised motor-vehicle, behind which sit simulated replicas of the century's major figures in popular music in their baroque-vaudeville phase. In that moment which temporarily freeze-frames the narrative with its iconographic power, Jackson the obsessive Beatles fan and Jackson the devotee of visceral splatter momentarily fuse to body forth Jackson the fashioner of arresting pop imagery. And to cap off this segment of the film, Jackson resorts to an iconographic parody of Leatherface in *The Texas Chainsaw Massacre* before lunging into a Keatonesque altercation between Derek and the alien which achieves an effect of 'violence' deflating into farce not dissimilar to some of Jean-Luc Godard's Frank Tashlin-inspired fight sequences.

V

Bad Taste climaxes in an excess of cinematic parody as Derek straps his brains (and freshly acquired additions) in with a leatherbelt (geddit!) while the chief alien, Lord Crumb, has difficulty fastening his seatbelt for lift-off from the planet in a bit of long-distance house moving. Upon waking in the airborne house, Derek looks out the window to find himself caught in a homage to the final section of *2001: A Space Odyssey*, and exclaims, 'Mummy!' Then, having cut a circular hole in the ceiling above Lord Crumb, he dives headlong onto him with chainsaw buzzing ('suck my spinning steel, shithead') and relentlessly burrows his way down and out through the alien's progressively degutted, eye-popping body. When he emerges at last from this travail, he is framed in direct address to camera: 'I'm born again, ha ha ha . . .', he says as the gore runs down his face.

And this statement has more than internal, intra-diegetic significance: it not only caps off a truly spectacular piece of splatter-fest but also adds the signature of a cinematic force at once thrust above ground into the arena of world genre film making and into a local film industry still largely looking to literary or painterly sources for its bearings. It is perhaps not only the hypothetical 'planet full of Charlie Mansons' that are at risk as the film draws to a close with Jackson, now encased in the dead alien chief's latex skin, chainsaw in his lap, shouting: 'I'm coming to get you bastards' – but the whole tradition of 'quality' New Zealand cinema.

And indeed Peter Jackson has remained true to his cinematic roots and made not one but three splatter movies. As he told *Fatal Visions* editor/*Fangoria* writer Michael Helms: 'I'm definitely not one of those guys who says they want to stop making horror movies to become a serious filmmaker. I fully intend to remain working in the genre.'[10]

VI

'Society takes its standards basically from the mother. The father may be used as a vague threat – "wait till your father gets home" – but it is the mother who sets moral standards.' – Lord Rees-Mogg, Chairman of Britain's Broadcasting Standards Council.[11]

Bad Taste has the kind of charm that only a film made over countless weekends with a bunch of mates can bring forth. Yet the very success of *Bad Taste* virtually guaranteed that Jackson would never again make a film quite like it. Using more non-actors than your average Bresson film, it possesses a covert quasi-documentary dimension in that it emerges directly from and is therefore an index of the milieu which produced it. In other words, this is Peter Jackson's repertory company, a repertory company of mates that for obvious reasons would not make another film with him.

Beginning with *Meet the Feebles*[12] and coming to fruition with *Braindead*, Jackson has joined forces with a group of writers and performers who come predominantly from various areas of New Zealand dramatic writing and performing. These include contemporaries such as Stephen Sinclair (playwright), Fran Walsh (TV scriptwriter), Danny Mulheron (actor-writer); and actors with a longer performance record: Peter Vere-Jones, Brian Sarjeant (a specialist in Teutonic impersonations: Peter Lorre's voice in *Meet the Feebles*; Erich Von Stroheim's face and voice in *Braindead*'s over the top reference to the recent claim that Nazi war criminals have taken refuge in New Zealand), Elizabeth Moody, Davina Whitehouse, Stuart Devinie, and Ian Watkin (who has worked on stage, TV, and in film from Geoff Murphy's *Wild Man* onwards).

Bad Taste has an all male cast, *Meet the Feebles* an all puppet one. *Braindead* is Jackson's first film to feature a male-female ensemble cast of professional actors. The film establishes its 1950s setting immediately in a pre-credit sequence which begins with the nostalgic sight of the New Zealand flag and the sound of the national anthem (an obligatory curtain-raiser then), before giving us an image of the youthful Queen Elizabeth II, an imperial mother on horseback in Buckingham Palace. Then it's straight into a Spielbergian spoof of gung-ho adventure hokum movies as Bill Ralston tells us: 'I'm a New Zealand zoo official and this monkey is going to Newtown.'

Following the credits we're plunged right into a fifties Wellington pastiched from New Zealand period movies (*The God Boy*, *The Scarecrow*) and fiction (*The Backward Sex*): a reconstruction of trams in the capital, Amber Tips tea, saveloys, and 'real Kiwi haircuts', sportscoats, and grey strides. Fairly quickly, the existence of two families, on opposite sides of the tramlines is established: on one side, the Latin Paquita (Diana Penalver), and her mother and father; on the other, the Anglo-Celtic Lionel and his WASPish mother. This Anglo-Latin contrastive pairing – retained so the story goes even after the Spanish co-production possibility fell through – enables Jackson, like Baz Luhrmann in *Strictly Ballroom*, to sidestep the unacceptable face of ethnic tension (i.e. *Broken Barrier* revisited) and indulge in a little bit of sub-Sauraesque Mediterranean colour.

And it isn't long either before two mother figures and two maternal residences are counterposed: Paquita's mystical seer, wise grandmother (Davina Whitehouse) in her spiritual den, the kitchen behind the shop; and Lionel's 'phallic', bad mother (Elizabeth Moody) residing in a huge two-storeyed house, introduced in a low-angle shot pattern which exactly echoes a corresponding one in *Psycho*. As Lionel enters the kitchen, the camera zooms into a close shot of his mother holding upright a huge knife in the manner of Piper Laurie in *Carrie*. In contrast to the soft tones of Paquita's mum, Mrs. Cosgrove's voice is loud, strident and authoritarian: the voice of maternal authority ordering Lionel to expel a minor instance of the 'abject'[13] (a beetle – 'the place is infested with vermin,' she shouts) from the borders of her kitchen.

A shot of a framed portrait of Lionel's deceased father (the film's producer Jim Booth), drenched with mother's crocodile tears, is soon followed by a flashback sequence triggered by the sight of an enclosed pond which Lionel notices during a trip to Wellington Zoo with Paquita. The source of the horror registered on Lionel's face will later be revealed in true *Marnie*-style fashion to stem from the childhood trauma of having witnessed the drowning in the family bath of his father and his father's lover by his mother. This then is a premonition of the film's ersatz 'primal scene' which locks its cod oedipal trajectory into place as surely as the following shot traps Lionel tightly behind the bars of an animal cage at the zoo.

This disturbing, barely repressed memory gives way to the sight of Mother spying on the couple, perhaps in the way she once did to her husband and his lover. And now we reach the narrative's moment of ignition as Mum is punished for her surreptitious voyeurism. She is bitten by the rat monkey and it won't be long before she goes the way of Harry the Hare in *Meet the Feebles*, thereby again raising the question of whether dubious AIDS references are a suitable subject for comedy.

From this point onwards, Vera Cosgrove transmogrifies from the authoritarian mother into the embodiment of the truly 'Monstrous-Feminine', '. . . totally dependent on the merging together of all aspects of the maternal figure into one – the horrifying image of woman as the archaic mother, phallic woman and castrated body represented as a single figure in the horror film.'[14]

Except that *Braindead* is not simply a horror film and we, the audience, are not simply horrified. It's a

'*The Wellington Lawnmower Massacre.*' *The gorily absurd piece de resistance of* Braindead *– cut from the R-rated US video version, known as* Dead Alive.

comedy in parodic and slapstick mode, right(?), and we're laughing at a massively foregrounded, second-degree hyper-representation of the 'Monstrous-Feminine' subtext of the modern horror film. Right! . . . Yet from time to time one does wonder whether the unremitting sadism shown by the film text towards the mother more than compensates for her crimes against the 'law of the father' (murder of her husband, a crime passionnel[?]); and the blocking of Lionel's entry into the symbolic order). In this regard, the credit 'original story idea – Stephen Sinclair' (co-screenwriter, too) uncomfortably reminds this viewer that the author of the stage play *Caramel Cream* is no stranger to the textual humiliation/punishment of women figures who for whatever reason fall foul of patriarchal imperatives. Is the suggestion of a residual streak of misogyny inappropriate here? Probably, after all the British Film Censor apparently refused to take anything in the film seriously.[15]

Soon, Mother isn't quite herself on any day, as she no longer polices the abject but is herself absorbed into it: her ear falls into her custard and she unwittingly eats it; she eats Paquita's dog; a section of skin on her face has to be super-glued back on. It isn't long before mother reaches the apparent terminus of the slide into abjection – death and reduction to the status of a corpse: '... the most sickening of wastes ... a border that has encroached upon every-thing. It is no longer I who expel. "I" is expelled.'[16] I say apparent terminus because this is a horror-comedy movie and mother gets a third act (Act One: maternal authority figure; Act Two: abject mother; Act Three: phantasmagoric mother as zombie-ghoul).

VII

'Q: Why is there so much blood in your films?
Jean-Luc Godard: That's not blood, it's red paint.' (Source unknown)
I would like to take a break from this infernal-maternal journey and discuss a particular-ly fine instance of Jackson the director of slapstick comedy.

Nurse McTavish's pronouncement of death over the prostrate corpse of Vera Cosgrove proves to be a faulty judgement as with a crash on the soundtrack mum rises from the dead to bloodily waste her. She then throws Lionel across the room, his foot hit-ting the radio switch, which provides a major component of the scene's soundtrack – a pastiche of *The Archers*, complete with theme music. Until the end of this scene, Lionel's frantic tussles with both mother and the nurse are intercut with shots of an oblivious Paquita blithely going about her business upstairs. Breaking free from mother's strangling grip and backing away from her, Lionel breaks a vase over her head as we hear these words from *The Archers*: 'Mother you're not looking well today, how about a nice cup of tea? (bang-crash; crash-bang). Sorry Mother, that were your favourite teapot; it slipped out of my hand.' After deftly ducking to avoid being caught in the two-way vice of an advanc-ing mother and nurse, Lionel hurls an item of kiwiana (a flying wall duck) into the nurse's forehead, and then manoeuvres the two of them (the nurse's semi-detached head is shot upside-down in blood gargling close-up) down into the basement. The scene ends with Lionel's manufactured laughter at the hugely cranked up volume of *The Archers* in order to drown out the cries and shouts from the basement (Paquita: 'where's your mother?').

The skilful *mise-en-scène* of this sequence turns on Lionel's double need to both evade the two newly minted murderous zombies and at the same time prevent Paquita from suspecting that anything is amiss. This is achieved by cutting between the blithe inno-cence of Paquita's calm, upstairs activity and the frenzied shenanigans downstairs, almost along the lines of bedroom farce.

VIII

In much the same way that the purpose of the narrative in, say, the musical film is to link together a number of spectacular song-dance sequences, the comedy-horror film is built around choreographies of splatter. The graveyard sequence, for one, easily outdoes the ceme-tery scene in *Return of the Living Dead*, with the Kung-Fu vicar, Father McGruder (Stuart Devinie, 'kicking arse for the lord') an especially inspired creation indeed. But in terms of sheer, all-out gory action with an awesome body count, the prolonged final sequence is the film's *piece de resistance*. It both tops previous efforts in the genre with an orgy of special effects and provides a resolution of the cod Oedipal conflicts in the narrative structure.

The mayhem of the finale lasts a staggering 35 minutes, at least a full third of the whole film and it appears to have been too much for some stomachs.[17] Rather than detail the inventive array of ways in which bodies are dismembered, rent asunder, etc., I will concentrate on tracing an ongoing set of images which threads its way through this largest section of the film.

As Lionel tries to escape from the extremely wired zombie (Jed Brophy) trapped on a toilet, by scaling up a rope into the attic, an 'umbilical cord'-shaped entrail wraps around his lower leg. Once in the attic he opens a chest, which reveals the secret of his repressed memories: photographs of his father with a lover, both of whom he now realises were drowned in the bath by his mother.

A desiccated skeleton is also in the chest and the 'umbilical cord' entrail suddenly springs out from it to begin strangling Lionel; his feet are caught, it goes up his trouser leg and then he crashes through the ceiling. As he hangs from the rope upside down, he bites through the 'umbilical cord'.

After Uncle Les's handiwork with a meat cleaver ('step right up you creepo bastards') and Lionel's travail with a trusty Masport lawnmower (rope conspicuously around his neck), he cautions Paquita thus: 'haven't seen Mum yet.' And he's right because Mum – all tooth, claw and breast, the ultimate phantasmagoric maternal monster – having dealt to Uncle Les, is not ready to let Lionel go without a fight. Lionel and Paquita escape up the 'uterine' passage of the chimney onto the roof where the final pre-Oedipal showdown occurs. Having seized the phallus (his workout with the Masport lawnmower) Lionel is now able to say: 'you don't scare me Mum.' In response her belly opens and reabsorbs Lionel back into it. However, by using the talismanic crucifix[18] from the 'good' mother he manages to make his way out in a showering heap of blood and guts. Mum falls into the burning house while Lionel and Paquita slide down a rope to safety and a happy ending.

Thus, in sum we get both the *coup de grace* in special effects gore (the climax of the film cycle beginning with *Blood Feast*) and parodic meta-commentary on the 'psychological' horror film (climax of the cycle beginning with *Psycho*). Textural 'horrality' (Brophy) runs riot inside, with sub-textual parody playing itself out up on the roof under the light of the moon. Alternately, Lionel is suspended upside down in the 'womb' of the house, within the grip of various surrogate umbilical cords, and is moving along uterine passages or being reabsorbed into his 'mother' as literally his entire world is defined as one hugely monstrous maternal space. With the 'uterine', 'monstrous–maternal' climax of *Braindead*, then, Peter Jackson circles back to the end of *Bad Taste* where, as I've already mentioned, travelling on the 'mothership' he emerges from the hollowed out interior of Lord Crumbs's body crying: 'I'm born again.'

At *Braindead*'s close, when the mother in Lionel's unconscious has been exorcised, presumably he is on his way to his rightful place in the symbolic order as he walks into the night with Paquita. But this is New Zealand in the 1950s, remember, a time when '. . . the cult of domesticity made mothering an all-embracing process, so that the young boy would grow up highly dependent on his mother. She would form his closest relationship and the most available role model.'[19] So that even as Lionel leaves the belly of his 'mother' for the arms of Paquita we should still remember that 'the excessive mothering of New Zealand boys left them permanently dependent on women'.[20]

But hang on a minute mate, this is an historian writing about the 'historical' mother whereas *Braindead* is pitched at the level of the 'psychic mother', the 'mother in the unconscious' who is theorised in Freudian discourse and later reduced in neo-Freudian revisionism and the popular media (including film).[21] It is the latter discourse(s) which the film picks up on and blows up to parodic proportions. Even so, it still manages to hold in place its 1950s sleepy hollow kiwisms alongside the dimestore Freudisms and the filmic meta-commentary. No mean feat. But then all Jackson's films have a strongly local flavour to their comedy; their props are from our garden sheds.

The first three features add up to a gore-nucopia[22] of comedy horror. But now Jackson has announced that he wants a rest from the Grand Guignol theatre of his imagination. He is working on *Heavenly Creatures*. Based on the Parker–Hulme murder case in 1950s Christchurch, at first it seems an unlikely subject for the director until one notes that it too contains two central mother figures. This time though they are genuine historical mothers. All the same they must still be appropriated in the frames and schemas of the symbolic. It will be interesting to see how Jackson and Fran Walsh (co-screenwriter on *Meet the Feebles* and *Braindead*) deal with this already highly overcoded story.

IX

'My [film] school loves Peter Jackson. Everyone knows me because I'm a New Zealander and that's where Peter Jackson's from.' – Chris Graham.[23]

Peter Jackson is an axiom . . .

NOTES

1. A treated sample from a 1950s *Cahiers du Cinema* piece by Michel Mourlet.
2. Roger Dadoun, 'Fetishism in the Horror Film', Translated by Annwyl Williams, in James Donald (Editor), *Fantasy and the Cinema*, London: BFI Publishing, 1989, p.44.
3. The most consistent and intelligent local commentators on Jackson's films have been *The Dominion's* film critic Costa Botes and Ian Pryor. In a review of the video version of *Meet the Feebles,* Botes writes: 'what Jackson has proved . . . is that it is possible for New Zealanders to make ambitious, and thoroughly entertaining genre films for the rest of the world, which aren't necessarily tainted by commercial compromise,' *The Dominion Sunday Times*, April 7, 1991, p.27.
4. Don B. Wilmeth, *The Language of American Entertainment*, Westport: Greenwood Press, 1981, quoted in Steve Neale and Frank Krutnik, *Popular Film and Television Comedy*, London and New York: Routledge, 1990, p.21.
5. For a discussion of these terms see Neale and Krutnik, section one.
6. Philip Brophy, 'Horrality – the Textuality of Contemporary Horror Films', *Art and Text,* Number Eleven, Spring 1983, p.87. This article and several subsequent ones by Brophy are indispensable to an understanding of the mechanics of the contemporary body-horror film.
7. Philip Brophy, 'The Body Horrible: Some Notions, Some Points, Some Examples', *Intervention* 21/22, 1998, p.59.
8. Linda Williams, 'Film Bodies: Gender, Genre, and Excess', *Film Quarterly*, Volume 44, Number Four, Summer 1991, p.4.
9. Raymond Durgnat, *The Crazy Mirror: Hollywood Comedy and the American Image*, New York: Delta, 1970, p.30.
10. Michael Helms, 'Action Jackson', *Fangoria* 121, April 1993, p.33.
11. Quoted in Valerie Grove, 'Standard Procedures', *The Dominion*, September 17, 1992, p.11.
12. *Bad Taste* and *Braindead* are the main focus of this article. For a detailed discussion of *Meet the Feebles* in relation to the animated and puppet film see Ian Pryor, 'Meet Your Creature Feature: Foam-Rubber Depravity in *Meet the Feebles*', *Illusions,* Number Thirteen, March 1990, pp.7-11.
13. The contemporary locus classicus of discussion of the 'abject' is, of course, Julia Kristeva, *Powers of Horror: an Essay on Abjection*, translated by Leon S. Roudiez, New York: Columbia University Press, 1982.
14. Barbara Creed, 'Horror and the Monstrous-Feminine – an Imaginary Abjection', *Screen*, Volume 27, Number One, Jan-Feb 1986, p.63. Creed's paper is the major, perhaps only instance of the application of Kristeva's theory of abjection to the study of the modern horror film.

15. See Helms, op.cit., p.29. Note too that *Caramel Cream* is a thoroughly realist work whilst *Braindead*, although illusionistic, cannot qualify for the epithet realist.

16. Julia Kristeva, op.cit., pp. 3-4; quoted in Creed, p.47.

17. For example, Brian McDonnell who writes of *Braindead*: 'by the end . . . we are reduced to repetitive, ultimately boring, hideous violence,' 'Viewing', *North and South*, September 1992, p.125. This comment echoes an earlier one by the same writer on *Meet the Feebles*: '. . . its nastiness is too unrelieved and the gore and sex and vomiting and bodily wastes become too much,' 'Viewing', *North and South*, December 1990, p.155.

18. Lionel has recourse to this talismanic crucifix at several moments of extreme danger in the final section of *Braindead*. Roger Dadoun's comments on the significance of the cross in opposition to the fetishistic form of the phallus (whether it be embodied as a blood-sucking vampire or a flesh-eating ghoul) are very interesting here: 'This antagonism between the cross and the vampire could easily be seen as the survival of a conflict between primitive religions attached to the figure of the mother, which maintain magic and mystical relations with the animal world*, and Christianity as the religion of the father and especially the son . . .', Dadoun, op.cit., p.58. *Note: Before Lionel's mother rises for the last time she receives a massive dose of animal stimulant mistakenly administered as a 'euthanasiac' poison.

19. Jock Phillips, 'Mummy's Boys: Pakeha Men and Male Culture in New Zealand', in P. Bunkle and B. Hughes (Editors), *Women in New Zealand Society*, Auckland: George Allen and Unwin, 1980, p.238.

20. Ibid, p.239.

21. The distinction between the 'historical' mother and the 'psychic' mother is elaborated in E. Ann Kaplan, 'Motherhood and Representation: from Postwar Freudian Figurations to Postmodernism', in Kaplan (Editor), *Psychoanalysis and Cinema*, New York and London: AFI/Routledge, 1990, pp. 128-142.

22. This phrase is taken from John McCarty, *Splatter Movies: Breaking the Last Taboo*, New York: Fantaco Enterprises, 1981.

23. A New Zealand filmmaker studying at New York's School of Visual Arts, quoted in Andrew Beach, 'Hollywood, Here I Come', *The Dominion*, June 8, 1993, p.7.

DEAD ALIVE (aka BRAINDEAD) Back
A Retrospective by Guillermo Del Toro

in 2001, when Peter Jackson's *The Lord of the Rings: The Fellowship of the Ring* was released, more than a few stunned filmgoers looked at each other in astonishment, asking, 'Who knew?'

Ahem . . . I did.

OK, others did too. Many remembered Jackson's deft turn with *Heavenly Creatures*. This film augured a prestigious future for a master storyteller.

But no kidding, I knew much earlier than that. I had seen *Dead Alive*.

In *The Name of the Rose*, Umberto Eco writes: 'Books speak of books: it is as if they spoke among themselves.' One could say the same about movies made by filmmakers who love movies passionately. Peter Jackson is that sort of director: His movies talk of other movies, essentially his cinematic obsessions. Miniatures, models, Harryhausen, gorefests . . . it's as if they all 'spoke among themselves'.

Of all the grotesque highlights of Braindead, *the blackest laughs come from the zombified nurse's mutated baby, Selwyn.*

Nowhere is this feeling more evident than in *Dead Alive* (*Braindead*, to the cognoscenti). Here, he took his passion to the limit. Even years later, it has never – and could never – go wilder than this.

The film opens on 'Skull Island' (Kong, anyone?), where we plunge into a frantic chase down a steep, dusty canyon somewhere 'near Sumatra' (yeah, right). Cavorting natives close in on a scholarly nerd and his ragged native assistant. They carry a cage containing a deadly creature, the monstrous, fierce 'rat monkey'. From the outset, Jackson's camera is frantic, unnaturally alive and infused with holy anger. After this brief Indiana Jones-style prelude, Jackson gets down to business. The malignant rat monkey – the carrier of a zombifying virus – bites the nerdy scientist, and he's gleefully chopped to pieces in order to 'save him' from infection.

The startling combination of comedy and the grotesque starts strong and builds by sheer force of will. If the paradigm dictates that the storyteller must top himself as the tale progresses, Jackson has set forth almost impossible stakes. Well, don't worry, he has plenty in store.

As a film buff, Jackson embraces beloved movie conventions with a tender, almost demented faith. He uses model planes against fake skies, prefiguring and surpassing the zest of *Kill Bill*. He crafts pus-oozing orifices that out-Savini Savini. He makes Sam Raimi's camerawork look like that of Yasujiro Ozu. The melodramatic love story and the actors' emotive gesticulations recall silent-film pantomime. Even the score seems to jangle from a silent-film pianola.

The film's 'Mother' is Mrs. Bates times ten. The hero's house looms over the town like the *Psycho* mansion. The rat monkey leaps out from a Harryhausen production. Hey, there's Forry Ackerman snapping pictures in the zoo scene!!

Here is Jackson's love for movies – all movies – exploding all at once on the screen. A furious, twitching spasm of joy. Remember the projectile vomit in *The Exorcist*? Well, maybe Jackson is possessed by Pazuzu and he's here to 'kick ass for the Lord' and create the gore movie to end all gore movies. His ambition was to bite big, but damn, does he chew it down. All the way to the bone.

Many moments in this film will live forever in my memory:

The merciless, fetishistic close-up of Mother's heel as it crushes the rat monkey's skull.

The obsessive zoom into Mother's pulsating, infected arm, paralleling her son's first lovemaking and the dire omens of the Tarot cards that the local oracle woman spreads.

The brutal dinner-table scene in which the zombified Mother decomposes into her guests' soup.

Paquita, our innocent heroine, realising that her future mother-in-law has just eaten her dog, raw.

The kung fu-fighting priest and his remarkable zeal.

The 'baby in the park' scene.

The lawnmower massacre . . . Ah!! How glorious!!

And finally, proving that he could in fact top himself, Jackson leaves the best for last: the 'return to the womb', which is not only unique in film history but reprises the main character's central conflict. Bravo!!

Dead Alive is a driven movie. An exercise in individual filmmaking that remains at the peak of its genre. If ever a movie could be accused of stylistic gluttony, of pushing the envelope and breaking *all* taboos, *Dead Alive* is that film. It showcases the joys of cannibalism as it devours every sacred institution: motherhood, church and state. Each scene is pregnant with invention, epitomising and concluding the wave of eighties gore cinema. First released in 1992, it stands tall as a reminder of better, braver times when we didn't hide behind political correctness and postmodern irony.

Back then, as the credits rolled, I realised that Peter Jackson was one of the most committed, detail-orientated, obsessive, brave and adventurous filmmakers ever to walk the Earth. A madman who could tackle and succeed in making the impossible. A man who tramples all institutions, only to cherish and celebrate love above all things mundane.

So, when people looked at each other and raised an eyebrow and asked, 'Who knew?' . . .

Well, sorry, guys – I did.

Guillermo Del Toro is the director of Cronos, Mimic, The Devil's Backbone, Blade II *and* Hellboy

HEAVENLY
CREATURES

HEAVENLY CREATURES
by Steve Braunias

Peter Jackson was still editing his latest feature when I spoke to him about the only death scene in *Heavenly Creatures*: 'It's done in a way that will give people an impression of what happened, without going into graphic detail. I filmed shots that I refused to use in the end because I felt too sickened to include them.'

Jackson and his long-time co-writer, Fran Walsh, have clearly had an attack of the sensitives. His buzz-words for the movie that will premiere at the upcoming Cannes Film Festival are 'Compassion, humanity and sympathy.' But there's no mystery to his approach. It just makes sense. Jackson's film deals with a sad and brutal murder which is still all too real for the citizens of Christchurch, the genteel New Zealand city spread out on the flat banks of the lazy Avon river, where a casual afternoon walk on June 22nd, 1954, ended when two teenage girls took turns at battering one of their mothers to death with a brick wrapped up in a stocking.

Juliet Hulme, fifteen, and Pauline Parker, sixteen, had been best friends for two years. They met at Christchurch Girls High School. Juliet's father, Henry, an eminent physicist, had emigrated from Britain to the colonies and became the Rector of Christchurch University College; Pauline's father worked as a fishmonger, and her mother ran a boarding house. While it seems that both families were embarrassed by their class difference, they had a stronger reason for trying to separate Juliet and Pauline. An extract from Pauline's diary. 'We have now learnt the peace of the thing called Bliss, the joy of the thing called Sin.'

Hence the screaming headlines in the local and international press: 'Lesbian Schoolgirl Killers'. During the trial, Pauline's secret diary became a matter of public record. It described how she and Juliet bathed together – and how they began their plan to 'moider Mother.'

April 29th, 1954: 'Anger against Mother boiled up inside me as it is she who is one of the main obstacles in my path. Suddenly a means of ridding myself of this obstacle occurred to me. If she were to die.'

April 30th: 'I told Deborah [her pet name for Juliet] of my intentions and she is rather worried but does not disagree violently.'

June 19th: 'We have worked it out carefully and are both thrilled by the idea.'

June 21st: 'Deborah rang and we decided to use a rock in a stocking rather than a sandbag . . . The happy event is to take place tomorrow afternoon.'

And so Juliet, Pauline and Pauline's mother Honora caught a bus to Victoria Park. They stopped for some scones at the tea kiosk. Then they ambled along a leafy path. Juliet secretly placed a pink brooch stone on the ground. At 3.05pm, as Honora bent down to look, Pauline hit her over the head. So did Juliet. The coroner later reported 45 discernible injuries. Honora died minutes after the attack. Both girls pleaded guilty. After sentencing, they never saw each other again.

Kate Winslet as Juliet Hulme and Melanie Lynskey as Pauline Parker (aka Rieper, her parents unmarried). Juliet's father (Clive Merrison) regards the Heavenly Creatures *(1994).*

Jackson says, 'We tried not to make *Heavenly Creatures* depressing. It is sad, but there's a lot of humour in it as well. Juliet and Pauline were people. We're not making a film about murderers – we're making a film about human beings.'

Filmed entirely in Christchurch over eleven weeks, starring Melanie Lynskey as Pauline and Kate Winslet as Juliet, *Heavenly Creatures* managed to pip two similar projects to the post although it follows other perspectives on the crime. A year after the trial, Kiwi playwright Bruce Mason performed *The Verdict*; Tom Gurr and H. H. Cox collaborated on a trash novel, *Obsession*, in 1958; while last year saw Michelanne Forster's stage play *Daughters of Heaven* and the book *Parker and Hulme: A Lesbian View* by academics Alison Laurie and Julie Glamuzina.

So what's new about *Heavenly Creatures*? Quite possibly, the truth. Jackson and Walsh have dug up more research than any previous efforts, the setting of events is certainly more realistic than the phony stage production (blood gushing from the floorboards!), and the leading players seem to be more, er, fleshed out than before.

That includes Honora – the victim who has been ignored in most accounts. 'For sure, that's the way we felt too,' continues Jackson. 'But we found people who had known her quite well, and we found the only photo of her that I've *ever* seen taken close to the time of the murder. Honora was basically a very nice person who came into conflict with her daughter, but that's not unusual. The thing that was ultimately clear to us is that there's nothing unusual about what happened – only the consequence of it all. When they murdered her, the girls thought they were doing what was best for them. We had to present that fact while showing they weren't justified at all. It's really a murder story without villains.'

Jackson says he and Walsh also spoke with fifteen of Juliet and Pauline's former classmates ('Only one had talked to both Forster and Laurie') as well as kiosk manageress Agnes Ritchie (the last person, other than the killers, to see Honora alive) and a retired policeman who had rescued the official mug-shots of the girls. 'Police history was his hobby. He knew the importance of the mug-shots and had them in a drawer by his bed. They are the only copies in existence.'

However, Jackson and Walsh were given short shrift at the girls' school. 'They told us to go away,' remarks Jackson. 'Their attitude is that they find it a personal affront to even mention their names. They've tried to wipe them out of existence. Their class yearbooks don't exist. They have class photographs going back two million years – oh, but not *those* ones! To me, the school was no different to the day after the murder when the headmistress got up at assembly and said, "No girl is to discuss a certain matter." A certain matter!'

The brush-off couldn't deter Jackson from filming in the girls' original classroom. Since the school moved, the old location is now used as a community centre. It only took a little effort to persuade the Women's Embroidery Guild to denude their walls and allow Jackson to transform it into a replica of Juliet and Pauline's 3A form room.

'It's not a political film. It has no agenda other than "This is what we think happened, and why,"' explains Jackson, referring to Laurie and Glamuzina's book. By contrast, their treatise examines the murder as a result of homophobia. Laurie writes in her introduction, 'These days, we would hope that two young lesbians in an isolated position could ring up Lesbian Line and get advice.' Jackson says *Heavenly Creatures* avoids any attempt at making a similarly glib conclusion.

The director also decided against making any contact with either Juliet or Pauline. After they had served five years in jail, Juliet is said to have left New Zealand immediately, and later worked for a US domestic airline. Pauline remained on probation until 1965 and is believed to be carrying out office duties in a Catholic institution.

Junior defence counsel Brian McLelland believed that both girls were mad. During the trial, they seemed more interested in the play they had written. 'They really believed it was so brilliant that it would be filmed in Hollywood,' he told the Christchurch press. 'They were going over there to arrange all this. The whole thing was so ridiculous.' With *Heavenly Creatures* coming to a multiplex near you soon, maybe not.

*H*EAVENLY *C*REATURES
reviewed at the Wellington Film Festival by Bill Gosden

Peter Jackson was outrageous before, but the outrageousness of his first G-rated movie is something else entirely: he catches us up in the heart-thumping breathlessness of two schoolgirls, giddy with joy and fright at the brilliance of each other's romantic aspirations. *Heavenly Creatures* is the whirling, soaring rhapsody that ensues when two misfit imaginations suddenly fit – and lock into a single empowering vision. Theirs is certainly not the Christchurch of punts and daffodils being perpetrated in the fifties *Pictorial Parade* with which Jackson introduces his setting. But it may be the equally improbable city where a schoolgirl choir imprisons the lilt of a gospel hymn in prim, clipped elocution: you can't always tell when Christchurch is being refracted through the protagonists' conviction that they live in the stuffiest city on earth.

But you know for sure when their romantic vision of the place prevails. Not since *Utu* have there been such ecstatic flights of fancy in New Zealand film making. And there's never been such light-headed delight in cinema magic. Special effects conjure up castles in the air, then rush you through their portals and up, up, up to the parapets. And just as you're thinking, whoooaa, this is getting nutty, there's the frisson as you remember: this 'intense' friendship between the teenage girls Pauline Rieper and Juliet Hulme is famous for a reason. Together they hatched a plot to murder Pauline's mother – and then, God help us, murder her is what they did. 40 years on, this story is still recalled in New Zealand as a warning of the dangers of 'unnatural' closeness between girls: what possessed these daughters of darkness? Jackson, who actively sought infamy in his earlier films, has had ample opportunity to test the starch of polite society's aversion. His own frenzied, transforming visions have not been found universally endearing. This may help explain the utter clarity of his imaginative identification with the girls. It does not account for the wonderful new fluency in this work, the assurance of tone, or the refinement and ebullient funniness of a script – co-written with Fran Walsh – which shows us plenty that the fantasists don't see. His heavenly creatures may have been tragically mis-

'He can be quiet, but he's an emotional man . . . I'm telling you, when we wept, he wept' – Kate Winslet. Jackson on the set with cinematographer Alun Bollinger.

understood, but we're given a fair and touching understanding of the decorous little English province that they so unnerved, and which they helped to unmake. For a film that takes its audience on such an emotional joyride, *Heavenly Creatures* is detailed and resonant on many levels. Every performance is securely and vividly etched into an apparently insecure surface. The two young leads embody their characters indelibly. The film appears to swirl about them: Alun Bollinger's breathtakingly fluid CinemaScope is an equally crucial player. There's no debate; this one was nourished all the way to startling fruition in New Zealand. And it is, in the best possible way, sensational.

HEAVENLY CREATURES
reviewed by Stella Bruzzi

The 1950s. Two blood-spattered schoolgirls run into the garden of a suburban house, crying out, 'Mother's terribly hurt.' The true story of how Pauline Parker and Juliet Hulme got to this traumatic point begins in 1953, with Juliet's first day at Christchurch Girls'

High School. Pauline, a native New Zealander who has been at the school some time, is a loner until she is put with Juliet, a new girl from England. Despite their very different backgrounds, the two strike up an immediate and exclusive rapport. They are linked by their childhood illnesses, their adulation of the tenor Mario Lanza and the fantasy world they create together: the non-Christian Fourth World of 'music, art and pure enjoyment'.

For Christmas, Pauline is given a diary in which she documents her life with Juliet and the imaginative realm of the 'novel' that they embark on together. The mythical Borovnia, a medieval tale of King Charles and Queen Deborah, soon consumes their real existence. When they discover, as Juliet puts it, the 'key' to the Fourth World, the extra part of the human brain that only ten people possess, this is where they escape to as fantasy and actuality become interchangeable.

At school one day, Juliet is rushed to a clinic to be treated for a recurrence of her TB. Despite their daughter's illness, the Hulmes spend the summer months in England, leaving Juliet alone. Separated for two months, Juliet and Pauline write to each other as Charles and Deborah, and when Pauline is allowed to visit she tells her that John, the student lodging in her house, is madly in love with her. Despite Juliet's protestations that this has broken her heart, Pauline allows John into her bed, only to be discovered by her father, who throws him out. However, she later loses her virginity to John.

On their return to New Zealand, Juliet's parents begin to sense that the friendship with Pauline may be unhealthy. The girls' time together is rationed and Pauline is sent to a psychiatrist. Due to the separation from Juliet, Pauline's schoolwork suffers. She decides to train as a typist, but meanwhile the two plot their escape to Hollywood where they hope to sell the rights to their novel. Juliet finds her mother in bed with another man, precipitating divorce proceedings from her father. It is decided that Juliet will stay with South African relatives; the girls' anguish at the prospect of separation reaches hysterical proportions. Pauline stops speaking to her parents and Juliet begs for Pauline to be allowed to go with her to South Africa. As compensation, Pauline is permitted to stay at the Hulmes' house; the girls sleep together and plan the murder of Honora, Pauline's mother. When the day arrives, the girls take Honora out to a local park where they hit her repeatedly over the head with a brick.

Captions tell us that the girls were found guilty of murder in what came to be known as the Parker-Hulme affair. They were released in 1959 on the condition that they never met again.

When she arrives at Christchurch High School, Juliet is brought into Pauline's French class, superciliously eyeing a sea of pupils with cardboard name tags tied around their necks – a penchant of the mistress who makes her classes use French names rather than their own. This kooky small-town fifties, with its obsolete rituals and garish pastel shades, forms the backdrop for what is essentially an exploration of the captivating and bizarre world of that even kookier phenomenon, the imaginative, pubescent schoolgirl. Like Tom Kalin's *Swoon*, Peter Jackson's film abandons the conventional investigative route and approaches a true-life murder case via the obsessive, private relationship between its central characters. Juliet and Pauline shroud themselves in a world of ritual and fantasy which increasingly severs its ties with the conformity of what lies outside, eventually repositioning fifties

Christchurch as one of the characters in their jointly conceived novel. Juliet and Pauline, the self-designated Heavenly Creatures of the title, script their own rites of passage, from kneeling at an altar to worship-worthy men to solemnly burning their Mario Lanza record collection on a funeral pyre after hitting upon the idea of killing off Honora.

Heavenly Creatures is a beautifully choreographed descent into the realm of the personal and therefore (to an outsider) the inexplicable. Initially we observe with curious detachment as the girls strip down to their underwear and dance around trees to a lush Lanza soundtrack proclaiming, 'She's the one for me'; but we are then jolted into their 'Fourth World', the real hills dissolving into their ornamental fantasy paradise. Such literalising of characters' fantasy worlds can have embarrassing results, as it did in *Sirens*, which made one wish that people never allowed their deepest sexual desires to surface at all. What disciplines the excesses of *Heavenly Creatures* is that the subconscious sequences are always clearly located within the teenage imaginations that concoct them; they're not some abstract, ashamedly adult vision of what Peter Jackson might assume constitutes dreamland.

It's significant, for instance, that Borovnia surfaces in both everyday life and the life of fantasy. In one evocative scene, Juliet and Pauline – as Charles and Deborah – are going through the birth of their son in the prosaic setting of Juliet's bedroom, a scene reminiscent of many a childish piece of role-playing. Scenes such as this (and the use of Pauline's diary entries as voice-over) ground the more outrageous flights of fancy into the animated Borovnia, a medieval castle populated by plasticine figures. Perhaps the most compelling and disquieting are the sequences in which the two worlds collide, as when Juliet imagines a figure decapitating a visiting vicar.

Whereas most films that deal with the relationship between the real and the unconscious (from *Spellbound* to *Sirens*) never lose sight of the dividing line between the two, *Heavenly Creatures* dwells on the smudging of those boundaries. The film's most intense, lyrical and absurd moment comes near the end, when Juliet mouths along to a Lanza aria, as a monochrome sequence shows her family united and happy. Although the film assiduously avoids making any definite comment about the girls' morality, their sanity or their motivation for the killing, such scenes capture the strange euphoric loneliness of their world of sword-bearers, matinee idols and self-glorification. As the girls repeatedly pummel Honora on the head, the vibrantly coloured violence is intercut with more black and white, now showing Juliet on a ship, joyously cocooned between her parents and waving to Pauline on the quayside. These are the last shots of the film, which ends therefore not with a neat return to where it began, but with an enigmatic, elliptical allusion to an emotional and psychological turmoil that remains unresolved.

This single idealised image sums up the strange sense of distance which pervades *Heavenly Creatures*: a distance which extends beyond the obvious separation between reality and fantasy, to touch on such diverse things as Pauline's detached third-person diary descriptions of 'these lovely two' or the way in which the camera, although often showing the girls in extreme close-up, always gives the impression of observing, of trying to understand but never quite getting there. Accompanying the details of the girls' sentence and subsequent release is Lanza's rendition of 'You'll Never Walk Alone', at once poignant and puzzling. For all its sensuousness, its detail and its affection, *Heavenly Creatures* leaves Juliet and Pauline as mysterious as they were at the beginning. Although difficult to attribute, this is somehow the source of the film's brilliance; without casting judgement over the girls' actions, it never seeks to explain them. After Pauline and Juliet sleep together, the diary entry refers to 'the joy of that thing called sin', which could be read as being specifically about sex or about everything besides. The whole film is a breathtaking blend of the particular and the opaque, a deft juggling act with the two undefinable notions of joy and sin.

Making a Film Out of the Horror of Mother Murder
by Bernard Weinraub

It remains the most sensational murder case ever in New Zealand. In 1954 two girls, Pauline Yvonne Parker, sixteen, and Juliet Marion Hulme, fifteen, were convicted of brutally killing Pauline's mother.

'What attracted me to this story,' said Peter Jackson, the 33-year-old New Zealand-born director of *Heavenly Creatures*, 'was that it was complicated, about two people who are not evil, not psychopaths but totally out of their depth. Their emotions got out of control.'

The film, recently released by Miramax Films, won prizes at the Venice and Toronto film festivals, and has opened to generally strong reviews in New York and Los Angeles. Writing in *The New York Times*, Janet Maslin said that its 'exaggerated sweetness is every bit as chilling as more familiar masculine reveries about violence and irrational revenge'.

During an interview the other day at a West Hollywood hotel, Mr. Jackson called the film 'a totally un-Hollywood concept'.

'Can you imagine me walking into an executive's office and pitching a film about two girls who do this cold-blooded, sort of premeditated murder and making them and their victim sympathetic?' he said. 'Can you imagine me saying I want to make a film where ultimately the motive for the murder is not that obvious?' (The film was financed by the New Zealand Film Commission and German financiers.)

The notion of making *Heavenly Creatures* began with the screenwriter Frances Walsh, who had collaborated with Mr. Jackson on his most recent projects, *Meet the Feebles*, an offbeat puppet film, and *Dead Alive*, a zombie film. The two have lived together for more than six years near Wellington, New Zealand's capital city.

'What the girls did was extreme, extraordinary and horrific,' said Ms. Walsh over the phone from New Zealand. 'But in some ways it's what other adolescents might fantasise about. Not only did they have a rich fantasy life, not only did they have an intense friendship, but they actually went through with their fantasy. It's heart stopping, I can't rationalise or understand or justify what they did. It's still a mystery.'

On the face of it, the reason for the murder was grotesquely simple: Honora Parker refused to allow her daughter, Pauline, to move to South Africa with her closest friend,

Pauline rains deadly blows on the head of her mother, Honora (Sarah Peirse). With unprecedented restraint, Jackson discarded some of the bloodier shots of the tragedy.

Juliet Hume. Mrs. Parker was then beaten to death by the two girls.

The so-called Parker-Hulme murder case returned to the headlines last summer with the news that Juliet Hulme, who had been convicted of helping murder her friend's mother, was living quietly in a Scottish village and successfully writing mysteries under the name Anne Perry.

The whereabouts of her friend, Pauline, is unknown. The two girls, after serving about five years in separate prisons, were given new identities and placed on parole for about another five years. The two have apparently not seen each other in more than 40 years.

Mr. Jackson said he deplored a continuing hunt by the news media for Pauline Parker. 'It's horrible,' he said. 'It's not that these girls are Nazi war criminals.' As for Miss Hulme, she has mostly kept to herself. She took no part in making the film and will not profit from it.

Though the murder seemed driven by inchoate motives, there was an intense passion – one that apparently never reached sexual involvement – between the two girls. And both of them maintained an almost feverish fantasy life that blotted out reality, something Mr. Jackson said he could identify with.

'If you're an only child you spend a lot of time by yourself and you develop a strong ability to entertain yourself, to conjure up fantasy,' said the director, who grew up in Wellington as the only child of a local civil servant.

In real life, the girls were both gifted writers with fertile imaginations. As their friend-ship intensified, they talked and wrote of what they called their 'fourth world', a fairytale kingdom called Borovnia.

'They used this world as an outlet for violent fantasies,' Mr. Jackson said. 'Their stories about Borovnia became increasingly violent and bloodthirsty.'

In *Heavenly Creatures*, this world is depicted in sequences that combine digital technology and, representing the often-violent 'Borovnian' populace, Plasticine figures.

Mr. Jackson said he had initially imagined using actors dressed in medieval clothes. Then he met someone who had visited Juliet's home in the 1950's and remembered seeing Plasticine figures that the girl had carefully constructed. 'I thought: "What a fascinating idea. Why don't we have Pauline and Juliet entering into a world populated by Plasticine figures rather than actors wearing costumes?"'

Mr. Jackson has long been enamoured of special effects. *King Kong* and *Batman* with Adam West were favourite films early on, and through his childhood and teenage years he constructed monsters out of rubber and wire, created fantasy forests around the family garden and, with a home camera, used his enthusiastic parents as actors in various movies.

He left school at seventeen, wanting to find a job in the movie business. To support himself he worked for seven years as a photoengraver on *The Wellington Evening Post*, a job that helped finance his first film, a dark science-fiction comedy called *Bad Taste*. The New Zealand Film Commission also chipped in, and the actors were Mr. Jackson's fellow photoengravers.

Next came *Meet the Feebles*, which became a hit in New Zealand, and then *Dead Alive*, which has won numerous awards at film festivals and has a cult following in this country.

Mr. Jackson will start making *The Frighteners*, a ghost movie and thriller, next year. Although Robert Zemeckis, director of *Forrest Gump*, is producing, and some prominent actors will undoubtedly appear in the film, Mr. Jackson insisted that he had not gone Hollywood. The movie will be made in New Zealand.

'Too often you see film makers from other countries who have made interesting, original films, and then they come here and get homogenised into being hack Hollywood directors,' he said. 'I don't want to fall into that.

'I have a freedom that's incredibly valuable,' he said. 'Obviously my freedom is far smaller in scale than people like Zemeckis and Spielberg have here. But it's comparable. I can dream up a project, develop it, make it, control it, release it. Could I get that here?'

It's All Frightfully Romantic!
Heavenly Creatures and the Horrors of Adolescence
by Peter N. Chumo II

Peter Jackson's *Heavenly Creatures* (script by Jackson and Frances Walsh) is an imaginative rendering of the Parker-Hulme Affair, the most sensational crime in New Zealand history, and a unique generic hybrid – a horror film for the art house audience. It is a true crime tale with a layering of horror conventions that enable the audience to go inside the minds of two schoolgirls, Pauline Parker and Juliet Hulme (who changed her name to Anne Perry and has gone on to become a best-selling mystery writer), who planned and executed the murder of Pauline's mother. In his review of the film, *Rolling Stone's* Peter Travers writes that the film's subject is the 'Sexual hysteria that drives two fifteen-year-old schoolgirls to murder.'[1] What Travers does not begin to suggest, however, is the different kinds of 'sexual hysteria' in the film – both the hysteria that overcomes the girls and the hysteria over sex that envelops their parents – and the ways in which the horror genre becomes the creative force in the girls' imaginative lives, particularly in the fantasy world they create in response to the cold, remote adult world.

The film begins with newsreel footage extolling the virtues of life in fifties Christchurch, New Zealand. Such sites as the manicured gardens, girls' school, and college all present a tranquil picture of a well-ordered community (where, according to the historical footage, 'daffodils bloom gay and golden') just before it faces the horror of a real-life murder.

The opening newsreel sequence presents a kind of impersonal, 'official' view of the city – a presentation of how the community sees itself and how it wishes others to see it. As the historical footage draws to a close, we hear the screams of Pauline (Melanie Lynskey) and Juliet (Kate Winslet). The film then cuts to a point-of-view shot as we race through the foliage of the forest, even though we do not yet know whose point of view we have assumed. The script gives the direction 'CAMERA CRASHES out of bush and races up a dark bushy track.'[2] This point-of-view shot that unbalances the audience comes straight out of the horror genre – it is, after all, a traditional way of presenting the monster or killer's view before showing us the monster itself. Metaphorically, the horror genre overtakes the newsreel (first on the soundtrack and then on the screen), the film in essence announcing that a supposedly objective form will not do justice to this story.

As the following shots reveal that 'their clothes, and Pauline's face, are splattered with blood,' our place in the horror genre is confirmed. Yet an interesting ambiguity surrounds these opening shots; an audience unfamiliar with the real-life events of the story would wonder if these two girls are victims escaping a bloody encounter or are criminals fleeing the scene of the crime. This ambiguity is emblematic of the film's overall theme, for while the girls have just bludgeoned to death Pauline's mother, Honora (Sarah Peirse), in a horrific scene we shall see at film's end, the film will also offer a sympathetic account of two girls coming to terms with their sexuality and, like many teenagers, feeling like victims to the sexual feelings they are experiencing (metaphorically, the blood running down Pauline's legs in our first glimpses of her could just as well be menstrual blood).

Intercut with the run through the woods is the girls' fantasy of a different run – aboard a ship that will carry them away to South Africa with Juliet's parents. The pre-title sequence, then, captures three levels of life for the girls: first the tranquillity of the city, then their post-murder frenzy, and finally their private fantasy of an idealised future. From the start, the script's inter-cutting sets up the conflict between the larger community and the girls' point of view and foreshadows violence as their direct reaction to the community's social norms. As the film progresses, the girls' increasingly violent fantasy life becomes both a reaction to their community (uptight, authoritarian schoolteachers and well-meaning but ineffectual parents) and a path to the murder itself.

Fantasy Worlds and the Allure of Horror

The shy, plain, lower-class Pauline and the self-assured, attractive, almost aristocratic Juliet (she chooses the name 'Antoinette' in French class) at first seem to have little in common. However, they are united by a passion for the arts and a history of childhood disease (bad chests and bone diseases are 'frightfully romantic' to Juliet in a turn of phrase that seems to sum up many of life's pleasures for her). Bodily illness, a kind of internal violence, becomes the catalyst for their friendship as Pauline shows Juliet the scars on her leg as if they were badges of honour. The girls retreat from the real world, create an imaginary kingdom called Borovnia, populate it with royal figures, and spin elaborate tales about their beloved characters. Moreover, they create clay models of their characters, as if their own bodies, with a history of illness, needed fantasy surrogates. Creating the body perfect, a horror trope that goes back at least as far as *Frankenstein*, is given a fresh twist in *Heavenly Creatures* – the creation takes place within Pauline's and Juliet's imaginations, which we are able to enter.

They even enact a mock birth scene in which Juliet, as their Borovnian heroine, Deborah, gives birth to a son, Diello, in a playful version of the classic 'birth of the monster' scene in so many horror films:

CLOSE-UP . . . Juliet's face twisted with pain. She gasps as if in labour. Short, harsh panting. Pauline looks panic-stricken.
PAULINE
   Push! . . . Breathe! . . . It's coming! . . . Oh, God!
PULL OUT . . . to reveal Juliet lying on her bed, in child-birth pose. Her pregnant stomach is pushing at the seams of her school dress. Juliet wails . . . Pauline pulls out a pillow from between Juliet's legs, her face a mixture of surprise and elation.
PAULINE
   It's a boy! Deborah . . . we've got a son and heir!
Pauline hands Juliet the pillow. She cradles it in her arms.
JULIET
   I shall call him Diello.
PAULINE
   You're such an incredible woman.
JULIET
   I couldn't have done it without you, Charles.

From the beginning, they imagine an active sex life for Deborah and her beloved Charles, in which he 'tries to have his way with her morning, noon and night', and a violent streak in Diello, who 'slaughters his nannies whenever the fancy takes him' and, according to Juliet, 'Although only ten, Diello has thus far killed 57 people and shows no desire to stop'; sexual desire and violence toward authority figures are linked in their imagination, just as their own desire for union will lead finally to matricide. Indeed, the violent details in their stories become the first hints of the violence they will bring to the real world.

What seems a kind of innocent role-playing (with Pauline as the father Charles) soon becomes a tool of revenge as a life-size clay figure of Diello comes alive in the girls' imagination to avenge them against their supposed enemies. For example, when Juliet is sick in the hospital and an unctuous clergyman comes to speak to her, she envisions Diello dragging him away to be beheaded:

During Reverend Norris's speech . . . **CAMERA** closes in to **BIG CLOSE-UP** of Juliet's face. Reverend Norris's voice fades away . . .
SUDDENLY!!!
A silhouetted figure rises up behind Reverend Norris . . . a lumpy hand closes around his throat!
REVEREND NORRIS
   Aaaaarghhh!!!
Diello - the Plasticine figurine, now life-size - drags Reverend Norris off his feet and across the room. Reverend Norris kicks and struggles as Diello hauls him through the doorway onto . . .
EXT. BOROVNIA CASTLE COURTYARD - DAY
. . . a scaffold in the town square of Borovnia. A medieval fantasy kingdom. **NICHOLAS** watches from a street corner.
Reverend Norris is grabbed by two **BURLY PLASTICINE GUARDS**. They hold him down, his neck on a chopping block.
Diello grabs a huge ax, swings it up above his head, and brings it crashing down onto . . .
REVEREND NORRIS'S NECK!!!

This passage illustrates how horror conventions are reconfigured in *Heavenly Creatures* through the imagination. We cut from a big close-up of Juliet's face to her monster, which is a product of her imagination and essentially her surrogate, rising up to execute the meddlesome reverend.

When a doctor questions Pauline about her attachment to Juliet to find out if they are lesbians, Pauline's imagination summons Diello to pierce the doctor with a sword just as he utters the last word of the line:

DR. BENNETT
   Perhaps you could think about spending more time with . . . boys -
Dr. Bennett stops in mid-sentence, a look of surprise on his face. He looks down at his chest . . .
A red bloodstain is slowly spreading across his shirt. Dr. Bennett twitches slightly as the blade of a sword works its way out of his chest!
Pauline's face lights up as . . .
Diello rises up behind Dr. Bennett.
DIELLO (Orson Welles voice)
   Bloody fool!

It is significant that Diello appears when the girls are at their most vulnerable — when Juliet's physical health is weak, Pauline's mental health is being questioned, and authority figures are bearing down on them. Through their personal creation, the girls are able to render powerless both religion and science, here represented as agents of repression that attempt to socialise the girls into their 'proper' roles.

Whether their relationship could properly be termed lesbian or whether it is the experimental play of two teenagers who do not have fixed ideas about sexuality, it is clear that the fear of homosexuality drives the adult reaction to them.[3] When Juliet's father, Henry Hulme, discovers his daughter and Pauline in bed together, he visits Pauline's parents on a stormy night – the traditional iconography for a horror film. The script explicitly states, 'Lightning flashes light up his face like something out of a gothic horror.' Unable to convey what he really fears, he talks around the central issue, at first calling Pauline 'imaginative' and 'spirited' and later deeming her relationship with his daughter 'unhealthy'. Finally, when he utters the words 'unwholesome attachement', the camera moves in on his face as the lightning outside illuminates him. The film thus develops another horror strand as Hulme becomes a monstrous threat to the girls' friendship. Likewise, when the doctor Pauline visits uses the word 'homosexuality' to describe her condition, his mouth is shot in extreme close-up and 'Honora looks horrified', as if he were a monster – and indeed he is to Pauline and Juliet's friendship. 'It can strike at any time, and adolescents are particularly vulnerable,' he points out, thus expressing a central anxiety over teenage sexuality in terms of a monster that strikes without warning the weakest members of the community. Pauline and Juliet are at odds with the adult world – both feared by the adults who see homosexuality as a disease for which 'There could be a breakthrough at any time' and fearful of parents, especially Honora, who is increasingly seen as a threat to their relationship.

The Horror Genre as a Refuge

The girls do not simply experience horror in their daily lives and respond to it as metaphoric horror filmmakers or animators who bring their creations to life; like many teenagers, they also face their fears through movies. Early in the film, they build a shrine to their favorite movie stars:

Three candles illuminate a little shrine, nestled into a flower bed in a remote corner of the Ilam garden.
Bricks have been stacked to form a miniature temple, decorated with flowers and tinsel.
Pauline and Juliet are kneeling on the ground, clipping pictures from film magazines. Clipped-out photos lie scattered about.
Pauline holds up James Mason's photo.
PAULINE (Enraptured)
   I wish James would do a religious picture . . . he'd be perfect as Jesus!
JULIET
   Daddy says the Bible's a load of bunkum!
Pauline reacts with a degree of shock.
PAULINE
   But, we're all going to Heaven!
JULIET
   I'm not! I'm going to the Fourth World! It's sort of like

Heaven, only better because there aren't any Christians.
Pauline giggles.
JULIET
   It's an absolute Paradise of music, art and pure enjoyment.
Pauline is entranced. Juliet plucks up some photos.
JULIET
   James will be there . . . and Mario! Only they'll be saints.
PAULINE (Giggling)
   Saint Mario!
Juliet places Mario Lanza' a photo in the shrine.
JULIET
   To be known as He!
PAULINE
   He . . .
Juliet places James Mason's photo in the shrine.
JULIET
   Him.
PAULINE
   Him . . .
Juliet picks up a photo of Mel Ferrer and places it in the shrine.
JULIET
   This.
PAULINE
   This. . .
Juliet places Jussi Bjoerling's photo in the shrine.
JULIET
   That.
PAULINE
   That. . .
Pauline places the last photo in the shrine . . . Orson Welles.
PAULINE
   It. . .
Juliet screws her face up and throws the photo into the stream.
JULIET
   Absolutely not! Orson Welles! The most hideous man alive!
Juliet dramatically sweeps her hand over the photos in the shrine
and bows her head.
JULIET
   We give praise to. . . the saints!
Candlelight flickers on Pauline's enraptured face.
The crumpled photo of Orson Welles floats down the stream. With
a sudden violent burst of sound, it is sucked into the weir.

This early scene plants the seeds for the idea of Orson Welles as a monster. His designation of 'It' is certainly the most impersonal, and his banishment from the shrine suggests that the girls are denying some part of themselves – the dark, monstrous side they even-

In love, but not erotically involved, the relationship of Pauline and Juliet earned them the prurient press tag 'Lesbian Schoolgirl Killers'.

tually express. Indeed, later in the film, they go see Welles in *The Third Man* and sit in rapt attention as if they were watching a monster. To Pauline, horror and sexuality co-exist in this one figure – augmenting Juliet's 'most hideous man alive!' comment, Pauline finds Welles both attractive and repellent: 'I have never in my life seen anything in the same category of hideousness . . . but I adore him.'

When they leave the theatre, a phantom of Welles confronts them wherever they go, and while they scream and run, they also seem genuinely excited by him, as if even the monstrous provided a dark thrill for them:

Pauline and Juliet run along dark, damp, atmospheric streets. Orson Welles steps out of the shadowy alley into the light. He leers at them. The girls scream! They turn to run, but Orson looms out of another alley.
Pauline and Juliet squeal and run about. **PASSERSBY** observe their antics with some alarm.
INT. ILAM/HALLWAY – NIGHT
The front door bursts open. Pauline and Juliet run in, still in a state of high excitement.
They charge up the stairs.
INT. ILAM/JULIET'S BEDROOM – NIGHT
Pauline and Juliet tumble into the bedroom, only to find Orson

lurking behind the door! They scream and flee along the balcony
only to be greeted by Orson at the other end! They run back into
the bedroom and collapse onto the bed, screaming and giggling.
PUSH IN . . . to Pauline's exalted face.
PAULINE (Diary V.O.)
  We talked for some time about It, getting ourselves more and
  more excited.
A huge shadow of a figure, dressed in hat and cape, rises on the
bedroom wall behind the girls, threatening to engulf them.
MUSIC SWELLS UP . . .
Pauline comes down on top of Juliet, kissing her on the lips .
. . Pauline's hands slipping Juliet's blouse off her shoulders.
PAULINE (Diary V.O.)
  We enacted how each saint would make love in bed.
Juliet heaves on the bed, Pauline leans over and . . . **MORPHS**
into Orson Welles!
CUT TO:
INT. BOROVNIA CASTLE — NIGHT
Diello thrusts and grunts, as if making love. He steps back hold-
ing a bloody sword. A slain peasant drops at his feet.
CLOSE UP . . . Pauline moaning and thrashing.
CLOSE UP . . . Diello swinging from side to side as he hacks a
peasant to pieces.
INTERCUT WITH SHOTS of Pauline and Juliet intertwined with Orson
and Diello. Pauline and Juliet sometimes change into their
Plasticine counterparts, Deborah and Gina.
PAULINE (Diary V.O.)
  We spent a hectic night going through the saints. It was
  wonderful! Heavenly! Beautiful! And ours! We felt satisfied
  indeed. We have now learned the peace of the thing called
  Bliss, the joy of the thing called Sin.

Welles haunts them like a supernatural monster who constantly appears out of nowhere
and cannot be avoided no matter where they turn. Like many traditional horror film
monsters, he is the other self – the dark side that keeps popping up and finally cannot be
repressed. The 'dark, damp' streets are the horror film's traditional setting, and the details
of Welles's appearance – 'huge shadow', 'hat and cape', the threat 'to engulf them' – consist of traditional horror hallmarks. The script thus builds a linkage between the boy-
genius filmmaker and villain of *The Third Man* and two precocious, creative girls who see
themselves as geniuses. He pursues them, but he is also their fantasy self, and indeed their
beloved creation Diello has Wellesian features and vocal tones. When sexuality reaches a
fever pitch, it is clear that their encounters with Welles have liberated them: the girls are
'intertwined with Orson and Diello' – the monster they fear and the monster they have
created, respectively. All of the film's themes – the attraction to horror, the thrill of violence, and sexual fulfilment through the imagination – finally come together in the
Borovnian orgy before the real-life murder that shatters everything.

Juliet in her fantasy life as Deborah, Queen of Borovnia. The realisation of the girls' imaginary kingdom, with its Plasticine courtiers, foreshadowed the epic Lord of the Rings.

Fantasy Becomes Reality

All along, the Borovnian fantasy world has in essence been a refuge from the horrors of adolescent sexuality. Pauline's first sexual experience is obviously very painful for her (with a family boarder named John, whose every thrust on top of her seems torturous), and so during sex she imagines herself entering the Borovnian kingdom, where a clay figure of her matinee idol, Mario Lanza, is singing, her creation Diello welcomes her and even kills for her, and Juliet is the fantasy figure Deborah. Here Pauline's fantasy life, particularly the special allure of Juliet, becomes a refuge from physical violence, namely John's sexual advances on her.

Later, the girls share a fantasy of John's beheading in Borovnia, in which a clay representation of John called Nicholas bends down to pick up a ring with a pink stone and Diello decapitates him: 'Diello slashes the rope with his dagger. Before Nicholas can react, the portcullis crashes down on him. His Plasticine body is crushed.' The pink stone falls out of the ring and is picked up by the girls. At this moment, Pauline declares, ''Tis indeed a miracle, one must feel, That two such heavenly creatures are real.' It is a moment of self-definition in which a rival for their affections has been eliminated and they are united in fantasy. More importantly, their self-definition is one of transcendence. To be a 'heavenly creature' is to combine opposites – heaven and earth, the ideal and the real, the ethereal Juliet and the average Pauline – in a union that, in their minds, can only be accomplished through violence.

When they kill Honora (in their minds another rival who threatens to split them up), the girls follow their Nicholas story. They plant a pink stone for Honora to bend down and pick up so that they can bludgeon her to death:

Honora's hand picks up the pink stone.
Pauline swings the brick down toward Honora's head.

Several more times Pauline 'swings the brick down' at her mother's head (Juliet does it once) in a gesture reminiscent of Diello swinging his axe in a Borovnian decapitation. The violence from the fantasy world has spilled over into the real world as the girls fulfil the role that Diello played in their imagination. Indeed, the killing of Honora is an extension of the violence of their fantasy life – the two become one in their frenzied adolescent imagination. *Heavenly Creatures* thus depicts a world in which violence becomes a refuge for the girls, even to the point where fantasy and reality are blurred in the girls' minds. (From the very beginning, the girls' fantasies are based in violence – Charles's killing of a rival frees Deborah to marry him in the early Borovnian stories – and thus become a model for how the girls dispatch their own rivals.)

The film's last shot is an unfulfilled fantasy: the murder having been committed, Pauline is unable to join Juliet on the ocean liner in the fantasy scene we saw at the beginning. *Heavenly Creatures* is full of foreboding close-ups of the girls, especially the brooding Pauline, usually with a cold stare that speaks of her isolation and dark fantasies. At the end, we are left with a

CLOSE-UP . . . Pauline looking devastated.
SLOWLY PULL OUT from Pauline's face . . . she stands alone, sobbing.

It is a final shot that speaks only of the horror that her fantasies have plunged her in.

Heavenly Creatures finally is a very paradoxical film. On the one hand, it purports to be the true story of an infamous crime (the voice-overs and the film's title are even taken from Pauline Parker's diaries). At the same time, it eschews the normal tabloid hallmarks of such a story – the trial and its aftermath – in favour of a look into the imaginative lives of the killers themselves and the way violence can inform and shape a teenage consciousness.

NOTES
1. Peter Travers, Review of *Heavenly Creatures* in *Rolling Stone*, November 3, 1994, p.104.
2. All script excerpts from Frances Walsh and Peter Jackson, *Heavenly Creatures*, in *Scenario* (Fall 1995).
3. Throughout the film, the girls' closeness suggests a very intense teenage crush. Juliet, for example, becomes very jealous when she learns of John's interest in Pauline, and small details like affectionate looks, hand-holding, and deep kisses support the idea that they are in love, even if they never explicitly declare it but rather use their fantasy world to express it. Jackson himself discounts the theory that Pauline and Juliet were really lovers, and comments: 'Fran [co-screenwriter Frances Walsh] and I felt very strongly that there was no sexuality, as such, beyond the fact that one girl would take on the role of James Mason, with the other pretending what it would be like to make love to James Mason.' (Edward Guthmann, 'A Heavenly Murder Most Monstrous', *San Francisco Chronicle*, November 21, 1994, p. D2.)

EARTHY CREATURES
by Michael Atkinson

A quivering bubble skin's breadth away from the millennium, it's no wonder that we're doped up on the torque of a life with movies: no other human creation ever let us step through a window into the rag-and-bone-shop of others' hearts, has allowed us to *see* ancient Rome or Satan or a man shake hands with himself or change into a wolf and back again, has altered the government of our dreams and the manner by which we view the passage of our own lives. Perhaps most of all, movies are sensory dynamos, hurricanes of compressed experience. Whatever chaos there is in life there is in movies tenfold: the simplest, stupidest action movie can become sublime through the choreography of extraordinary mayhem, and any argument against it is an argument against cinema. Formally, movies can make our perspectives their warped own in the passing of a frame, make nonsense of body tissue, space, and time, use visual momentum itself as a bludgeon. Sometimes we are made to feel we're choking on our own hearts, frozen on the dark brinks of complete bedlam. It's that taste of burnt nerves and raw pleasure that is one of movies' primal selves.

It's an excessive mind state, one predicated on vertiginous risk and the queasy comedy of catastrophe, and Peter Jackson has made it his own. Just as Busby Berkeley trucked in the utopian geometrics of success and love, Jackson contemplates in a similarly absurd fashion the texture of disaster, albeit on a personal level that in *Braindead* exceeds and violates any notion of physical intimacy movies may still keep faith with. Hapless ruin, be it visualised as the gargantuan horror of *Akira*, the amusement park thrill-machines of *T2*, *Speed,* and *True Lies*, or the miniature mano-a-mano nightmares of *Tetsuo*, *Evil Dead II*, and Jackson's films, has a seductive charm that suckles the sadist in all of us. And this includes *Heavenly Creatures*, visually conceived as it is like a fever-dream, and constructed so intimately around the heroines' obsessions that we, too, begin to look forward to the liberation of bloodshed.

Make no mistake, this is a time-honoured sensibility: the 'sick joke' midnight between farce and savagery can be traced (*pace* pop cult maven David J. Skal) to Jacobean death jokes like Cyril Tourneur's 1606 *The Revenger's Tragedy*. Of course, what makes Jackson stand alone in this killing field is hardly *Braindead's* passionate devotion to out-helter-skeltering the competition: it's *Heavenly Creatures*, a masterpiece that simultaneously marks a quantum leap from the crude emotional syntax of zombie comedies, and expresses Jackson's topos even more eloquently. For Jackson's earlier films are freshmanic, take-no-prisoners taboo-busters, built for shock and speed, fuelled by a very real and reckonable will to power and punkish hunger to usurp authority. They make trouble like a smart, bitter sixteen-year-old anarchist dizzy with his/her new sense of misunderstood self, of independence, of subversion and fearlessnes. They're films the girls of *Heavenly Creatures*, in another time and perhaps gender, might've made themselves. Jackson simply transferred his furious instinct for Dada thumb-nosing onto his Christchurch teenagers. In this way, and especially regarding the matricidal imagery of Jackson's earlier work, *Heavenly Creatures* can be read as autobio, New Zealand punk style.

Jackson's first film, *Bad Taste* ('88), is a clumsy, cheap, and sometimes hilarious shotgun wedding betweeen alien-takeover film and cannibal farce, notable for little beyond its intermittent Three Stooges riffs and seminal use of explosive birth/womb jokes. The type of movie that's often financed by the crew's frequent trips to the blood bank, *Bad Taste* was actually shot over three years, and looks it. Still, Jackson's consistent fondness for fish-eye compositions, loopy landscapes and biocombustibility is unmistakably present. It's apprentice work, and indicative of where a subversive spirit can lead you if you haven't developed the legerdemain and style necessary to speed the profane imagery across the screen like bullets out of a hundred guns.

From the first, *Bad Taste* quite apparently interfaced with the gory post-Stooge sensibility of Sam Raimi – Jackson's filthy blood-chuckles are the direct progreny of Raimi's first two *Evil Dead* movies, which simply carried the work of Herschell Gordon Lewis, Paul Morrissey, George Romero, and Frank Henenlotter to its logical extreme. What Raimi introduced to the sub-subgenre of body-assault comedy was a breathless degree of formal dementia, often abandoning his stories altogether for giggly jags of jet-propelled visual fury. That, and his deep understanding of physical comedy – the outer limits of which are represented by, of course, Moe, Larry, Curly & Co. – and its proximity to pain. (Note that all Raimi movies, even *The Quick and the Dead*, have cast credits for one or more 'Fake Shemps', homage to the decidedly un-Shemp-like dummies that often got hurled out windows in the aging Stooge's place.) Comparisons between Raimi and Jackson are unavoidable: co-opting the protean charge and pace of Raimi's films while maintaining a particularly NZ trashiness, Jackson had attempted to outgrue Raimi from the gitgo (consider Jackson Curly to Raimi's Moe, reacting in frantic fury to every eyepoke and brickbat), and after *Braindead* even Raimi has implicitly admitted that cannibal slapstick has seen its *Intolerance*.

Their careers have counterpointed from the moment brain matter began falling comically out the back of one of *Bad Taste*'s protagonist's skulls. Although Raimi is the pioneer and technically the more polished moviemaker, Jackson has proven to be the more imaginative, and the least genre-constricted. Whereas Raimi ascended to the exhilarating comic-book hyperbole of *Darkman* (his best), Jackson tangoed into savage media parody with *Meet the Feebles* ('89), an enthusiastically bloodthirsty rip through the Muppets and showbiz fables in general. That there are no humans in the film doesn't prevent Jackson from studying the arc of viscera, vomit, and disease as it invades a preposterous TV fantasyworld.

The Muppet Show per se may be an easy target, and the subjection of puppets to the foulest of human inequities a one-note joke born of a film majors' beer-flooded dorm caucus, but Jackson hits every comic note and never takes his foot off the insult-throttle. The various felt and vinyl bottomfeeders inhabiting this particular theatre of cruelty include: a satyric rabbit dying slowly of a sex disease; a knife-throwing junkie frog given to 'Nam flashbacks (the cruellest and funniest persona); a big-boss walrus caught more than once screwing a cat on his desktop; a huge, drug-dealing wild boar; an elephant saddled by a chicken with a paternity suit (he insists the child isn't his, but it *is* half chicken, half elephant); a toilet-loitering fly reporter who patrols the theatre for scandal; a rat who shoots s&m porn loops in the sewers with an udder-ringed cow and a cockroach, etc. Most of the madness is seen through the wide eyes of a method-acting, lispy hedgehog new to the Feebles and caught perfectly between cuddly and mortified, especially once the obese and much-abused hippo starlet picks up a machine gun and plows through the company like a postal worker on the first day of unemployment.

The pure excess of crude invention, devastating character assassination, and wicked visual vaudeville (the shivering frog's brutal POW nightmare, *à la The Deer Hunter* and complete with Vietcong gophers arguing Marxism around the campfire, is breathtakingly ballsy) is formidable and exhausting, as is Jackson's *mise-en-scène*, which makes hay out of the Muppets' below-the-belt neverland by emphasising the Feebles' sexual and excretory activites. Indeed, it seems the paradox of hand-up-the-ass puppet architecture, from Mortimer Snerd to Svankmajer's Punch and Judy to Alf, may have been what stimulated Jackson in the first place. Despite so much suffering (the AIDS-haunted rabbit's final on-the-air vomit is the outer limit), the nasty anthropomorphism never graduates onto a sober *Maus*-like plateau, and good thing: excessive anti-authoritarian stances like Jackson's are always built on the most delicate and treacherous of artistic urges. Pussyfoot, and it collapses into a lie. As in a good bar brawl, if you wonder where the door is, you've already lost the fight.

Jackson never lets us up for air, and so *Meet the Feebles* can seem relentless and unkind – an observation Jackson would have surely taken as a rave. His first three films carry an unmistakably Sadean attitude: we crave narrative balance, and so triumphant disrespect for the vox populi is often best expressed as ceaseless, irrational battering. Sade, Jarry, Céline, Genet and Burroughs, the Dadaists, Surrealists, and Lettrists, acid rock, punk and rap: Jackson's lineage runs back to Bosch (especially in *Braindead*), and through every college room, postered hideaway and teen hangout in the land, *FUCK 'EM*, the secret culture howls at a world constructed of duty, safety, and sense, then laughs, hard, when normal people don't seem to understand why.

Indeed, *Braindead* ('92) laughs louder at death than any movie ever has, and the titanic scope of dismemberment and butcher-shop slapstick pales all other attempts at blood humour, no matter the medium. It out-Raimis Raimi, and seems more human than Raimi's films besides – especially the more or less simultaneous *Army of Darkness*, the slight, cartoony close to the *Evil Dead* trilogy. Truly, *Braindead* is the most haemophiliac of movies – once it begins geysering plasma, it just can't stop.★ Still, this bloodshot bouillabaisse comes off as buoyant and invigorated with its own reckless nerve. Before the zombies attack the Norman Bates-ish hero's house en masse in a Spike Jones replay of *Night of the Living Dead*, we're treated to: the hero's zombie mum obliviously eating her own detached ear and spitting out the earring; the same Mum rising from her grave just in time to bite a gang thug in the crotch (yes, while he's pissing on her grave); a kung-fu fighting priest slamming his foot right through undead torsos ('I kick ass for the Lord!'); two drugged zombies copulating and speedily generating a pure-bred zombie toddler, who descends on the local playground, and much more. In terms of textual chutzpah, it's like watching someone walk out onto the wing of an airplane.

Once the climactic attack gets underway, the walls are literally painted red with movie blood – and it's the movieness that's the crucial issue. Jackson is crazy in love with bad taste (watch out for the self-ambulating pile of intestines, complete with farting anus) and his élan compounds every frame. For anyone with eyes, the wit and ocular tumult of *Braindead* proved that Jackson had more than visions of exploding tissue in his heart –

Pauline displaying wild joie de vivre *in the private world she shared with Juliet. Its threatened loss was the key to the murder of her mother.*

compare it to the equally ghoulish but insipid and lugubrious rot-fests of Jorg Buttgereit (*Nekromantik* et al). *Braindead* is a delirious hootenanny celebrating the rush of movies themselves, their potential for realising unimaginable imagery, their subversive spirit, their ability to bring breathless joy to the most harrowing and scatological material, their mad hubris and scorched-earth defiance. It's a wild-eyed party movie, and cinephiliacs everywhere are invited.

Viewed this way, the Tasman Sea-sized leap to the comparatively restrained and sober *Heavenly Creatures* doesn't seem so huge, though it shouldn't for other reasons. For one thing, *Heavenly Creatures* is, objectively, hardly a restrained or sober work – indeed, its portrait of *l'amour fou* is brilliantly eccentric, passionate, and risky. For another, the rebel-yell authorial dynamics of Jackson's earlier movies are sublimated as *HC*'s heroines' warped and frustrated world-view; the amphetaminic escalade of rage and manic humour belongs to the girls, coming from the inside out, not so much to Jackson's film. The infamous 1954 New Zealand murder of Honora Parker by her daughter Pauline and Pauline's schoolmate Juliet Hulme (real-life mystery author Anne Perry as a youngster) must have been a magnet to Jackson's particular jones for psychosexual damage and mother horror. (*Braindead* climaxes with a hellish primal scene, as the hero's mum transforms into a giant Moloch and swallows him up her uterine canal: cinema's most graphic episode of *vagina dentata*.) Hulme and Parker are half-lost in the hermetic, mock-medieval world of their own gland-powered reveries, an extreme intimacy – not unlike Jackson's fondness for the hidden interiors of body works – that's taken as overtly sexual by the girls' unlucky parents. Jackson clearly identifies with his misunderstood teenagers, and what may have seemed simply devilish japes in his previous films are used here to detail a deeply felt inner life.

I am loath to shrug off Jackson's earlier films as merely vicious yock tantrums, yet it must be admitted that gore comedy is not, in the end, a particularly challenging mode. Jackson knew he had run that jalopy right into a brick wall, which is where it belonged. So, in one lovely, graceful twist, he abandoned the company of Raimi, Henenlotter, et al, and expatriated to the country of earnest art films, style trumps, and Oscar nominations. (Raimi's contemporaneous genre defection, *The Quick and the Dead*, merely transfers the same *Evil Dead* heehaws to a static frontier farce.)

Heavenly Creatures displays good taste no one had the right to expect from Jackson, but it still crackles with a try-anything overload of visual ideas. The girls' fantasyworld is filled with life-size clay figures, distant castles, unicorns, and ordinary Christchurch landscapes that morph into flamboyant storybook gardens (the most creative use of morphing I've ever seen); adults are shot like matinee villains, but remain sympathetic; the camera's careening flights and suffocating closeness to things evokes a swollen, pubertal anxiety the true story can only half-express. What may be more of a surprise is Jackson's handling of the actors, eliciting laurel-ready performances, in two tough roles, from nonvets Melanie Lynskey and Kate Winslet. Surprising, too, are the purple, righteous, painfully desperate entries from Pauline's real diary, read as narration. To imagine for a moment the naked, expressive anguish and ardour that *Heavenly Creatures* contains bursting from an American movie is to glimpse an unknown, unrealised, and probably impossible Hollywood.

As a treatment of a real murder case, Jackson's film is uniquely empathic and fleshy; set it against the crude shortcomings of the (nevertheless fascinating) Leopold-Loeb threesome, *Rope*, *Compulsion*, and *Swoon*, and Jackson positively glows with humanism. *Heavenly Creatures* is many things to many people – a docudrama on microdots, a hellza-poppin opening of old wounds and plumbing of mad love, a valentine to all of us run over by the ten thousand cruel stories of youth – but it's never less than a crazed and earnest testament to how movies can express emotion by the creation, and manipulation, of vision. As per Hitchcock's attestation of what makes great cinema, we would still know exactly what *Heavenly Creatures* is about, textually and viscerally, even if the soundtrack were dropped out. Jackson may be the man to definitively film *Madame Bovary*, *The Castle*, DeLillo's *Libra*, even – dare we fantasise? – J. G. Ballard's *Crash*. That he can so adroitly use hot-diggity horror movie conventions to drench us so effortlessly in the sweaty madness of adolescent angst and matricide is an ordinary miracle not only for the filmmaker but of the medium itself. After a century, we may take cinema a bit for granted. In our placid thrall to a star's sexual aura or our routine expectation of plot zigzags, we may fail to fully grok the rare and momentous journey we're on, where a minute alteration of the focal plane can reveal a human truth, and where a camera swirling over the heads of schoolgirls can speak to us of their giddy hungers and precarious grip on reality. We live with this second language every day, and are encouraged to think of it as 'information'. Jackson's right: we should think of it instead as rapture, as sorrow, as flight.

*Beware renting the cut, R-rated version on video. The film is titled *Dead Alive* in the US, thanks to a copyright tiff; Jackson considered calling it *Everlasting Rot*.

FORGOTTEN
SILVER

HEAVENLY FEATURES
by Denis Welch

Film-maker Peter Jackson still can't quite believe it. It's nearly two years now since he finally yielded to his mother's urgings and promised to look at some old films a neighbour had stashed in a garden shed. 'I was expecting possibly some old home movies, that I would politely say, "These are fascinating," and go and drop them off at the Film Archive and that would be the end of it,' Jackson recalls. Instead, he found a treasure trove that has changed his life, and – he believes – the history of cinema, not just in New Zealand but worldwide.

His first inkling of the significance of the films came when he saw they were 35mm, not 8mm. 'My pulse quickened. That told me that, whatever these were, they were not home movies.'

The tins of film had sat for more than 50 years in an old chest belonging to Hannah McKenzie, a longtime neighbour of Jackson's parents in Pukerua Bay, north of Wellington. What had not been widely known was that she was the widow of pioneer film-maker Colin McKenzie, whose work was thought lost after his tragically early death in the 1930s.

Knowing nothing of McKenzie, Jackson called in friend and colleague Costa Botes, who identified one of the films from a description he had come across years before in an old newspaper article; and then archivist Jonathan Morris, who immediately set about transferring the crumbling nitrate films onto modem safety stock.

It was only after months of laborious preservation work – for which Jackson gives Morris full credit – that the three men realised the full extent of what they were sitting on.

'Shorts, features, newsreels, experimental films – you name it, McKenzie did it,' says Botes, who together with Jackson presents the three men's findings in the final *Montana Sunday Theatre.* 'That alone would have been an amazing find, just in terms of our history – but what really amazed us was the technical innovation.'

Neither Jackson nor Botes will be drawn on the exact nature of the innovations – all will be revealed in the programme, they say – but Jackson has no doubt about their importance.

'He really deserves a place among the luminaries of early cinema, like Edison, Meliés and the Lumière brothers. Because none of his films were thought to have survived, it was impossible to actually ascertain where he belonged in terms of cinema history. But this discovery puts him up there among the pantheon.'

Morris backs up this view. 'Most of the early films from the turn of the century were of parades, babies on lawns, family picnics, that sort of thing,' he says. 'Cinema was strictly a novelty. Yet here was someone in New Zealand who was not just using film as a novelty, but in an artistic way, and that is very rare.'

Given the recent resurgence of interest in New Zealand's film history, it still seems extraordinary that no one approached Hannah McKenzie about her husband's work. Botes says she did seek advice about the contents of the chest from time to time, 'but no one took her seriously, perhaps because her experience of Colin was such a brief one.'

Hannah McKenzie, now 77 – she married McKenzie shortly before his death, when

Unsung Kiwi cinema pioneer Colin McKenzie. This early twentieth-century genius was at last celebrated in Peter Jackson and Costa Botes's documentary Forgotten Silver *(1996).*

she was nineteen, and has never remarried – prefers not to dwell on the past.

'The suitcase of films was just part of his estate that I inherited,' she says. 'It was just prior to the war and then the war happened and the films were just put away. It wasn't till I knew that young Peter was somehow involved in films that I thought of getting in touch with him.'

By piecing together not only the films but the facts of McKenzie's life, Jackson and Botes have also been involved in a kind of detective hunt. Their discoveries form the basis of much of the programme, beginning with McKenzie's early days in Geraldine, where his first experience of a traveling cinematograph show inspired him to start making films while still in his teens.

'All the other kids were glued to the screen,' says Botes, 'but he would be looking the other way at the magic box making the picture – the projector. He was always mechanically adept.'

There are parallels here with Jackson's own precocious development as a director – parallels that have caused him to identify closely with his pioneering predecessor.

'I've got to say that researching Colin's life is the most exciting thing I've ever done,' says Jackson. 'In a feature film you can tell a story, you have a lot of artistic licence to invent things, but when you're telling the true story of a man's life you have to honour the facts.

'It all adds up to an experience totally different to fiction – you end up bonding with the guy. There are a lot of things in Colin's life I recognise in my own, even seven decades later. In a lot of things Colin did or tried to do – he wasn't always successful – I recognise my own passions.'

What now, then, for the McKenzie heritage? Sunday's programme could be just the start of an explosion of interest in the man from Geraldine. Jackson confirms that Harvey Weinstein of Miramax Films – the American company that backed *The Piano* and Jackson's own *Heavenly Creatures* – has secured the international distribution rights to McKenzie's films and plans to launch them at next year's Cannes festival. After that . . . Jackson wants nothing less than full recognition for McKenzie.

'After this documentary, this guy should be appearing on our banknotes. They should create a $3 banknote just to put his face on it. He is postage-stamp material.'

Hannah McKenzie, while sorry that her husband's work was never recognised in his lifetime, is just grateful that his genius has finally been acknowledged.

'He would just be so pleased,' she says, looking out the window of her Pukerua Bay home, where her favourite photograph of Colin sits on the sideboard, along with other mementos of his career. 'He was such a modest man, who never sought the limelight. I know that, wherever he is, he would be so proud.'

And to viewers wondering what a documentary – however sensational – is doing in the Sunday Theatre slot, Jackson explains: 'It was actually the Film Commission which suggested it. They had already got involved in funding it and they felt that the *Montana Theatre* would be just right for it.

'There was some pressure on us at first to possibly dramatise some aspects of Colin's life, but frankly, even though it's a documentary, the events of his life were so dramatic that the word drama is not inappropriate.'

Adds Botes: 'It's as gripping as any fictional story.'

GONE NOT FORGOTTEN
by Geoff Chapple

The question finally came down to this: was gulling the national television audience better than dulling it? Film-makers Peter Jackson and Costa Botes had no doubts – go for gulled. Their *Forgotten Silver* documentary – New Zealand's biggest-ever hoax – took as its subject an undiscovered film genius, Colin McKenzie from Geraldine.

On October 29 1995, 400,000 people watched on *Montana Sunday Theatre* and the collective Kiwi breast swelled with pride. Even overseas experts acknowledged, face-to-cam, that the early history of cinema would have to be rewritten to make way for McKenzie's contributions.

The letdown later was severe. Some people laughed, but some got very angry.

Says Jackson: 'Some people were upset, but nonetheless they had an entertaining time on television for an hour, which is rare. I don't watch television myself – it's usually so dull.'

Says Botes: 'This was fiction, but it was a full-blown celebration of Kiwi ingenuity, asking people to wake up and see what's in their backyard. Picasso said, "We all know that art is not truth. Art is a lie that makes us realise truth."'

Not everyone was that subtle. The reaction, as measured by phone-ins and letters to those who broadcast, funded or produced the film was – aside from TVNZ's claim of majority support for the programme – often negative.

Facts, the anti-*Silver* contingent said, should be always and only facts. But, by marketing measures, *Forgotten Silver* was an unqualified success. It has won a repeat screening on TV1, although when is not yet decided, and the New Zealand Film Commission is currently negotiating a distribution deal with Miramax Films in New York, which may recoup most of *Silver's* $620,000 budget.

The documentary – now revealed as part of the esoteric 'mock-u-mentary' genre – was based on film-stock recovered from an old chest in Pukerua Bay. In the years 1901 to 1927, McKenzie, the film genius, invented tracking shots, grabbed footage of the March 1903 flight of Richard Pearse at Temuka, shot the first colour film and the world's first sound feature, then built a vast set in deep bush for his masterwork, *Salome*. He fell in love with Maybelle, the female lead of *Salome* and, when she died in 1931, left New Zealand forever.

'People said to me they cried when Maybelle died, and that's what film should do,' says Jackson. 'It is about emotion. It is about the suspension of disbelief. In *ET*, the audience cried when he had to go home – and he was a little rubber alien.'

Colin McKenzie was, in the end, no more than a home-grown rubber man, a reminder that what walks like a duck, and talks like a duck, is still not necessarily a duck.

Some guessed quickly – either because of the absurdities, or by the sheer force of femaile intuition. Says NZ On Air's programme manager Jane Wrightson: 'A friend of mine called and said she knew it was a hoax – no one could have achieved all those things, and been called Colin.'

Others, and they included top executives at TVNZ and Creative New Zealand staff, were still enthusiastically expounding Colin's talents the next day.

'It's not that you made a jerk of yourself if you believed,' says Jackson. 'It shows a healthy imagination. They haven't shut their minds off. They're not cynical. The world is a bitter and dull enough place, and if you have some fun for some of the time, that's great.'

The idea came originally from Botes, who says he has one regret. A grand-niece of Richard Pearse, the man who really may have flown before the Wright brothers, watched *Forgotten Silver* in great excitement. The Botes/Jackson 'computer enhancement' of a newspaper in someone's back-pocket at the flight scene purported to establish the Pearse flight at March 1903 – nine months before the Wright brothers.

But, for the rest – there is no apology. Both filmmakers, by a neat inversion, say the people who have dumped on them are the same who would have dumped on McKenzie had he been real. Nor do they believe that they have diluted, by mock-u-mentary, the cherished national myth of backyard genius.

Says Jackson: 'There's a lot of Colin McKenzies out there, and a lot of such backyard people are nobbled in New Zealand. They're nobbled by the "go out and get a proper job" brigade. The negative reaction to our programme seems a very good example of that.'

And there were, of course, the many who loved it. Of all the letters that came into Wingnut Films after the production, Botes most liked the one that said, 'One Network News admitted that last night's *Montana Sunday Theatre* was a hoax. Well, all credibility has gone down the tubes – I won't be believing in TVNZ's news anymore.'

FORGOTTEN SILVER
Interview With Peter Jackson
by Pauline Adamek

Presented as factual, *Forgotten Silver* is a film that documents the extrordinary life of Colin McKenzie, a fictional pioneer New Zealand filmmaker. With co-writer Costa Botes, Jackson explores McKenzie's rich and at times tragic life. The film also follows the extraordinary story of how the work of this forgotten genius was brought to life.

Forgotten Silver *is an elaborate mock-documentary, how did it all come about?*
It was a joke, really. It was one of those fun type of movies, that you're not doing it for any serious reason other than you were lucky enough to be given some money to have a good time and stage this prank. The basis of the idea was a little newspaper story that I read in a New Zealand newspaper, maybe six or seven years ago, concerning a group of film historians in California who had gone out into the desert and had scraped away the sand and uncovered one of Cecil B. DeMille's sets from the 1920s, made of wood and

plaster. They revealed this Biblical city in the desert. So just that idea, transposed to a New Zealand setting, was the attraction of getting *Forgotten Silver* together.

What about the early films of Colin McKenzie – did they exist before?
I worked with a co-writer and co-director, Costa Botes, and once we had the initial idea we developed it into a story that chronicled this guy's life. So, as part of the twist in the story, we uncover a whole cache of his early films that have been forgotten so we had to recreate those films, yeah.

What was your budget?
The budget was around $600,000. I shot all the recreated stuff over two weeks. We did it very quickly. Then I handed it over to Costa who shot all the documentary stuff and I'm not sure how long he took. It was all happening just before *The Frighteners* started. I would check in with him from time to time to see how he was putting it all together and maintaining some sort of input at the weekends while *The Frighteners* was underway, so it was a bit full-on for me doing two movies at once.

You've really done it as cheaply as possible, is that right?
We got the amount of money that we needed to make it, but yeah it was pretty tight. Apart from a few existing documentary clips of Stalin and a couple of other bits and pieces, everything we used was shot for the movie.

What techniques did you use for the so-called early films?
You just had to work backwards from where we are today. We didn't use any old cameras or anything, we used completely modern cameras so everything is rock steady and perfectly sharp and the technology today operates in exactly the opposite way to what they were used to so it was just a case of deteriorating the film and copying it and deteriorating it again. We used chemicals to stain it and we scratched it. We dragged it across the floor and through sandpaper and made it unsteady in the camera and played around with fluctuating the exposure all the time during the shots. We just studied old movies and looked closely at what they looked like. People often try this and they think so long as it's black and white and it has some scratches down it that it looks like old film but old film has a lot more subtleties, such as the size of the grain and the contrast ranges that it picks up. We were very careful to go into a lot of detail to try to make our stuff look as realistic as possible.

But not to the extent of mixing egg whites to make your own emulsion, much like Colin McKenzie allegedly did.
No, no – we didn't use any of his techniques.

What about the casting? You've got some people there who really look as if they were around in the early part of the century.
You've just gotta be careful. Casting is very important and you can't just grab your friends and stick them in front of the camera. You've got to look for the right faces and there are some faces that look as if they belong in the 1920s more so than some others. We looked

at hundreds of photos from the different agencies until we found the right ones. This was one case when acting skill wasn't the primary factor.

Where did the sets come from that we see in the film?
They were sets that we built and sometimes we used a little bit of computer trickery to make things look a little bigger.

Forgotten Silver was first aired on television in New Zealand. How was it received?
Most of the people that saw it seemed to actually fall for it, which surprised us in a way. We didn't intend that. The publicity before the screening made it sound like a true programme. We deliberately didn't want to give the game away but we were quite sure that there's enough silly stuff in there and enough over the top humour that at some stage during the course of the film people are going to start to twig to the fact that it's not real. But it did actually surprise us how many people in New Zealand actually fell for it.

Why do you think that is?
People want to believe in heroes. They push all the unrealistic, over-the-top stuff out of the back of their mind in a desperate need to believe that this is actually true. It's very sweet, really.

When do most people cotton on, though?
I don't know. I think everybody's different and I haven't seen it enough times with an audience to actually know. I guess different people cotton on at different times, depending on how sharp you are.

There is not really a tradition of this kind of deceptive, phoney documentary. There's Zelig – were you at all inspired by Woody Allen's film?
Not really, no. That wasn't the reason for doing it although once we were doing it we were wanting to achieve the same kind of seamless, cinematic tricks that that film contained.

But with less computer trickery, perhaps?
We used computers for a few shots. But we were very much aware that we wanted the film to be more than just a one joke movie. It also has to stay entertaining for people who know the joke. There's no point spending all this effort and making this film if as soon as people know the joke it becomes a pointless exercise screening it. The film has to operate on some level of drama beyond the fact that it's a pseudo documentary. We actually took quite a bit of care in trying to make his story as dramatic as possible and as entertaining as possible so that even if you know it's not true, it actually doesn't destroy your entertainment of the film.

Isn't it possible that in time more people will look at your film as an historical account rather than a joke?
No. I think that as time goes on the fact that it's a joke will become more and more well known, so I think it's the reverse of that, really.

It's really cheeky that you've got Leonard Maltin, Sam Neill and Harvey Weinstein giving interview sound bites and endorsing your deception. How far were you prepared to go with this deception?

You go as far as you need to make it real. We were very lucky that those guys agreed to do it. They both saw the humour in it and realised it was a bit of fun. You have to take this all with a sense of humour and have some fun with it. It certainly makes a change from all the usual straight movies that we see all the time.

Was there a backlash at all, from those who were duped?

People either laughed at it when they found out or they got angry, depending on how stupid they looked. Some people were angry but that doesn't matter. Don't take it too seriously. Loosen up a bit. People have to realise that just because they see something on film, in a documentary format, that it doesn't necessarily have to be real.

It's funny that you've only just now made that point.

It just shows you how easy it is to fool a lot of people with something that is incredibly over the top and unrealistic. The intention wasn't to make people feel stupid, it was for us to have some fun and create a documentary about someone's life, complete with archival material. There are no rules that say that person had to actually exist.

But you're not going to change the way you promote the movie?

That's all out of my hands. I have no idea what's going to happen. If people can still perpetuate the myth for a while then it makes it more fun. It would be a shame if every time it was screened it had advance publicity that it was fake.

It's not as if it makes everyone run into the streets and panic, like Welles' **War of the Worlds.**

No one gets hurt. It's a harmless thing.

SILVER MAGIC
by Jane Roscoe and Craig Hight

In an article on generic transformation, John Cawelti has presented the idea that when a genre exhausts itself it can take on a number of different modes, one of which is 'the use of traditional generic structures as a means of demythologisation'.[1] From Cawelti's argument, there is the suggestion that as an audience becomes more familiar with a particular form of representation, that audience is prepared to accept transformations which can include the deconstructing of the myths and assumptions on which the original form is based.

It is debatable whether or not documentary modes of representation could be seen collectively as a genre. Bill Nichols[2] suggests that it is possible and illustrates this argument by the identification of three ways of defining documentary. First, it is suggested that there is a community of practitioners (the 'documentrists') who all work within a particular framework of institutional practice. They share a language and a similar set of objectives and assumptions which frame their screen practices. They can be seen as constructing a specific screen product, the 'documentary'. Second, there is a corpus of texts that share similar structures and conventions. Nichols argues that all documentaries take shape around an informing logic. In this way the documentary can be identified as a specific screen form. Third, there is a constituency of viewers who share a set of expectations and assumptions about their relationship to these documentary texts. In this way, viewers engage in a documentary mode of engagement. Taking these points together it is possible to think of documentary as a specific screen genre. From this starting point, Cawelti's arguments on generic transformation can yield an interesting avenue of investigation.

In this article Cawelti's arguments are applied to *Forgotten Silver*, the mock documentary made by Peter Jackson and Costa Botes. It is our contention that this programme represents something of a maturation of the documentary 'genre' in the New Zealand context, and, as such, it can offer a number of valuable insights into what could be termed the cultural status of documentary forms within this context. The analysis presented here examines *Forgotten Silver* at three different levels: first, the immediate context of its production; second, its use of documentary codes and conventions to demythologise the form itself; and third, the programme's public reception within New Zealand.

Contextualising *Forgotten Silver*

There are a number of aspects to the immediate context in which *Forgotten Silver* was produced which effectively served to reinforce the text's documentary credentials with its audience. First, the programme was screened (by Television New Zealand on Sunday, 8 November 1995) in the 'quality drama' *Montana Sunday Theatre* slot. In previous weeks, this slot had screened a series of original New Zealand dramas and the finishing of that series with a documentary about an apparently forgotten New Zealand film maker seemed appropriate, if somewhat unusual. A wider cultural context also served to further legitimate, justify and authenticate the programme and its subject matter. New Zealand is celebrating 100 years of cinema, with the Film Commission spending much time, effort and resources in promoting an awareness and celebration of this milestone both nationally and locally.

One such activity organised through the Film Archive has particular relevance here. Over the last couple of years the Film Archive has been conducting a nation-wide film search, encouraging the public to hand over old films which had largely been left to disintegrate in garages and attics. Peter Jackson makes specific reference to this search at the start of *Forgotten Silver* when explaining how he first encountered the work of Colin McKenzie. While most of the material collected by the archive has been home-movies and similar short excerpts of film, it was certainly the hope (if not the reality) that the search would uncover material of historical importance. *Forgotten Silver* claimed to be presenting a film 'find' that matched, and even exceeded, the dreams of the Archive and of the many people who had contributed to the search. Given this context, it seemed rea-

McKenzie with silent comedian 'Stan the Man' (right), another supposedly forgotten New Zealander who anticipated Hollywood.

sonable to accord the announcement of the discovery and a presentation of McKenzie's work a place in a slot known for its promotion of high quality and original material. The fact that the Film Commission and New Zealand On Air had supported the project financially only served to reinforce the legitimacy and significance of the programme. It was, then, with some excitement and curiosity that an estimated audience of 400,000 viewers tuned into TV1 that Sunday night to learn more about a pioneering New Zealand film maker.

This first screening was preceded by a significant amount of publicity focusing on the importance of its find. *Forgotten Silver* was first brought to the attention of the New Zealand audience in an article in the *New Zealand Listener*[3] which 'broke' the story, claiming to herald a 'sensational find' with the discovery of a hoard of long-lost films by a previously unknown New Zealand film maker, Colin McKenzie. The article placed Peter Jackson and Costa Botes in the role of discoverers and celebrants of McKenzie's assumed legacy. In hindsight the article contains a number of cues as to the real nature of *Forgotten Silver*[4], and in fact is written in the same tones as the discourse of *Forgotten Silver* itself; excitement at the importance and relevance of the work of McKenzie, and of the implications which this discovery seemed to hold for both New Zealand and world cinema history.

The first public screening of *Forgotten Silver* was not unprecedented in New Zealand television broadcasting. The programme could in fact be seen as part of a well-established 'tradition' of mock New Zealand television reports. Perhaps the most well-known examples have been the numerous mock reports of agricultural developments or inventions featured on *Country Calendar*.[5] The two main nightly news programmes also produce mock news items immediately before the conclusion of their April 1 broadcasts.[6] What was perhaps unique was the level of secrecy which went into maintaining the pretence that the programme was a legitimate documentary, and the publicity surrounding this first screening. Here *Forgotten Silver* went beyond this tradition of spoof news items to enlist the complicity of a national print publication (the *Listener*) which generally enjoys a reputation for responsible journalism.

Documenting Colin McKenzie

Forgotten Silver also worked effectively itself to reinforce the claim that it operated within the bounds of conventional documentary-making. The programme presents a sophisticated simulation and parody of the documentary genre. To take part in this parodic exercise, the audience has first to engage in a documentary mode of viewing. Viewers need to watch as though it were a documentary, drawing on certain well-established expectations concerning what documentaries in general can offer, and in particular how documentary texts represent the historical world. We expect the people, places and issues to be 'real' and documentaries to treat these subjects with seriousness and authority. These expectations effectively frame the manner in which viewers approach and engage with these programmes.

The success which *Forgotten Silver* had in convincing its audience of its claim for documentary status reveals the complexity and sophistication with which it presented its subject matter through the language, practices and conventions that define documentary as a specific screen form. In a very accomplished way, Jackson and Botes utilise all the codes and conventions of documentary to turn a fiction into an authentic and plausible truth.

Forgotten Silver utilises the expositional mode of documentary, the form that relates most closely to the traditional expositional essay. It is a mode which seeks to offer an argument about the social world, incorporating a variety of editing devices designed to reinforce this argument. This mode also commonly employs a narrator, either on screen or in voice-over (the 'voice of God') and uses expert testimonies to legitimate or develop specific parts of its argument.[7] Its structure can perhaps be likened to a scientific experiment, with the narrator as 'scientist' working from an initial hypothesis, gathering data and facts, testing the hypothesis and finally presenting a set of findings designed to support an accurate and truthful conclusion.[8]

Although structured by the logic of an underlying argument, the expositional form nevertheless remains couched within the rhetoric of objectivity. The presentation of its argument still involves retaining the appearance of an adherence to the prized quality of 'balance'. Above all, this means expositional documentaries tend to present interviews from a range of sources, and a variety of materials claiming to be original and authentic references to historical events serving to locate the text within a temporal reality.

Forgotten Silver begins with Jackson in his backyard, locating him, and the story of McKenzie, in real and identifiable surroundings. As Jackson tells of his role in the story and the initial discovery of the forgotten films, Polaroid snap-shots of the film canisters fill the screen. Documentary has used such photographic evidence to the point where it has become a cliché. An interesting difference here is that the photographs are colour shots, in direct contrast to the 'original' and 'authentic' black and white photographs seen later in the programme.

Before the listing of the title credits the audience is presented with a line-up of clear-ly-labelled experts: Jonathan Morris, film archivist, Costa Botes, film maker, Harvey Weinstein of Miramax Films, film historian Leonard Maltin and actor/director Sam Neill. All make claims regarding the historic importance of the films found and of the place of McKenzie himself as a pioneer in the history of film. They all play the role of film 'experts' and as such their testimonies serve to both 'authenticate' the find, and, importantly, give credibility to *Forgotten Silver* itself. Throughout the film we return to these experts, with their interviews being used to reinforce the arguments presented by Jackson.

Another key player in the documentary is McKenzie's 'widow' Hannah. She plays the role of 'eyewitness' whose testimony serves as a compliment to the sobriety of the other, more expert, testimonies. As the film progresses she reveals vital clues which help Jackson and viewers piece McKenzie's story together. However, true to the expositional style, the programme builds tension and drama by pacing these revelations at regular intervals.

The rhetoric of science, and in particular of scientific discovery, is utilised throughout the film to further enhance the objectivity of Jackson's findings. The revelatory nature of scientific discovery is used as the basis for much of the narrative of the film itself, and, more overtly, in the manner in which various forms of evidence are presented. Examples could be when describing McKenzie's early inventions, such as his experiments with egg whites he supposedly used to make film stock, or his complex attempts to develop colour film.[9] These inventions are authenticated by the 'experts' who explain the chemical reactions or the technological aspects of these various inventions. Without specialised access to these scientific discourses, these claims are difficult to reject outright.

These events in the McKenzie story are constantly being validated by the use of authenticating material, such as the black and white photographs which show McKenzie as a young man, with his family and with his inventions. These 'documents' provide external validation for the argument promoted. They have the appearance of being 'real' and 'original' and, as mentioned earlier, photographs of this sort are used so often within documentaries that we take them for granted. We expect them to be real. There are also stills taken from old newspapers which chart McKenzie's progress in the film making business. Taken together, these 'documents' provide a seeming wealth of authenticating material to support Jackson's claims for the significance of McKenzie's accomplishments.

Perhaps most convincing are the extracts from McKenzie's own films, both his fictional work (*Salome*) and his 'reportage' films of Gallipoli and of the Spanish Civil war. The latter films are of particular importance to the argument of *Forgotten Silver* because they ground its rhetoric in the real world. In a sense, these references to historical events and McKenzie's footage work to reinforce each other. The programme offers McKenzie's films as further documentation of historical events, which in turn helps to establish McKenzie's presence at these points in history.

Forgotten Silver also features Jackson and Botes organising an expedition into the West Coast bush in an attempt to find the location of the filming for McKenzie's masterpiece, *Salome*. Here history is almost treated as an accessible realm, in the sense that it has left tangible remnants which can be used in its reconstruction. The journey of Jackson and

Botes into the New Zealand landscape deliberately mirrors that of McKenzie. These are the same conventions which historical documentary relies on.[10] In utilising the codes and conventions of the genre and in inviting viewers to join in a documentary mode of engagement, Jackson and Botes have succeeded in presenting a film with the appearance of an authentic historical reality, a 'true' story. On the surface, *Forgotten Silver* looks and operates like any other documentary.

The Appeal to National Myths

One of the more interesting aspects of *Forgotten Silver* is its relationship to myth, and to New Zealand myths in particular. A perhaps central part of the effectiveness of the programme with New Zealand audiences is the subtlety and variety of ways in which its film makers exploited cultural stereotypes and accepted notions concerning the nature of New Zealand history and society. This was combined with the more general conventions of documentary-making, forms of representation which, as discussed above, in themselves draw upon naturalised myths concerning notions of 'objectivity' and 'truth'. Outside of the use of outside experts (such as film historian Leonard Maltin) and scientific knowledge to validate the claims made by witnesses and the historical record, a second and more interesting feature, in terms of myth, has Jackson as a reporter performing the roles of both detective and tourist for the audience.[11]

Jackson operates as a detective in the sense that he presents a number of mysteries to the audience, which are then solved by Jackson and Botes throughout the course of the programme. The mystery of why Colin McKenzie remained unknown until discovered by the film makers serves as perhaps the dominant narrative device of *Forgotten Silver*. Much of the narrative structure of the programme serves to unfold the story of McKenzie's life, presenting a biography with references to a number of already known historical events (such as the two World Wars). How McKenzie died is one of a number of smaller puzzles solved as this story unfolds.

A central part of the solving of the over-arching mystery of why McKenzie remained undiscovered involves the search for a huge set supposedly built by the film-maker in the West Coast bush for his masterpiece *Salome*. This search, which forms the second major part of *Forgotten Silver*'s narrative (regularly and expertly intercut with McKenzie's biography) allows Jackson and his colleagues to also perform the role of reporter as tourist. In terms of myth, here the film makers act as representatives of the audience on a journey into the unknown, in terms of both space (into the 'jungles' of the New Zealand bush landscape) and time (into the past to establish the authenticity of McKenzie's achievements and hence his legacy to cinema history).[12]

This journey into the New Zealand bush is one of the more important ways in which *Forgotten Silver* draws specifically on New Zealand myths to make its narrative so compelling. In New Zealand popular culture the native bush and its associated landscape plays something of a similar function as the Western frontier does in American folklore. Here it is the bush which served as a frontier for early European colonialists, and as the place where the more admired aspects of a supposed New Zealand character were forged. The resilience, independence, and persistence of McKenzie in the face of the natural obstacles provided by the West Coast bush appeal to such well-established stereotypes in New Zealand culture.

Other aspects of McKenzie's character also draw upon stereotypes established by the colonial period of New Zealand history. He is one of the legendary backyard inventors supposedly at the heart of New Zealand's development, and both he and his brother Brooke serve as soldiers in the various conflicts claimed to have forged the beginnings of the nation itself. It is Brooke, with a camera built by his brother, who provides the first footage from the very cradle of the nation itself, Gallipoli. *Forgotten Silver* succeeds here by not just appealing to an important myth of the origin of the birth of the nation, but reinforcing this myth by providing the first documentary (and hence 'real' and concrete) evidence of the hardships suffered by New Zealand soldiers.

Above all, the character of McKenzie is the epitome of the dogged inventor-genius who perseveres despite a wealth of natural, personal, financial and political hardships. Although McKenzie's endeavours are in vain in terms of recognition for himself during his lifetime, they serve as a kind of historical lesson for the audience of the way things should have happened. In doing so, the narrative of *Forgotten Silver* both draws on and subverts some of the more basic value systems inherent to New Zealand mythology.[13]

The Public Response

From a cursory survey of responses reported in the media, the New Zealand audience apparently reacted to *Forgotten Silver* in a number of varying and interesting ways. The written responses to the *Listener* itself, which featured the original article publicising *Forgotten Silver*, demonstrate a range of these audience reactions to the programme. The magazine states that of 'the writers of the 24 letters the *Listener* has received on the *Forgotten Silver* hoax, sixteen express disapproval, five approve, and three still believe.'[14] This public response could be divided roughly into the three categories listed below. These are by no means exhaustive, nor mutually exclusive, but they do serve as a useful starting point for any discussion over the willingness of the New Zealand audience to allow, in particular, for the subversion of many of the basic assumptions exploited by documentaries, and news services in general.

A. Uncertain: Some viewers evidently still felt some confusion over whether or not Colin McKenzie could be considered a New Zealand historical figure; whether *Forgotten Silver* was in fact a documentary.[15] These kinds of audience responses to *Forgotten Silver* testified to the effectiveness of Jackson and Botes in perpetrating their hoax, and to the quality of the craft which went into the programme itself.

The confusion of some viewers was perhaps also due to an expectation that there is a clearly demarcated line between reality-based television and fictional programmes; that there should be something either preceding or during the programme which makes this division obvious to the viewers. *Forgotten Silver* does have a degree of reflexivity – it does features a number of clues as to the nature of its subject[16] – but these were very subtle and perhaps overwhelmed by the effectiveness of the programme's other devices. These viewers were apparently unaccustomed to being asked to judge the validity of an entire programme itself.

B. Positive: A portion of *Forgotten Silver's* audience, apparently initially a minority, expressed some appreciation of the degree of directorial ability which went into the making of the programme, and to some extent supported the idea that there were some national myths which New Zealanders should be able to laugh at:

'Congratulations to the perpetrators – it was the best New Zealand entertainment in ten years!'[17]

'The producers have done us all a service by showing how easy it is to hoodwink a viewing public that has been conditioned to believe that anything labelled "documentary" is necessarily the truth. Viewers should bear this experience in mind, and keep a pinch of salt handy, when watching supposedly more serious documentaries or "infodocs" on current issues, especially controversial ones.'[18]

In a follow-up article in the *Listener*, Botes offered the following response as his favourite: 'One Network News admitted that last night's *Montana Sunday Theatre* was a hoax. Well, all credibility has gone down the tubes – I won't be believing in TVNZ's news anymore.'[19] These viewers could perhaps be termed 'televisually sophisticated', in that they did not automatically assume that information structured within a documentary discourse was accurate, or even non-fictional. In Cawelti's terms, they were prepared to engage in the programme's effort to demythologise the documentary form itself.

C. Negative/hostile: The most interesting responses to the programme were those which expressed anger at having been taken in by the hoax, and especially at the willingness of the film makers to play with some of the more central aspects of the rhetoric of objectivity which serves as the basis for television documentary and news texts (as discussed above).

'I do not wish to reveal my score on a gullibility rating of 0 to 100 percent. Suffice to say, I was not entirely surprised to discover it was a hoax, but was also profoundly disturbed by the discovery that I had been duped. If on this, then on what else? God, the Pope, the integrity of *Fair Go,* Richard Long, Judy Bailey, the last shreds of Paul Holmes; all disappearing down a gurgling plughole of lost credibility.'[20]

'I can't express my disappointment at having lost a genius and gained another "clever" film maker. A wise film maker of yesteryear (when standards were more stodgy) warned against tricking or insulting your audience. Whatever its motive, this film could not be said to be in sympathy with its audience. I doubt if I'll ever look at the work of Peter Jackson (or the *Listener*) in quite the same light again.'[21]

'Because of the damage to true documentary and the misuse of that honoured term, I for one, after a lifetime of interest in film, have resigned my membership of the Film Society.'[22]

'Peter Jackson and his Silver Screen conspirators should be shot.'[23]

These types of responses seem to be representative of viewers who positioned themselves in relation to the programme with a number of basic assumptions in mind. They seemed, first of all, to be unable or unwilling to accept that documentary techniques are themselves conventional forms of representation, rather than being able to serve as tools capable of revealing some pre-existing reality. Given the constructed (and hence partial and relative) nature of audio-visual texts, the attempt to treat visual and audio-visual documents as 'evidence' or 'remnants' of this reality is inherently problematic. The makers of news and documentary texts, however, often (or perhaps invariably) prefer to adhere to the professional ideology mentioned above, one which constructs a role for journalists and documentary front-persons of balanced, objective and politically neutral observers of the historical world.

The implicit acceptance of viewers of this same ideology apparently led many to express a feeling of betrayal at having their expectations and assumptions in some sense 'violated' by *Forgotten Silver* not having been labelled as fictional. In this case the violation is of an apparent trust which these audience members feel exists between themselves and Television New Zealand as an institution, a trust which is itself a legacy of TVNZ's history as a BBC-styled public broadcasting service.[24] The programme itself violated some of the more 'sacred' myths of New Zealand history, in particular those surrounding the experiences of New Zealanders in war, and, perhaps significantly for some viewers, did so within a serious drama timeslot on a Sunday.[25]

A perhaps third aspect of the negative reaction to the programme could also be a degree of anti-intellectualism – the idea that this was a hoax which was just too clever, that it could not have been unravelled except by the most visually sophisticated viewers. Here the anger seems to be directed at film makers who would supposedly play with some of the more treasured popular New Zealand legends (such as the alleged pre-Wright brothers flight of Richard Pearse) largely for their own amusement.

Discussion

The challenge which Jackson and Botes made, in producing *Forgotten Silver* and perpetrating the hoax of its documentary status, was not just to the acceptance of a form of representation, but to a climate of adherence to assumptions concerning the 'truthfulness' of documentary texts. As audience members, we do not turn away from a documentary and say, 'it's just a film.' Documentary invites you to act upon the knowledge it presents, and as it is embedded in and representative of the historical world it requires such a response.

The most significant legacy of *Forgotten Silver* is not its status as a hoax. It is the programme's exercise in engaging us in a documentary mode of viewing in such a way which causes us to reflect upon the way in which these modes appropriate important aspects of myth. This appropriation has implications for the very screen form which documentary texts utilise in their effort to establish themselves as 'documents' of the historical world. As some viewers commented, if Jackson and Botes can make us believe in a fiction, then what are the implications for other film makers, and other texts, which attempt to do this on a day to day basis? Documentary has continued to retain something of a sacred place within contemporary society, despite widespread acceptance of the notion that experience, and its representation, is extremely, and inherently, relative.

This relativity of experience should also be applied to representations of the historical world. Documentary texts, even in a purely formal sense, can be difficult to distinguish from drama. The argumentative nature of documentary modes of representation, as Nichols suggests, distinguishes documentaries from fictional texts. The logic underlying such arguments, however, necessarily involves an appeal to a partial and selective understanding of the historical world which they claim to reveal. The 'truth' contained within documentaries is always relative. As Jackson claimed in his own defence – in a television news story on *Forgotten Silver* the day after its first screening – he is 'in the business of creating illusions', a *raison dêtre* which could be extended to the very form which his film effectively attempt-

Colin McKenzie stands in front of costumed extras on Salome, *his 'forgotten' silent masterpiece. Jackson and Botes's mock-ups of early cinema made their hoax convincing.*

ed to demythologise.

This is perhaps a fear of some of the audience members who reacted so negatively to the first screening of *Forgotten Silver*. One of the more interesting public responses to the programme was the following:

'The connection with Richard Pearse was tasteless and left many in South Canterbury disappointed and angry. It also may have the effect of discounting any claim that he might have of being the first to fly, for many may now dismiss his life as part of the hoax that the film has perpetuated.'[26]

The undermining of a special status for documentary forms of representation is not a matter for purely academic debate. Documentary texts attempt to offer us a series of insights and revelations concerning the nature of the historical world, and the forces which shape this world. The knowledge they impart, however relative, necessarily serves as the basis for how we make decisions, individually and collectively, on the extent of our social, economic and political engagement with our part of this realm. In a discussion of the Spielberg film *Schindler's List*[27], Weissman argued that in choosing not to represent on film certain events of the Holocaust, Spielberg was in effect allowing those events to 'disappear from history'. In a similar way, the letter above suggests that the truthful elements contained within *Forgotten Silver* will in fact now be considered as false and, as such, removed from history. However, this argument could be turned on its head to produce a very different conclusion. The fact that the life and work of Colin McKenzie has been immortalised on film (whether authentic or not) allows it to enter into the realm of History. In effect, he now has an existence within a historical reality which is external to the film. For better or worse, Colin McKenzie is forever located within the public consciousness in New Zealand. The fiction has become a 'truth'.

NOTES

1. J. G. Cawelti, '*Chinatown* and Generic Transformation in Recent American Films', in G. Mast and M. Cohen (editors), *Film Theory and Criticism: Introductory Readings*, Third Edition, Oxford University Press, New York, 1985, p515.

2. B. Nichols, *Representing Reality*, Indiana Universiy Press, 1991.

3. D. Welch, 'Heavenly Features', *Listener*, October 28, 1995, pp31-32.

4. In the article Jackson is quoted as stating that there 'was some pressure on us at first to possibly dramatise some aspects of Colin's life, but frankly, even though it's a documentary, the events of his life were so dramatic that the word drama is not inappropriate,' and Botes apparently offers the claim that 'It's as gripping as any fictional story.' Among other clues, the article also specifically highlights the fact that *Forgotten Silver* was to be featured within a programme slot reserved for dramatic productions.

5. These have surfaced occasionally during the long run of the series, and have included 'reports' on a remote-controlled sheep-dog, protective gumboots for turkeys, a farmer using his fence as a musical instrument, and an episode featuring the lifestyle of 'farmer' Fred Dagg.

6. These are not explicitly labelled as such, but the news frontpersons always provide quite blatant signals for their audience to read, and effectively these items are separated from the remainder of the news content.

7. J. Corner, *Television and Public Address*, London: Edward Arnold, 1995 .

8. See for example, R. Silverstone, *Framing Science: The Making of a BBC Documentary*, London: BFI, 1985. Also, B. Winston , 'The Documentary Film as Scientific Inscription', In M. Renov (Editor), *Theorizing Documentary*, London: Routledge, 1993.

9. Or even the computer 'enhancement' of the newspaper date in the Pearse flight footage.

10. P. Rosen, 'Document and Documentary: On the Persistence of Historical Concepts', In M. Renov (Editor), *Theorizing Documentary*, London: Routledge, 1993.

11. R. Campbell, in 'Securing the Middle Ground: Reporter Formulas in *60 Minutes*' in R. A. Avery and D. Eason (Editors), *Critical Perspectives on Media and Society*, New York: The Guilford Press, 1991, offers a break-down of the various narrative formulas commonly offered by (American) programmes centred around reporters. These are reporter as detective, analyst and tourist.

12. Ibid, pp.280-287.

13. In a completely unconscious way, the local television coverage of the last Americas Cup competition appealed to this same mythology. Here it was the supposed small-town technology which defeated that of the American superpower, and in a fashion acclaimed as being true to some of the basic values of the country itself (hard work, persistence, and a sense of fair play).

14. Letters to the editor, *Listener*, November 25, 1995, p12.

15. The Film and Television Studies Department at the University of Waikato, for example, received calls from viewers anxious to know whether or not the programme was actually a hoax, and where they could view a copy of McKenzie's *Salome*.

16. Such as the tenuousness of the 'scientific' basis to the egg and plant chemistry experiments from which McKenzie supposedly developed film stock, an interview with an Alexandra Nevsky at the Russian embassy, the numerous references to Taurus (bull) symbols, the sign on the wall, over a bucket, in one shot of the Film Archive restoration room which reads: 'Spillage Response Kit', and so on. The final image of the programme itself has McKenzie grinning while filming himself in a mirror, with credits for the writing and direction of Jackson and Botes superimposed.

17. J. Chadwick, (Orewa), letter to the editor, *Listener*, November 25, 1995, p12.

18. K. C. Durrant (Upper Hutt), letter to the editor, Ibid.

19. C. Chapple, 'Gone, Not Forgotten', *Listener*, November 25, 1995, p26.

20. I. McKissak, (Hamilton), letter to the editor, *Listener*, November 25, 1995, p12.

21. G. A. De Forest, (Te Atatu Peninsula), letter to the editor, Ibid.

22. W. J. Gaudin (Christchurch), letter to the editor, Ibid.

23. S. Anderson, (Herne Bay, Auckland), letter to the editor, Ibid.

24. It is interesting to speculate whether TV3, the much younger rival to TVNZ, would have received the same degree of vilification from members of its audience if it had been the channel to broadcast *Forgotten Silver*.

25. Our thanks to Dr. Mike Goldsmith at the University of Waikato for pointing out that the comparatively close-knit nature of New Zealand society, together with the, for Pakeha, shallow time-depth to New Zealand history, means that many historical events attain a sacred significance.

26. W. J. Gaudin (Christchurch), letter to the editor, *Listener*, November 25, 1995, p12.

27. G. Weissman, 'A Fantasy of Witnessing', *Media, Culture & Society*, Volume Seventeen, 1995, pp293-307.

FORGOTTEN SILVER
The *Variety* Review by David Stratton

This wickedly clever hoax 'documentary' is a highly amusing satire on the recent spate of historical documentaries made to celebrate the centenary of cinema. Top Kiwi director Peter Jackson (*Heavenly Creatures*) and film critic Costa Botes collaborated on this lavishly produced labour of love, which provoked complaints from deceived viewers when it aired on NZ television late last year. Now available on 35mm, it's a must for film fests, TV programmers and audiences interested in film history.

The film deals with the career of a supposedly forgotten pioneer of international cinema, Colin McKenzie, who was allegedly born in rural New Zealand in 1888. McKenzie had been completely forgotten until decomposing reels of his films were discovered in a shed in the garden of Hannah McKenzie, his second wife, who happened to be a neighbour of Jackson's parents.

According to the film, McKenzie became fascinated with all things mechanical at an early age, and invented a motion picture camera in 1900 when he was twelve; unlike other early cameras, this one was mechanised by being attached first to a bicycle and later to a steam engine, allowing for trailblazing tracking shots.

McKenzie produced his own film stock from raw eggs; it evidently took twelve eggs to produce one minute of film. He filmed the first flight of a New Zealand aviator who, his footage now reveals, preceded the Wright brothers. In 1908, he made an 84-minute feature, *The Warrior Season*, which employed a primitive soundtrack; unfortunately, the actors were Chinese, and McKenzie had not invented subtitles, so the film was not a success.

In 1911, McKenzie discovered a way to make colour film stock from a type of berry found only on one of the Tahitian islands. He shot some test footage there, but some dusky, topless Tahitian maidens appeared unexpectedly in front of the camera, and when McKenzie returned to Kiwiland, he and his brother, Brooke, were convicted of exhibiting a lewd document and sentenced to six months' hard labour.

McKenzie then worked on a series of slapstick comedies with a vaudeville comedian known as Stan the Man; the pair invented a type of violent slapstick involving custard pies, later copied by Mack Sennett and others. There was more trouble when Stan, who liked to attack passersby with his pies, inadvertently assaulted New Zealand's prime minister, who was not amused.

McKenzie's greatest achievement was the epic *Salome*, which was filmed on and off over a number of years in a remote location, where a vast set was built for large-scale battle scenes. When money ran out, funding was provided by the new Soviet government, on condition some ideological changes were made to the script.

McKenzie went to Spain in 1936 to cover the Civil War and managed to film his own death in 1937.

The supposedly aged film material has been created with tremendous skill and care. Scenes from *Salome* look as if they could have been made at about the time of *Intolerance*;

acting styles, colour tinting, use of circular frames and irises, and even the intertitles are astonishingly close to the real thing. It looks as though hundreds of extras were used during the staging of this fake footage.

Several well-known personalities appear in the film. Leonard Maltin enthusiastically, and with a commendably straight face, explains McKenzie's historical importance. Harvey Weinstein lauds *Salome* as 'the greatest film discovery of the last 50 years'; actor Sam Neill adds authenticity, commenting on McKenzie's importance to NZ film history.

The pic identifies none of the actors who appear in *Forgotten Silver*, not even the actor who plays the mythical McKenzie, but he certainly looks the part.

This exceptionally elaborate hoax will provide plenty of appreciative chuckles, especially from film buffs. Produced in the $500,000 range, this little gem is a remarkable film in its own right.

The
FRIGHTENERS

THE FRIGHTENERS
Peter Jackson Interviewed by Michael Helms

Peter Jackson admits to a lot of weird things about *The Frighteners*. Like the way he and Fran Walsh had been labouring over the script, thinking that Robert Zemeckis was more than a good possibility to direct it. Then came the phone call. Zemeckis really liked the script but would Jackson be interested in helming *The Frighteners*? 'It was actually the first time I'd ever thought about directing it – which was kind of weird since we'd written the script; so I ummed and ahhed,' laughs the bearded triple-threat filmmaker. 'The story is quite weird. It's been around for a long time and the script was written during the shooting of *Heavenly Creatures*. *Heavenly Creatures* was written during *Braindead*, so one movie has had its birth during the previous one,' he states incredulously. We're firmly ensconced in the haven that is the director's Quiet Room, high above several expansive sets of *The Frighteners* in the Wingnut Films offices, and Jackson has taken part of his afternoon off to chat to *Fangoria*. It's a mere week from the end of principal photography on this epic production and, although it's hard not to hide the rigours of a full-on writing and filming schedule that has now entered its seventh month, Jackson does begin to look more relaxed as he gets stuck right into the gestation story behind his ghostly comedy.

'Some time after *Braindead* was finished, Fran and I were mucking about with story ideas. We wanted to see whether we could get some spec scripts sold in Hollywood. As far as making them, we wouldn't have anything to do with them. They'd just be a bit of work we could do; like in between movies. It's the sort of thing I'd like to do. I still haven't really done it, but from time to time just to do a little bit of script writing instead of filmmaking – just to have a break from all this craziness. So we came up with this idea and wrote a two-page outline which we sent to our agent in Hollywood. If he thinks it's a good idea to show it to anyone, he does. Not long after, he heard that Robert Zemeckis was looking for story and script ideas for a series of *Tales from the Crypt* movies. The plan then was that the guys who developed the *Tales from the Crypt* show – Zemeckis, Richard Donner, etc. – they were all going to direct a feature film and all had scripts except for Bob. So our agent duly fired the outline across to his office. He liked the story idea and we had a meeting. He said, "This sounds like a neat idea but I don't think it's necessarily *Tales from the Crypt*. It doesn't quite fit but I like it anyway, so let's develop it."'

Suddenly Jackson changes the tone and pace of his conversation, breaking into a broad smile as if preparing to deliver a major punchline: 'The call to direct *The Frighteners* actually came in about Jan/Feb 1994. *Heavenly Creatures* wasn't finished. I eventually said to Bob, "Yes. I'd like to direct *The Frighteners*. But how about doing it in New Zealand?", and he said, "Okay. If you can make it look like middle America."' Talking with Jackson, it's not hard to understand that this is the most salient factor behind his directorial involvement in *The Frighteners*, and a point that he's positively proud of even if the film is actually set in America. Whatever the results, it's a facet of the film that's sure to differentiate it from previous studio product.

Jackson continues, 'We immediately sent someone around New Zealand taking pho-

Jackson and animatronic hound, during shooting for The Frighteners *(1996). This tongue-in-cheek horror story saw the director and his team merge CGI with more literal special effects.*

tos of small towns. Bob and Universal were happy with the stills and the whole thing came together relatively quickly. Fran and I wrote more drafts and had more meetings, and we were still taking *Heavenly Creatures* through its final stages of post and into festivals. That about sums up '94, that and getting *The Frighteners* ready to shoot.'

But that's not really all. Jackson almost had to be coaxed into mentioning two other film projects made in between *Heavenly Creatures* and *The Frighteners* that he's been associated with. *Jack Brown, Genius* is a low-budget fantasy flick starring *Braindead*'s Tim Balme, who plays an addled inventor obsessed with self-propelled human flight. Largely the work of writer/director Tony Hiles, who previously produced the rarely screened documentary about the making of *Bad Taste* titled *Good Taste*, which did appear on British TV during 1995, *Jack Brown, Genius* will have Jackson listed as its executive producer when it finally extricates itself from post-production Hell. During a shooting lull on the next day, the perpetually cheery Sue Rogers, publicist for *The Frighteners* and producer of *Jack Brown* (alongside *The Frighteners* co-producer and editor Jamie Selkirk) takes us for a quick trip to a downtown Wellington sound studio, where they proceed to hammer out the details of the *Jack Brown* score while we get to witness several sequences from the film. Even though it's aimed at a more than slightly youthful audience, *Jack Brown, Genius* does heavily feature the fantastic work of Jackson's effects company Weta Ltd, and specifically the prosthetics and model making of Richard Taylor with digital dynamics from George Port. Both are frequent Jackson collaborators and have integral positions in *The Frighteners*.

Speaking of TV, we also get to witness the hour-long documentary entitled *Forgotten Silver*, which Jackson co-directed for New Zealand TV. Purportedly documenting New Zealand's (and the world's) first feature filmmaker and universal cinematic innovator, the massively unheralded Colin McKenzie, *Forgotten Silver* not only presents Jackson as an authoritive talking head (he will appear in *The Frighteners* as he does in *Heavenly Creatures*), but also drags in such luminaries as movie mogul Harvey Weinstein and critic Leonard Maltin to gab on about the wondrous Mr. McKenzie. Jackson elaborates, 'We shot *Forgotten Silver* early in '95, just before we started work on *The Frighteners*, and that was fun. Shooting 30 set-ups a day with a small crew was great.' Sweeping his hands around the room he reasons, 'I certainly love being in the middle of all this, but the concept of doing a little film with a small crew certainly has its appeal.' Wherever you are and whatever you do, don't pass up any opportunity to catch *Forgotten Silver*, which does for film history what *Spinal Tap* does for rock'n'roll.

To questions regarding his relationship with Universal, he answers in several ways: 'Firstly, I've got nothing but good things to say about working with a major studio, especially if they leave us alone to make the film as Universal have. The way things ended up going was that we wrote a script for Bob, who saw it and liked it before the studio ever knew anything about it. Bob had a development deal with Universal. In other words, the studio didn't even know the project existed until they saw that script, by which stage Bob obviously liked it and wanted to go ahead with it, so he came to them with an enthusiastic approach. I'm sure the studio reaction to the project would have been very different if it had just been me hammering on their door saying, "Read this, and I want to make it in New Zealand." Because it's Bob Zemeckis it softens the nerves a little bit, I think. One of the things that has been great has been Bob's confidence in us all the way through, which has rubbed off on the studio. "Bob's happy; Bob likes the dailies; Bob likes the footage he's seen" – so the studio like it. I'm sure it's had that kind of effect.'

Answering further questions re Universal, Jackson re-emphasises his relationship with his executive producer: 'I don't have final cut on the film, but I knew that going in. But Bob's got final cut, so I have no qualms about that. The guy's made some great movies, so I'm quite happy for him to have that sort of control. But it's not really like that. Bob's been very definite all the way through that I should make the sort of film I want to make. His feeling is that he wants me to make this because of my previous movies, and he does n't want anything, either from him or the studio, to intrude on what I want to do, because otherwise it's not my film: it becomes some weird hybrid. So, he's been very supportive and given me freedom. I've never had a discussion with Bob at any stage about whether I should shoot this differently or that differently – he's just left me alone. Where he has been very useful has been with suggestions in terms of scheduling and budgets and the nuts and bolts of getting the film made. Certainly he's never attempted to really have major creative input, which is great, because I guess it means he's happy with what he's seen. If he wasn't happy I suppose it would be a different story.'

Jackson constantly refers to *The Frighteners* as a collaborative work, and goes on to relate a decidedly unique aspect of the film's production: 'Fran and I have re-written the script all the way through the shoot, which is the way we like to work. We see the rush-es and see how the film is developing and then re-write. Just about every week we've been inserting new pages. All the time we just try to stay ahead of ourselves and to keep improving it. The guys at Universal say this is the first time this has ever happened. Usually they don't re-write much because, if they finance a film, then, in a year's time, that's the film they want to see. But the folks at Universal have been really pleased, because they have seen that we've been improving it and so they say, "Great. If you want to change this – OK." So that experience has been very good. I don't feel that at any point they have tried to influence me in any way at all. I've had total freedom,' says the director almost disbelievingly.

Concerning differences between his usual style and that of *The Frighteners*, Jackson gives his response: 'My style, I guess, is just me making a movie and saying, "I think it would be really neat to do this or to do that." Certainly I have no reason to think my style's been impeded. *The Frighteners* does contain a reasonable number of visual gags but it's a different type of genre. Obviously it's not a splatter genre so it's not style, it's a genre thing. In terms of my filmmaking style, this is just another movie I'm making. I certain-ly haven't consciously changed my style or done anything differently on this one. It's just a character comedy really. A psychological black comedy. It's got ghosts and some hor-rific stuff in it – some monsters and some psychos. It hasn't got the graphic gore because it's a studio movie and we're not trying to make *Braindead 2*. We're trying to make a dif-ferent type of movie. It has the same sensibility and the same black comic feel. It's a sim-ilar mix but without the gore. Michael [J.] Fox describes it as Truffaut meets *The Mask*. Bob Zemeckis was going on a description of it as a combination of *Ghostbusters* and *Natural Born Killers*. Hollywood always has to categorise you and has to mix the films to try to explain it,' laughs Jackson.

Asked to nominate a personal favourite aspect of *The Frighteners*, Jackson responds

Psychic con artist Frank Bannister (Michael J. Fox) pursued down a dark corridor by FBI Agent Milton Dammers (Jeffrey Combs).

thoughtfully: 'At the end of the day, this has been a real performance movie, which has been fun for me. *Heavenly Creatures* was in a sense, but it was about other things as well. This film is based totally on character and story. There's special effects, but we don't ram them in people's faces. It's like there's 400–550 special effects shots – about half the movie probably – but it's ghosts as characters, and kind of fun. The cast have been fantastic; great cast, best I've had.'

This observation leads Jackson to a Michael J. Fox anecdote: 'Michael really gets into character. There's a ghost in *The Frighteners* called The Judge [John Astin], an old character who's now mummified. Rick Baker has done the make-up for The Judge. In the movie, Michael's relationship with The Judge is that of a wise old guy who imparts all this information to Michael, but he's also a crazy, bug-eyed, mummified sort of guy. A vaguely similar relationship to that between Christopher Lloyd and Marty McFly. Twice it's happened that Michael has to say "Hey, Judge," and on take one he says, "Hey, Doc," and then, "Oh, damn," as he suddenly realises he's got the wrong guy. Like I said, the film has been fun to make.' Broaching the subject of casting, Jackson again cites Universal as being completely supportive. 'Fran and I obviously took the casting very seriously, and they didn't try to put anyone on the film. If you get the script right and the casting right it becomes very difficult to make a bad movie. We liked the script and we just wanted to be sure we got the very best cast for the characters. The role that Michael plays is a difficult combination of straight drama and comedy. We came up with names of various comic performers, because we could see that this character is funny but we wanted him to be a real person, not a goofy clown. So we needed to find an actor who could do the dramatic role and also deliver the comedy. When you start thinking in those terms, it's hard to think of people. It's a straight role in a sense, but the guy gets caught up in such ridiculous circumstances that he just has to acknowledge the humour whilst not actually creating it, not playing up to it – similar to Lionel in *Braindead* really. We thought of Michael and mentioned him to Bob. Bob has a relationship with him and said, "If you want Michael, I'm happy to give him a call, send him a script and see what he says." I met Michael in Toronto, at a film festival there, and he was immediately willing to sign on and give it a go.'

Casting his mind further afield, we couldn't resist asking Jackson about his response to the American R-rated version of *Braindead*, which immediately gets a big laugh. 'I loved the version where they removed about eighteen minutes. I think it's a real laugh. A bunch of us sat down with beers and watched it and laughed every time it got cut. The lawnmower sequence is virtually gone – Lionel walks in the front door and then, the next minute, he's standing among these piles of bodies. I don't take any of that stuff seriously. The whole rating system in America is totally stupid. But it doesn't worry me because the unrated version is easily available. The fans who want to see that sort of film can get copies anywhere in the world, which is just great. So who cares if someone puts out the R-rated version? Too bad.'

Conversely, Jackson welcomed the opportunity to reduce *Heavenly Creatures*. 'Miramax wanted it to be a bit shorter for America, so Fran and I looked at it again and thoroughly tightened it. Now we actually prefer the American version to the NZ one, which is ten minutes longer. It just takes some of the sluggishness out of it,' observes the director. Jackson went on to talk about the Oscar nomination for *Heavenly Creatures*: 'It was surprising. I didn't think films like *Heavenly Creatures* got any attention by the Oscar people and the Academy. That was very good,' he says with a huge smile. But in the same breath, he also describes as a complete debacle the controversy surrounding Anne Perry, the real-life character portrayed in the film. 'I wish it had never happened. We were aware of her identity as we were making it. We didn't tell anybody, thinking it was best. At the end of the movie, when we have the trailer credits explaining what happened to people, we didn't say that Juliet wrote under the name of Anne Perry. We felt an obligation to respect her privacy. In all the interviews I've done, I've never told anyone. But, eventually, it was uncovered by this journalist. I regret it, because no one who's basically lived a private life for 40 years deserves to have someone go around and uncover these aspects of their private life. Especially as she served her time in prison. It wasn't as though there was some outstanding debt to society that had to be paid. She'd done that, so it was completely unnecessary,' says the director, getting as close to anger as this interviewer has ever witnessed.

Quickly changing the subject, Jackson expresses delight in owning a poster for the somewhat belated North American theatrical release of *Meet the Feebles*. He's also keyed up for the first-time US theatrical release of *Bad Taste*.

Declining to name any film jobs Hollywood's offered in the wake of his previous films ('Just a bunch of stuff – different movies. I shouldn't go through a list of movies I've turned down because it's a bit embarrassing'), Jackson can allude to what might be consuming him in the future. 'What I've ended up doing is getting a deal with Miramax – a development deal that lets me develop my own projects, and they have a first look at them for anything they like. And that's the sort of deal I like, because I'm interested in scripts. I'm still not enthusiastic about shooting other people's scripts. It doesn't appeal to me: I find it hard to get worked up about other people's material.'

As to whether Jackson would ever attempt a straight horror film, the filmmaker replies in the negative: 'I don't think so. I find it hard to keep a straight face. To do a straight horror film you have to take the whole thing seriously, and I find it hard to take a lot of things seriously – especially in filmmaking. If you took all this seriously you'd go crazy. Actually we've got one or two ideas for a couple of low-budget films – a psychological thriller and two or three character films. Right now, I don't know when I'll make another film, because 1996 looks like being totally with this [*The Frighteners*] still. And then I'll have a rest,' he says hopefully.

As for *The Frighteners*, Jackson must have the last word: 'This is one movie I can't wait to see finished. Unlike any other movie I've worked on, where you cut it as you shoot, so by the time you finish shooting you've a fair idea of what you've got, this movie, because it's blue screens, it's going to take months to put it all together, to do the CGI effects to be added on to make some shots really impressive. I just want to see the finished movie. I'd love to be able to click my fingers and walk into a cinema and watch it,' says the director, as he's called back to the set. Yeah, you and the whole *Fangoria* readership, Peter.

THE FRIGHTENERS:
The Thrill of the Haunt
by Mark Cotta Vaz

Some ghosts only go bump in the night. But in *The Frighteners*, a Universal summer release, one malevolent spirit takes the form of the hooded, scythe-wielding Grim Reaper to embark on a virulent killing spree. Only psychic con man Frank Bannister (Michael J. Fox) stands between the evil spectre and the living.

For director Peter Jackson – who also wrote the script with longtime partner Fran Walsh – *The Frighteners* was an opportunity to not only spin a supernatural thriller but indulge a lifelong love of the magical possibilities of visual effects. 'We wrote this ghost story with the ghosts being the principal characters,' Jackson related. 'I wanted them to be realised through visual effects – but the effects definitely had to service the story. My hope was that audiences would respond to the movie like they would to a roller-coaster ride through a haunted mansion.'

The spectral players included the Reaper – the killer ghost who would go through several transformations in the film – as well as Bannister's trio of spirit sidekicks and a number of graveyard ghosts. The effects were even slated to provide a glimpse of heaven and hell. In all, 570 shots would be produced at the computer workstations of Jackson's

Ghostly gunfighter The Judge, played by John Astin. Astin is familiar as Gomez from creepy TV comedy The Addams Family, *while his son, Sean, would later play Samwise Gamgee.*

own effects company. Other renaissance filmmakers had taken this course – most notably George Lucas, whose seminal *Star Wars* effects unit became Industrial Light & Magic, and, more recently, James Cameron, who co-launched Digital Domain – but Jackson organised *his* effects house in his native New Zealand, far from the stateside talent pool and technological resources.

Jackson began dabbling in computer generated effects with his 1994 feature *Heavenly Creatures*, a true tale based on a notorious mid-fifties case of matricide in New Zealand. Jackson's cinematic account of the murder pact between teenagers was an unlikely CG project; but having created the effects-laden *Dead Alive* with longtime associate Richard Taylor, he was determined to come to terms with the digital possibilities presented by such breakthrough films as *Terminator 2* and *Jurassic Park*. 'I was aware that CG was the way effects were heading,' Jackson noted, 'and that both intrigued me and scared me. Part of the fun of doing *Dead Alive* was that Richard and I had been able to do the effects in-house. I wanted to keep making my movies in New Zealand; but I was worried that, with CG, I wouldn't be able to do my own effects, that I'd have to farm them all out to the States. With that in mind, Fran and I deliberately wrote the *Heavenly Creatures* script to include some CG sequences. We'd write something like, "The girls run across a barren hillside, which magically morphs into a beautiful garden," with the word "morph" actually in the script.'

Jackson earmarked several hundred thousand dollars of his $2.5 million *Heavenly Creatures* budget for the hardware and software he would need to start up a digital effects department. Freighted to New Zealand was an Oxberry Cinescan 6200, a Solitaire film recorder, a Silicon Graphics Indigo computer, along with appropriate software. To get things rolling, Jackson hired his computer savvy friend George Port, who spent some four months setting up, then single-handedly produced about 30 CG shots for the movie.

During this start-up period, Jackson and his associates officially organised Weta Ltd., incorporating the computer graphics department and a creature effects shop headed by Richard Taylor. Following *Heavenly Creatures*, several more workstations and digital artists were added as the CG unit ramped up to produce 150 shots for a New Zealand feature called *Jack Brown, Genius*. At the onset of *The Frighteners*, the CG crew expanded further to twenty artists, who started producing images that were almost too successful. The early effects rushes so enthralled Universal executives that the planned Halloween '96 release date was moved up to summer, shortening the original work schedule by three to four months.

At that nexus, the studio proposed farming out shots to stateside effects facilities – which would have deflated Jackson's dream of keeping the work in-house. At last, the studio agreed to increase the film's effects budget, allowing Jackson to infuse his New Zealand base with more talent and technology. That breakout creative period was capped with the hiring of Wes Ford Takahashi – a former ILM effects animation supervisor – to supervise the visual effects. 'When I hired Wes, it was a turning point,' Jackson stated. 'Our approach of growing slowly as an effects unit, which we'd taken with *Heavenly Creatures* and *Jack Brown*, had finally caught up with us. We were working with talented CG people, but no one was experienced in running a big CG department. We needed someone to come in and tie the whole thing together. Wes also had contacts in the States, and was able to get some people to come to New Zealand. We finally got another fifteen experienced CG artists to complement our core New Zealand group, ending up with 35 artists and 35 workstations.'

One of the major effects challenges facing the revamped Weta was the killer ghost. Revealed as the spectral remains of executed mass murderer Johnny Bartlett (Jake Busey), the ghost worked in dark communion with his still living accomplice Patricia (Dee Wallace Stone). In addition to his Grim Reaper form, Johnny's ghost would have two further incarnations: a character the crew dubbed Wallpaper Man, which undulated underneath the walls and floorboards of Patricia's old house, and a dripping blob-like figure. All three characters would be conjured up as ingenious CG creations – although the Reaper was originally envisioned as a practical effect. 'We set out with the intention of doing the Reaper as a rod puppet,' commented Jackson, 'maybe shooting it in a water tank. We even thought of shooting someone, dressed in costume, at different camera speeds. We did a lot of tests, but the Reaper wasn't coming across as menacing and predatory. By the time we started shooting the movie, we still hadn't achieved any success with the Reaper puppet or our other practical approaches. I shot plates of Michael J. Fox reacting to the Grim Reaper, allowing space in frame for the character, but not yet knowing how we were going to create it.'

With the practical approach going nowhere, the production turned to a computer graphics solution. Taking the lead in creating the synthetic figure of death were Takahashi and CG supervisor Gray Horsfield, one of a supervisory team that included Wayne Stables, John Sheils and Matt Aitken. Softimage was used for walking and other primary animation, with Wavefront's Dynamation package providing such secondary animation effects as the spectre's rippling robe. That company's Explore software was used for rendering and lighting.

With nearly 100 Reaper shots required – many of which would have to be composited in with real actors and settings – the production shot its live-action plates motion control at 24 frames per second. 'We'd take the data from the computer operated motion control camera,' explained Matt Aitken, 'and use it to describe the path of the virtual camera for the computer graphics element. Other times, when Peter wanted to use a hand-held camera – which is part of his visual style – we'd just do a visual match-move to come up with the appropriate position of our CG camera.'

While the computer generated effects were usually achieved with off-the-shelf software, more specialised effects required customised software. A case in point was the Wallpaper Man, who opens the film in grand style as dizzying camera moves follow his form scuttling through the ceiling, wall and carpeted floors. 'The running ghost began with the animation of a 3-D human form,' Aitken explained. 'Then we'd use a piece of code that I wrote to wrap a surface over the 3-D figure. After that, it was a case of classic computer graphics techniques like texture-mapping a carpet pattern over the shape and applying shadows and lighting to match the scene.' A shot of the Wallpaper Man rising up from the hallway carpet and dragging Patricia from behind required the compositing of an element of the actress being handled by a blue-suited performer – ultimately replaced with the final CG-carpeted figure – and a motion control plate of the hallway set.

The blob man, which required additional proprietary code, made its appearance in a graveyard scene wherein Bannister's astral form battles the Reaper. The Reaper is finally reduced to a bubbly blob of tar-like goo, a piece of which forms the face of Johnny Bartlett. To achieve the shot, a plaster cast of Jake Busey's head was digitized, with actual photography of the actor's face texture-mapped onto the base geometry. Spattered pieces ultimately drip into an underground crypt where the ghost coalesces into the blob character.

While the killer ghost was manifested in spectacular incarnations, other ghosts in the film were rendered as humans who had clearly gone beyond the mortal pale. 'I wanted the human ghosts to be transparent and glowing,' Jackson explained, 'but still reasonably traditional. I didn't want some weird, shimmering thing that was so unique it would distract from the story.'

What Jackson and his team came up with was a look reminiscent of light refracting through water. 'The backgrounds warp as the ghosts pass by,' said Aitken. 'We combined that with a glow emanating off the characters.' The ghost actors were shot bluescreen, with the resulting elements manipulated to produce the glowing spirit effect. 'Since the ghosts were shot bluescreen, they could be composited with a variable opacity. Colour grading and consistency were also big issues since the ghosts were transparent and were being added onto backgrounds that changed in colour as the ghosts moved past them. We had to compensate for those changes in the colour of the ghosts themselves.'

Other prominent ghost characters include the trio with whom Bannister runs a haunting con. The most distinctive among them was The Judge (John Astin), a gun-sling-

Con man Bannister with his spectral accomplices Stuart (Jim Fyfe, left) and Cyrus (Chi McBride). The Frighteners *concentrated more on ghostly comedy than gore.*

ing wraith from the Old West. While Bannister's two other spirit partners, Stuart (Jim Fyfe) and Cyrus (Chi McBride), were somewhat recently deceased, The Judge was very old, even by ghostly standards – evidenced by his withering ectoplasmic skin and a jaw-bone coming off at the hinges. Because of the peculiar physical qualities Jackson envisioned for The Judge, the director called in Academy Award-winning makeup artist Rick Baker to design the character's visage. Baker then trained Brian Penikas to apply the makeup at the shooting location in New Zealand.

Baker started his work by inviting Astin to sit in a makeup chair still warm from an Eddie Murphy *Nutty Professor* makeup session conducted earlier that day. 'I wanted to see how much I could do out of the kit, without putting a bunch of appliances on him,' Baker recalled. 'I built up some old-age stipple here and there to see how much his skin would crinkle up. Since The Judge was going to be a double-exposed ghost effect, we had to be pretty theatrical. The shadows were darker, the highlights were lighter and the overall makeup was punched up so it would read through. We probably could have done the entire makeup without appliances, but for continuity and to save time we decided it would be best not to fabricate stuff on his face every day. Ultimately, the makeup was a combination – 50 percent out-of-the-kit and 50 percent appliances, such as an acrylic lower teeth piece and a jawbone.'

The finale of the film takes place on the edge of heaven, with a downward look at a gargantuan worm swallowing up the ghosts of Johnny and Patricia and diving down into the fires of hell. In the scene, the two evil spirits – floating in a tunnel of light – are about to return to their murdering haunts when the tunnel transforms into the fleshy interior of the worm. Hundreds of serpents writhe out from the wall of flesh to rip through the damned characters. Gray Horsfield headed up the sequence, producing CG snakes and using photos of fresh meat taken at a slaughterhouse as texture maps for the worm's inner body.

In a brief glimpse of heaven – where Bannister is joined by Stuart, Cyrus and Frank's deceased wife – a soft blue sky dotted with clouds and a halo of light surround the characters. 'At one stage, we were trying to figure out what heaven would look like,' Aitken noted. 'We finally went for something indistinct and suggestive. We created cloud effects using the particle rendering capabilities of Dynamation and composited them with blue-screen elements of the actors. We used Alias for the halo because its atmospheric rendering effects are very good. For shadows, we used virtual cutout copies of Michael J. Fox and the others – a 3-D outline to match the flat, 2-D photography – with a burst of light rays coming out from behind them.'

By the end of production, the fledgling effects company had succeeded in completing one of the biggest visual effects productions ever conceived and tackled outside the United States. With the baptism of fire of a big Hollywood production now behind it, Jackson and his Weta unit have begun preparing for their next film – a remake of the classic *King Kong*. Having established a core group of experienced computer graphics effects artisans in New Zealand, Jackson will, no doubt, use the *Kong* experience to expand on what he has learned and what he has built. 'I'm not intimidated by CG,' Jackson affirmed, 'I'm intrigued by it. When I saw the CG T-rex in *Jurassic Park*, I felt as if I was twelve years old again. I had feelings of awe and wonder watching that movie that I hadn't had since I was a kid watching the original *King Kong*. As a guy who loves effects and making movies, I'm amazed and excited by what we can actually do now.'

THE FRIGHTENERS
The *Variety* Review by Todd McCarthy

The Frighteners is a two-tone scarefest, the first half a facetious, aggressively jokey send-up of the supernatural, the second an attempt at some legitimate thrills. After his brilliant breakthrough two years ago with *Heavenly Creatures*, his new pic reps a step back into infinitely less interesting genre work for New Zealand auteur Peter Jackson, with an added reliance on elaborate, almost continuous special effects. Horror and f/x fans may go for it, but this smirky retreading of familiar haunted ground looks to scare up just moderate box-office, although a strong promo push could generate potent openings.

The story was originally conceived as an episode of *Tales from the Crypt*, and that is perhaps what it should have remained, as the thinness of the conceit shows throughout,

Jeffrey Combs – previously the title role in cult horror pic Re-Animator *– as obsessed FBI Agent Dammers.*

painfully so in the first half. The film does rebound significantly in the second hour, but not enough to redeem so much initial silliness.

With New Zealand standing in for coastal California, the yarn serves up a shock opening, as a fast-moving form within an obviously haunted house terrorises a shrieking woman. This is just one of many inexplicable events in the town of Fairwater, whose healthy citizens are being afflicted by a string of mysterious heart attacks some years after the local hospital was the scene of a horrible mass murder perpetrated by Charlie Starkweather fan Johnny Bartlett (Jake Busey), since executed.

Enter self-styled 'psychic investigator' Frank Bannister (Michael J. Fox), a down-and-outer who hustles up a little business from local medic Lucy Lynskey (Trini Alvarado) and her obnoxious hubby Ray (Peter Dobson), whose home has seemingly been invaded by a poltergeist.

Frank, it turns out, can actually see ghosts, while others cannot, due to a traumatic accident some time before in which his wife died in a car that he was driving. Three friendly spirits – an Old West gunman named The Judge (John Astin), a loud, large, seventies-attired black man named Cyrus (Chi McBride) and the studious Stuart (Jim Fyfe) – help him in his work, although they can't prevent the perplexing heart attack monster from strikng.

Scenes with these three aren't as funny as intended, and the pic reaches its nadir in a dinner scene in which Frank acts as an intermediary between Lucy and her now-dead mate, who continues to rant at her about what she should do even though she can't hear him. In these sections, Jackson's direction seems nervous, even frantic, as if he were desperately trying to compensate for material he knew wasn't much good.

Already viewed as a suspicious character due to his weird behaviour and repeated presence when people die, Frank is locked up when yet another woman perishes after a ride in his car. But by now we've seen the spectre of Death zipping all around town in a cape, possessed of the traditional scythe, so it's only a matter of time before Lucy helps Frank escape from prison so he can do battle with Death, who is stalking both of them.

In the way that the story eventually ties in with the shade of psycho killer Bartlett and the crazy woman in the house, who was his lover and accomplice in crime but got off much easier, *The Frighteners* shares with *Heavenly Creatures* a preoccupation with murdering teams. This time, however, the approach is cartoonish and conventional rather than insightful and unsettling.

It would seem, then, that the *raison d'étre* behind this new tale would be Jackson's desire to play with a hefty budget and sophisticated digital effects and creatures, with which the actors must interact in a great number of the scenes. The ghosts themselves are milky white see-through figures, while the most impressive moves come from the walls, carpets and other portions of the musty old house. Effects aside, the pic is garishly designed and lit, just as the direction, sound and Danny Elfman's score are busily in your face and ears.

Fox's combination psychic seer and con man is a difficult character to warm up to, a reckless schemer accidentally blessed with a vision so esoteric it's hard to know what to do with it. Alvarado survives with some dignity intact as the bright doctor, while off-the-wall supporting honours go to *Re-Animator* favourite Jeffrey Combs as a scarily lunatic FBI agent on Frank's case. R. Lee Ermey pops up to reprise his *Full Metal Jacket* performance as a shouting military commander, only this time as a ghost.

THE FRIGHTENERS
reviewed by Stella Bruzzi

A mysterious heart disease is sweeping through the town of Fairwater. Frank Bannister, a self-styled ambulance-chasing psychic investigator, offers his 'spirit clearing' services to the afflicted inhabitants. After crashing his car into the fence of newly arrived resident Ray Lynskey, Frank leaves him his business card, and is called out to Lynskey's house that evening following an unexplained poltergeist disturbance. Frank is only partially able to clear the house before the sceptical Ray asks him to leave, but not before Frank sees a number imprinted on his forehead, an omen signalling his imminent death. The following day, leaving a house where he has been spirit clearing, Frank runs into Ray's hearse. Lynskey's widow Lucy, wanting to communicate with her dead husband, has dinner with Frank. In the washroom Frank witnesses a Grim Reaper-shaped spirit kill another man, and by virtue of being at each murder scene, becomes the prime suspect. At the police station he encounters the Federal agent assigned to the case, Milton Dammers, and during the interrogation it surfaces that Frank's wife was killed in a car accident some years before.

Frank now decides to actively seek out the murderer, but is again arrested for the murder of a woman he is trying to save. As Lucy and Frank – by now romantically attached – kiss in the Sheriff's office, he sees a number on her forehead, and realises she is the next intended victim. Frank now believes that the only option is for him to become a spirit himself, and, to facilitate his near death, Lucy – a doctor – locks him in a hospital freezer, but is handcuffed by Dammers, who still believes Frank to be the murderer. On the point of death, Frank's spirit is released from his body, following Dammers and Lucy to the cemetery, from where the spirit and Lucy manage to escape. It is now obvious that the murdering spirit is that of Johnny Bartlett, who a few years earlier had killed

Horror veteran Dee Wallace Stone, as serial killer Johnny Bartlett's girlfriend, is best remembered for cult horror movies The Hills Have Eyes *and* The Howling.

thirteen people in one spree. A manic chase ensues at the disused hospital where these murders occurred, during which Bartlett's spirit and his still living girlfriend finally die. The real Frank awakes from near-death in Lucy's arms.

Most films centred on the wish-fulfilling dialogue between the living and the dead (*Ghost* say, or *Truly Madly Deeply*) sink whole-heartedly into the saccharine, romantic fantasy of the two worlds meeting. Peter Jackson's far more visceral and ironic film includes a reference to this maudlin tradition, as the almost dead Frank is briefly transported to heaven and reunited with his deceased wife Debra, even saying, in true melodramatic fashion, 'I'm home.' The fatuous bliss of this moment is immediately dispelled, however, by Frank's hardened spirit friends telling him to start living, and propelling him back to earth. *The Frighteners* refreshingly refuses to conform to the belief that the spirit world is a cosy imaginative extension of terrestrial mundanity – that it is exciting but ultimately containable. There is a fierce unpredictability about the intrusive, truly frightening spirits in Jackson's film, exemplified as early as the title sequence in which a malevolent force stretches and strains the walls, carpets and paintings of a haunted house almost to bursting point.

At the core of *The Frighteners* is an interesting and symbolic juxtaposition between the friendly spirits who assist Frank Bannister and the anonymous, omnipotent 'Shadow of Death' who almost destroys the small-town tranquillity for good. Frank's dubious career as a psychic investigator is aided and abetted by a fanciful trio of ghosts of horrors past (Stuart, a cardiganed, bow-tied nerd; Cyrus, a throw-back to the age of funk; and The Judge, a trigger-happy wild-Westerner) who deliberately wreak spooky havoc in people's houses so as to prompt them into calling Frank in to protect them. This is the fun bunch who can make beds levitate, Elvis float and kids fly (and who recall the trio of wicked uncle ghosts in *Casper*). Their counterpart is Bartlett's alter-ego, an amorphous, cloaked Grim Reaper who stops people's hearts.

What elevates *The Frighteners* beyond the tricksy horrors of the conventional paranormal is its tense existence in the gap or fissure between the real and the symbolic. It is significant, for instance, that the malign spirit is somehow linked to the real terror that was Johnny Bartlett, a modern reincarnation of the senselessly destructive youth examined from *Gun Crazy* to *True Romance*, and the perpetrator of the actual murders that occurred in Fairwater years before. It is equally important that this figure of death recalls the undefinable, shadowy evil of Expressionist nightmares, that he neither results from nor is defined by the fertile imaginations he invades. His swooping, hooded silhouette is an evocative cliché, recalling (if this is not too grandiose a comparison) Nosferatu's distorted shadow ascending the stairs to Nina's bedroom and sliding up her virginal nightdress to claw at her heart in Murnau's 1922 film *Nosferatu*.

There is something strangely powerful about the focus on the capture of the heart in *The Frighteners*, again because this is a connecting point between the corporeal (the victims literally die from heart failure) and the metaphoric. As anyone who has had to suffer productions of the Jacobean splatter-tragedy *'Tis Pity She's A Whore* will attest, whilst the symbolic ensnaring of the heart can be an intense and moving experience, the ripping out of a real one is almost invariably trite.

Like the sister in the 'Snow Queen' fairytale who succeeds in saving her brother's heart from being permanently frozen, Frank is up against a force that is at once tangible and intangible. What Jackson's film does best is to convey the terror of an entity that can, at will, penetrate the boundaries of the body without leaving a trace and subsequently decompose into thin air. The times when the Reaper figure swoops into cars or rooms from nowhere (thus also invading the surface of the film) provide the most frightening moments, particularly during the final frenzied pursuit of Lucy.

In a film so overtly dominated by special effects, it's inevitable that the style dominates over everything else, and *The Frighteners* is far flashier than Peter Jackson's last feature *Heavenly Creatures*, as befits his transition to Hollywood. An obvious similarity between the two films is the interweaving of fantasy and reality, but whereas in *Heavenly Creatures* there was a slightly uneasy fusion between the social world inhabited by the protagonists and the animated figurines their pubescent, naïve imaginations created, in *The Frighteners* the cohesion between narrative and visuals is complete.

Notable in terms of style is the film's use of the camera to convey the terrors of the story – it is forever moving, sweeping, in a constant state of empathic agitation, a disturbing effect sustained by the edits usually occurring on rather than after an action. In fact, *The Frighteners* is possibly only coherent because of its overall style: the plot is breathlessly labyrinthine at times and the acting and characterisation very much of subsidiary interest. If there is an obvious flaw, therefore, it is that the characters remain undeveloped and two-dimensional. While this might not be a bad thing when it comes to Michael J. Fox as Frank, it doesn't give much room to the zealous over-acting of Jeffrey Combs as Milton Dammers, whose array of twitches, neuroses and illogical, incoherent outbursts steals the show.

The
LORD of the RINGS

RINGS BEARER
by Michael Helms

To borrow an analogy from writer Richard Matheson, J. R. R. Tolkien's *The Lord of the Rings* is the Mount Everest of fantasy novels. There's no easy way around it. Upon reading the book at age eighteen, New Zealand filmmaker and *Fangoria* Hall of Famer Peter Jackson came away with a similar response – especially with regards to turning it into a movie.

'I never really thought it would be possible to make that film,' comes Jackson's voice, wavering down a phone line way too early one morning from his base in Wellington. But twenty years after reading it, he did indeed find himself co-writing, co-producing and directing a version of *The Lord of the Rings* that, at the very least, is comparable to the novel in terms of the extent of its ambitions.

When finished, and remaining faithful to Tolkien's three-volume work, *The Lord of the Rings* will consist of a trio of FX-studded features (all released by New Line) which were shot back to back (something never done before) with a major cast all over New Zealand, a relatively small country whose previous experience with such big-budget productions (*Rings* reportedly cost $270-300 million in total) mainly consists of Jackson's *The Frighteners*. The only thing the screen trilogy doesn't automatically share with its source material is the global audience that has consumed over 50 million of the copies published in 25 different languages since the mid-1950s. But surely that's bound to be a matter of course when *The Fellowship of the Ring*, the first of the trilogy, sees the light of international projectors December 19, 2001.

For those readers who have yet to be touched by the *Lord of the Rings* books, it is an epic tale of good vs. evil set within a place called Middle-earth that is both incredible and entirely credible. Meticulously crafted by Tolkien over a period of fourteen years, Middle-earth is populated by numerous creatures of different and complex cultures (from Elves to Orcs to Wizards), who are at once not entirely human but immediately recognisable as bearing all the traits of humanity. The trilogy grew out of the author's desire to elaborate on a world he had constructed for another book, *The Hobbit* (which New Line has also acquired the rights to), and was informed by his interest in linguistics, and simply in creating completely engaging storytelling.

Of greatest interest should be the ongoing attention to the different shades of evil and the growing aura of doom that is present from the outset. The book contains a palpable sense of growing menace; it may revolve around an unlikely hero of a Hobbit named Frodo, but it's a story of survival in a strange yet familiar world that never skimps on confrontations of the terminal kind. Deep, dark and composed of many intertwining relationships, the original hardcover version contained various appendices and an index of 130 pages. It is a road trip, a head trip and a questing journey, and bonding does occur in Middle-earth, but as written in the book, it's hardly a love story (which has been a serious source of concern for *Rings* traditionalists worldwide, many of whom support what is estimated to be around 1,000 websites devoted to Tolkien's writings).

'One ring to rule them all.' Frodo (Elijah Wood) grasps the Ring of Power at the climax of the trilogy, The Return of the King *(2003).*

Fangoria speaks to Jackson while the director is well into the final phase of post-pro-duction on *The Fellowship of the Ring*, which will be followed by *The Two Towers* at Christmas 2002 and *The Return of the King* in December 2003. Jackson can't hide the strain in his voice that indicates enormous encircling pressures, but true to form, the obliging filmmaker's basic enthusiasm soon bursts through as he discusses his personal attachment to this megaproject.

'Well, it wasn't really a long-held ambition of mine; the ambition was to make a fan-tasy film,' he reveals. 'I grew up with *King Kong* and Ray Harryhausen movies like *Jason and the Argonauts* and *The Golden Voyage of Sinbad*. The intent one day was to make a fan-tastical adventure story with monsters. For a long time I thought I'd have to create an original screenplay from something we'd dream up ourselves. But when we were mak-ing *The Frighteners* and had all this CGI facility, we felt the time was right. We made an inquiry into the rights to *Lord of the Rings* because ultimately, we thought that would be the most exciting type of fantasy film to make.

'It took some time, because we discovered that the rights were with Saul Zaentz [who produced Ralph Bakshi's ill-fated animated *Rings* in 1978]. This was 1995, and we were in a deal with Miramax. So we had to go through a process of talking to Miramax about doing it, because our deal was that we had to take any potential projects to them first. Fortunately, Miramax head Harvey Weinstein knew Saul very well, so he was able to start talking about the possibility of getting the movie rights. But that process in itself was lengthy and discussions took over a year. It wasn't really until 1997 that Harvey was able to say that the deal was done with Saul and that we now controlled the rights, so we could start work. We had this very agonisingly long wait just to see if it would happen.'

Along the way, Jackson and his wife and writing partner Fran Walsh became involved in a new version of another fantasy epic. 'We had these legal discussions about *Lord of the Rings* that were going on and on and on; meanwhile, Universal wanted us to make *King Kong*,' the director recalls. 'Eventually, a deal was struck where Universal and Miramax would co-finance both movies. Miramax would co-produce *King Kong* and Universal in turn would get to be a partner on *Lord of the Rings*. It was always an intention to do these films back to back. Then, four or five months into the prep and scriptwriting of *King Kong*, Universal got cold feet.

'This was the year that *King Kong* would have to come out with *Godzilla* and *Mighty Joe Young*,' Jackson explains. 'Universal had just won a very expensive race against 20th Century Fox between *Dante's Peak* and *Volcano*. There was only going to be room for one volcano film on the market. Universal won that battle, but it cost a huge amount of money to fast-track postproduction. They looked at this race in terms of the three giant monster movies, and another ape film that was a little further behind in development did-n't add up. Unless *King Kong* could be the first one out, they didn't want to do it.'

Jackson changes tone as he discusses different problems he had with Miramax, which led to the *Rings* project being picked up by New Line. 'After about a year of developing it with Miramax, where we had the go-ahead, we found ourselves developing two scripts. Miramax didn't want to make three movies; they only wanted to do part one and part two. We wrote scripts and did a lot of effects research and development. As the scripts were coming together, we were able to budget them, just wondering how much they were going to cost. But as time wore on, the budget was getting a little too high for what Miramax was prepared for. It got to a point in 1998 where they said, "Well, we can't do two movies; we now only want to do one." So we said, "Does this mean that we shoot the first one, release it and only if it's successful do we get to shoot the second part?" They said, "No, we just want to condense *The Lord of the Rings* into one two-hour film."

'They had a plan for how we were going to do that, and for all the characters we were going to lose, the story we'd lose,' Jackson continues. 'They were fairly adamant, because it was all they could afford. We said that we really didn't want to do that, because we weren't interested in being part of a *Lord of the Rings* that did not represent what people were expecting if they'd read the books. So we came to a parting of the ways, and Miramax said they were going to make the movie with another filmmaker. Then our agent, Ken Kamins, negotiated a four-week window of opportunity where we would try to find someone else who would accept three films as a condition. If we didn't find a partner, then it would go back to Harvey and they'd continue with whatever plans he had, which wouldn't involve us.

'So we went to LA and had a lot of meetings, and things were looking pretty grim. Most people had no interest or simply didn't want to get involved. We had a meeting with New Line and showed them videotape of some tests that we'd done and designs we'd been working on, because we had a lot of visual material. At the end of the meeting, Bob Shaye, the head of New Line, said, "I don't get it," and our hearts sort of sunk. But he went on to say, "I don't get it because there are three books, so why aren't you thinking about three movies?" And that was the moment that we realised New Line not only wanted to make it, but wanted us to go back to our original dream and do three. It was an unbelievable thing that we didn't expect to happen.'

Not surprisingly, tackling an adaptation of *Rings*' magnitude was a daunting job, and the director wound up taking on a second screenwriting partner. 'At the very beginning, Fran and I were working on the script, and soon after that a friend of ours, Philippa Boyens, joined us,' he recalls. 'She's an ex-president of the New Zealand Writers Guild, but we also knew she was a huge Tolkien fan. We invited her on board just to help us wade through all the material and figure out how to tell the story. The biggest challenge with the script was that we were adapting a very complicated 1,200-page book. The advantage and disadvantage was that we were doing three movies. Obviously the advantages were fantastic, because we were able to include most of the characters and events we wanted to and still have ample screen time to tell the story. The disadvantage was that we had to write three scripts at the same time. That tripled the amount of work and the amount of brain-twisting problems. Stephen Sinclair, one of the co-writers of *Dead Alive*, helped us out on parts two and three. But the first one was just the three of us.'

Then came the shoot – over a year of work on locations and in studios in New Zealand, with a huge cast and epic action scenes. 'It has gone very smoothly,' says Jackson of by far the biggest movie he has ever directed, 'but it has been the single hardest thing any of us has ever done. Just in terms of the physical endurance, mental endurance, the stress and sheer size and scope of it. From that point of view it has been like a siege, a marathon – it has been gruelling. On the other hand, as opposed to everything else I'm doing on this film, as the guy who walks on set each day to direct actors, it has probably been the easiest and simplest experience, which is a tribute to Barrie [*The Matrix*] Osborne, our producer.

'As a director, my focus is to come to the set each day prepared for what I'm going to shoot,' he elaborates. 'But also, the actors have to be there in costume, the crew has to be there and that crane or whatever we need for that day has to be there. The effects equipment has to be there, 250 horses have to be there, complete with trainers and feed and the accommodation for housing them. Whatever the huge logistical problems were, they never impacted on me on set. In terms of how Barrie put the film together and how it ran on a day-to-day basis, it was the most smoothly organised and easy experience I've ever had. I also had a great cast, and the other thing that made it such a pleasurable experience was the fact that normally, you meet actors and work together for ten or twelve weeks, and then say goodbye and everybody goes home. That's usually just enough time to get to know someone – and just when that happens, you have to go your separate ways. In this case, we had our cast with us for the best part of fifteen months.'

The *Rings* ensemble is led by young actors Elijah Wood, Sean Astin, Dominic Monaghan and Billy Boyd as the questing Hobbits, Sir Ian McKellen as Gandalf the Wizard, Christopher Lee as the sorcerer Saruman, Viggo Mortensen as the warrior Aragorn, Liv Tyler as his Elf love Arwen and Cate (*The Gift*) Blanchett as Lady Galadriel. It was a huge cast to become familiar with, even on an uncommonly long schedule, but Jackson notes, 'Twelve weeks into the fifteen-month shoot, I got to know these people really well, and six months into it we had a wonderful shorthand way of communicating. We totally trusted each other and became very good friends. By the time a year was up and we knew we had several months to go, we had this incredibly tight, family-like team going where everyone liked each other, we hung out socially together and it felt good.

'There was no room for anyone to be a prima donna or to be difficult, because we were all together for so long,' he continues. 'That was just not an option for anybody – the only option was to get on well with each other. And it became a wonderful family-like feeling. We've ended up with an incredibly strong group of friends. It's an experience we've all been through where no one else will really know what it was like.'

Jackson's film work has ranged from the outrageous gore of *Bad Taste* and *Dead Alive* to the FX-heavy horrors of *The Frighteners* to the dark, unsettling drama of the Oscar-nominated *Heavenly Creatures*. When asked whether *Lord of the Rings* will contain specifically recognisable elements or mark a complete departure, the director steers the conversation away from self-analysis. 'I'm always the worst person to judge these things, because I don't consciously think about style,' he admits. 'I have a way of shooting, of looking at a page of script and trying to figure out how to shoot it, where to put the cameras, how to cut it together and what I want the actors to do.

'You're talking about something that totally comes down to the taste and the sensibilities of the director, and how I would imagine that scene playing. That same taste and sensibility is consistent throughout all my films. I am the same guy, it's as simple as that. I'm not trying to reinvent myself with each film I make. I simply have my preferences of how I want things to look when I'm on set, so I'm sure people seeing this film will absolutely recognise it as being the same style from the same mind and imagination that was behind the rest of the films I've made. I can't be specific or more analytical than that.'

Wizard Gandalf (Ian McKellen) and Hobbit Pippin (Billy Boyd) in the Rings trilogy. It marked Jackson's progression to Hollywood A-list director, without leaving New Zealand.

Jackson's approach to *Lord of the Rings* inevitably revolved around the multitudinous FX shots required for everything from shrinking normal-sized actors into three-and-a-half-foot Hobbits to epic battle scenes. 'What was good preparation for this project was the fact that I grew up always loving visual effects in different forms, whether they've been stop-motion animation or ultimately CGI. I love the tricks of making films, I love the magician's sleight of hand, and so I sort of walked into what is possibly the most complicated effects exercise of all time, being not just one heavily effects-laden film. [While working on] one movie with 500 visual effects shots, I've got two more going at virtually the same time. The one advantage is that I went into this with absolutely no fear of visual effects. I've got a very good knowledge of how things can be accomplished, either practically or using computers.

'We were also able to think on our feet incredibly well,' Jackson adds. 'When different thoughts came up on set, we were able to adapt and figure out ways we could shoot scenes and achieve the effects very, very quickly, right there on the spot.'

The director can't hide his enthusiasm for his FX team, which includes one of his oldest collaborators. 'Richard Taylor, who has worked with me since *Meet the Feebles*, is one of the cornerstones of the film,' Jackson says. 'We have absolutely wonderful conceptual artists in Alan Lee and John Howe, and our production designer, Grant Major [a veteran of *The Frighteners* and *Heavenly Creatures*], did great work. But Richard and his Weta team were the group that really made it all happen. All the designs that came from Alan, John or Grant, if they involved weapons or armour or special costumes, miniatures, prosthetics, anything at all, got channelled into Richard's department. He ran a huge operation in an incredibly smooth way. If we wanted 100 archers, we'd have no doubt they'd be there with all the support and backup they required.

'Just giving the filmmakers a bunch of swords or costumes wasn't really the limit of Richard's job,' Jackson continues. 'He also had to provide technicians on set who could dress these people and make running repairs. When someone's sword broke during a take, there'd always be a Weta technician there with the tools ready to go. The logistical backup, in addition to actually building the stuff, was huge. I can't imagine anyone else in the world being able to pull it off as well as Richard did.'

With *Fellowship* ready to charge into theatres worldwide, Jackson has no time to sit back and await the response. 'We've already done assembly edits of the second and third films,' he reveals. 'We're now going into heavy postproduction on the second. We've already done some of the CGI work. We are going to be refining the cut over the next few months and then we go on to the third movie. So really, I'm with this for two more years. Two more years from now sees the release of *The Return of the King*, and that will be it,' he says with no small sense of relief.

The *Rings* trilogy marks the first time Jackson has worked below the R-rated level, and rumour has it that more violent editions will surface when the movies hit DVD. 'At this stage, I haven't cut anything for DVD,' he notes, 'but if the studio is willing to give me a free hand to do a true director's cut of *Lord of the Rings*, I'd certainly tend to put more of the fighting in there. We haven't filmed anything exceptionally violent, since we're aiming for a PG-13, but I believe we could slip a few things in on the DVD that wouldn't allow it to go out with that rating.'

As for whether his version of *King Kong* stands a chance of revival, Jackson maintains a hopeful tone. 'Universal owns the rights to our script, so it would have to be something they want to do, but let's just see, I guess. If *Lord of the Rings* is successful, it may inspire someone to look at the project again. I'm definitely inspired to be connected with it. *Kong* is my favourite film of all time, and I certainly liked the script we wrote. I was very pleased with it, even though it needed a little bit more work. It was a faithful yet slightly original homage that would've been quite fun to make.'

Before the director returns to his over-the-top work schedule, a wistfulness comes over his voice when he's asked whether he's likely to be involved in any hardcore horror projects again. 'Yep,' he says. 'Every time you're in the middle of doing something, you think of what you'd like to do next, or certainly what your ambitions are. Fran and I have quite a few ideas, and I'd like to adapt some more true stories in the *Heavenly Creatures* vein, because we found that such an enjoyable experience. Certainly, having spent all these years on something as fantastical as *Lord of the Rings*, going back to real-life material appeals to us.

'And somewhere down the line, I'd love to do another splatter film, another zombie-type film, a guerrilla filmmaking exercise. I'd love to do something I'd finance myself and shoot on weekends, without a studio on board. You see, one of the tricks with that type of film is that as soon as they get too studio-involved, they never seem to satisfy, because too many people start to get nervous about the content. I certainly like the idea of shooting a film with a bunch of friends on weekends over a long period of time, and am seriously contemplating that as a possible thing of the future. I've really got no interest in becoming a guy who does big-budget effects films forever; I certainly get an equal amount of pleasure out of doing small films as well.'

ONE RING
by Harry Knowles

December 22, 2000. 6.00pm. Wellington, New Zealand. It's the last day of the fourteen-month shoot for the *Lord of the Rings* trilogy. On the set of Minas Tirith, the fortified outpost on the edge of Middle-earth, Viggo Mortensen's Aragorn is being strapped into his armour, while Peter Jackson – the man behind this $180-million behemoth – barks final orders: 'Viggo, look mean, like you can't wait to go kick Sauron's ass!'

Mortensen nails the take, and a low murmur starts. A crew member shouts, 'Checking the gate!', people start giggling nervously. Then, 'That's a wrap!' Champagne corks shoot into the air, and the crew begin hugging and consoling one another. Elijah Wood, the star of the three-movie series as Hobbit hero Frodo Baggins, and Sean Astin, his comrade Samwise Gamgee, are smiling through tears. Orlando Bloom, the young British actor who plays the Elf Legolas, runs onto the set. He is already crying. The emotional outpouring is too much even for an outsider like me. Because this moment means that I'll be going home as well. And I don't want to leave either.

Peter Jackson is standing off to the side, smiling like a cherubic kid in a toy store. Suddenly his cellphone rings. It turns out that the second-unit crew are running behind schedule. They're shooting a scene set in the camp of the Rohan riders! Peter grabs me and says, 'Harry, want to come see the real last shot?' And so we hop into his sports utility vehicle and dart across Wellington, swerving in and out of the traffic. During the entire journey, we reminisce about what has been a long and fantastic voyage . . . And where it all began for both of us.

So just how did an internet movie geek like me, from Austin, Texas, end up rushing through traffic in New Zealand with the director of the most ambitious film project the world has ever seen?

It began on 3 November, 1997. I was contacted by some folks inside Peter Jackson's New Zealand-based special-effects company, Weta, who said they were working on a live-action adaptation of J. R. R. Tolkien's fantasy epic *The Lord of the Rings*. For those who haven't read the book, it relates the quest of Frodo to save the world from the forces of the evil Sauron. To this end, he must travel to the heart of Sauron's territory, Mordor, and destroy The One Ring – the source of the malevolent overlord's power – aided by a fel-

Aragorn (Viggo Mortensen), the 'True King' who ascends the throne of Gondor at the trilogy's climax. Rings *made Mortensen recognisable throughout the world.*

lowship of Hobbits, Dwarves, Elves and Men.

Well, that afternoon I posted a story that said, quite simply: 'By the way, it looks solid that Peter Jackson's next project IS . . . *The Lord of the Rings*. I've been hearing this from a bunch of Weird Educated Tall Apes that purport to be insane and busy bodies. So you know you can trust it.'

A pretty non-spectacular start to what has been the best story I've ever covered at *Ain't It Cool News*. It might not seem like much, but that insignificant paragraph was the first time that *The Lord of the Rings* had been mentioned outside of New Zealand or the offices of Miramax. Yes, Miramax, the Disney-owned mini-studio behind movies like *The English Patient*, *Good Will Hunting* and the *Scream* trilogy. Because, in those days, Miramax held the reins, and New Line, the films' eventual producers, hadn't even heard of the protect.

During the next couple of months, all kinds of rumours leaked out. It was claimed, for example, that second-lead Hobbit, Samwise Gamgee, was going to be turned into a female to avoid any homosexual undertones, that DreamWorks and George Lucas were trying to buy the rights, and that it was actually Tolkien's first book, *The Hobbit*, that was going into production. One spy even heard from Sean Bean's agent in early 1998 that the Brit actor was all hot and heavy to play Aragorn, the mysterious ranger who comes to Frodo's aid. Of course, Bean later took on the role of the proud warrior Boromir, with Viggo Mortensen stepping in to play the heroic Aragorn.

In fact, most fans don't realise how close this trilogy came to death. By 23 February 1998, the project was only four days away from snuffing it completely. Word was that Miramax wanted to condense the entire three-book series into one film, that they'd lost confidence in Peter Jackson, and that they were looking at other directors. A Weta employee leaked me the entire sad story. He said that Peter was planning an incredibly faithful adaptation, that Samwise was remaining a male Hobbit, and that Peter and Miramax had agreed to make two films, *The Fellowship of the Ring* and *The War of the Ring* (the latter an abbreviated version of Tolkien's second and third books, *The Two Towers* and *Return of the King*). But he also said that Miramax had got cold feet, and were about to pull the plug.

'They say Peter Jackson is tearing his hair out,' I wrote in a browbeating editorial posted later that day on *AICN*. 'He is so pissed off with Miramax about their lack of support, he's about to move onto another film. A source close to Jackson says that he has been offered a sci-fi movie and may sign onto it before the end of the week.'

The day after the editorial went up, Peter received a phone call from a screeching Miramax executive: 'Have you fucking read the internet today!?' The executive was livid, but Peter insisted the article was accurate – until the executive told him he had another three months of pre-production financing on the film.

Peter and I first struck up a cyber-space relationship a couple of years earlier when he contacted me to find out if my original issue 1933 *King Kong* one-sheet was for sale (it wasn't). At the time, he was working hard on a new version of *Kong*. He had a finished script, set designs and effects test – he was ready to go. Universal Pictures, however, canned it because they were afraid of going up against Roland Emmerich's *Godzilla* and Disney's *Mighty Joe Young*. Jackson was devastated and stopped replying to my missives.

But after *Rings* was granted a reprieve, he got back in touch – this time by phone. He seemed genuinely thankful for what had taken place. And very surprised. But his joy didn't last long. Sources at both Miramax and Disney were murmuring that Miramax didn't have the dough to make the film and that Disney was opposed to the project anyway because they didn't want their sister studio competing with them in the Big Film Category. Miramax was also still insisting that Peter make one film out of the whole series. In August 1998, the company gave him a limited window of opportunity to shop the project around at other studios. As far as they were concerned, *The Lord of the Rings* was dead.

Thank God, then, for Bob Shaye, head of New Line Films. Shaye topped Peter's list of potential saviours, but even he was surprised by the New Line chief's enthusiastic welcome. Shaye not only gave the greenlight, but also chose to make three films rather than two. New Line's commitment – both logistically and financially – was enormous. Suddenly, the *Lord of the Rings* movie adaptation became a reality. There are millions of Tolkien fans in the world, and most of them dream of a great film of his books. But their first reaction was one of fear, which they began voicing on *AICN*, questioning why any-one would trust Peter *Braindead* Jackson with what many feel is one of the greatest works of modern English literature.

On 26 August, 1998, Peter decided to address their concerns, saying, 'I was a little nervous about the job ahead of me . . . now I know the feeling of true terror!' He want-ed to set the record straight, and above all stress that he wasn't seeking to make yet anoth-er bad fantasy film. Specifically: 'I do not intend to make a fantasy film, or a fairytale. I will be telling a true story – just as I feel when reading the books.'

That statement began to win the hearts of fans. He then charged my readers with the opportunity to ask twenty questions. Within no time, my mailbox was flooded with e-mails. In all, over 14,000 questions came in from Tolkien lovers around the world. Not just hippies or fanboys, but questions from literature professors and other fantasy authors. It was insane.

Even after sending him an abridged version of the questions, he wrote back: 'Jesus! Give me a day or two.' Sure enough, two days later, he had the answers. He explained how he was going to shrink normal-sized actors on screen to play Hobbits and Dwarves. He dealt with the budget, the special-effects questions, the benefits of shooting in New Zealand. But the key to the entire Q&A was the following query: 'What are you dying to capture in these films, and how will you do it?'

And Peter answered: 'I want to take movie-goers into Middle-earth in a way that is believable and powerful. Imagine this: 7,000 years have gone by since the film started. We take a film crew to Helm's Deep. It's looking older, but still impresses as a mighty fortress. The Art Department set to work, patching up holes and removing tourist signs. The cur-rent owner strikes a hard bargain, but New Line money finally gets us permission to film there for six weeks. Archeological expeditions have unearthed an incredibly preserved mummified Orc carcass. We make exact prosthetic copies of these vicious killers and use CGI to give us a 10,000 strong army. We have cast actors who look like Aragorn and Gandalf. In an amazing casting coup, Legolas has agreed to return to the human world with Gimli to recreate their part in this cinematic retelling of the events at the end of the Third Age. They stand on the battlements of the Deeping Wall, wind blowing in their hair . . . Orc drums roll up the valley . . . Huge lighting rigs flash simulated lightning . . . Rain towers send gallons of water into the air . . . On an assistant director's signal, twenty 35mm cameras start rolling simultaneously . . . The battle of Helm's Deep is about to be captured on film.'

'Sure, it's not really my *The Lord of the Rings*,' Jackson concluded. 'But it could still be a pretty damn cool movie.'

The imaginations of Tolkien fans were stoked. Perhaps this Kiwi film-maker was the right man to helm this epic after all.

The *Lord of the Rings* shoot kicked off at the end of 1999, and I knew that I had to get onto that set in New Zealand. Eventually, I wrote to Peter and asked his permission to come down for the final ten days of shooting, at my own expense. He agreed. I was elated.

On 12 December, 2000, I landed in Wellington, and, walking into the airport, spotted a familiar form in the distance. 'Harry!' a voice shouted out. Elijah Wood was there to greet me. Elijah and I became friends years earlier on the set of 1998's *The Faculty*, in which I had a cameo role. When Elijah had time off from the *Faculty* shoot, he came over to my

The forces of Mordor wage their war against the people of Middle-earth. The Lord of the Rings *is awash with monsters – like the earthily grotesque Orcs, led by the Wizard Saruman.*

house in Austin to eat barbecue, watch films and talk about how cool it would be if Peter Jackson really did make *The Lord of the Rings*. Elijah was a huge fan of *The Hobbit*, but also knew enough about the *Rings* trilogy to know he wanted to play Frodo. I even mentioned in an e-mail to Jackson around that time how Elijah would kill to play Frodo.

And now here he was, one year and six months into playing the part he had dreamed about for so long. Far from appearing tired or worn down, Elijah was still gripped by the excitement of being part of such a huge epic.

During the journey to the hotel, Elijah told stories about being evacuated off a mountain due to a blizzard and surfing along the New Zealand coast. He was totally in love with what he was doing. And so was every other cast and crew member I met. The sense of pride and achievement was huge, which was unsurprising given what I saw during the next ten days . . .

The first day on location, I was taken to a rock quarry outside Wellington, where the gates of Minas Tirith rose above a truly imposing set. After passing through the looming stone gateway into a courtyard, I was confronted with a huge bronze-effect statue of one of the Kings of Gondor (the land leading the fight against the Dark Lord Sauron). As I walked up a cobblestone hill, it struck me how much attention went into every last detail, right down to the tiniest carving.

Then, right in front of me, was Gandalf himself – the Wizard who sets Frodo on his

Dwarf warrior Gimli, one of the heroes of the Fellowship. Like the Hobbits, strapping six-plus-footer John Rhys-Davies was cut to size by forced perspective and diminutive stand-ins.

journey and leads the war against Sauron. I expected some deep words of wisdom to boom out, but instead all I got was: 'Feeling jet-lagged?' The spell was broken and Gandalf suddenly became a heavily made-up Ian McKellen. Throughout my time on the shoot, it seemed as if McKellen enjoyed shattering the illusion of Gandalf's sorcerous gravitas. Right at the end of one battle scene, fresh from blasting Orcs with his magic staff, he suddenly opened a large red-and-blue umbrella to keep the afternoon drizzle from drenching his costume. That surreal image is one of my favourite on-set memories.

Of course, most of the cast were given the prosthetic treatment. The actors playing the Hobbits, for example, had to wear curly wigs, pointy ears and the Hobbits' characteristically huge, furry feet. When I humped into Billy Boyd, who plays Frodo's cousin Pippin, I found those feet incredibly distracting. The toes wiggled and reacted to the ground in a very real way. Boyd explained that the prosthetics had a 'strange, spongy, squishy feeling . . . I wear the same pair all day except when I have to run around lots. Then I usually get through two pairs.'

Fortunately, Peter didn't restrict my on-set wanderings too much. I watched him controlling the action on five different sound-stages simultaneously, barking instructions into his cellphone, witnessed animatic tests of Gandalf riding astride a giant eagle, wandered through the dark Fangorn Forest, and met the animatronic recreation of Treebeard the Ent (a half-human, half-tree creature) – even getting to feel his strange, mossy beard.

This was easily one of the most ambitious movie projects ever undertaken. Not only did Peter have several units to co-ordinate at once, and not only were most of the cast covered in delicate prosthetics, but so much of what was being 'seen' by the cast and crew would not be filled in for months. But, from what I saw, none of this dampened anyone's spirits.

Take the scene from *The Fellowship of the Ring* which takes place at the gates of the Mines of Moria - a dangerous and evil place which our heroes cannot avoid. There beside a lake was the door, with its Dwarvish runes giving off a golden glow. In front of it, Peter was shooting the moment when Frodo has his leg grabbed by a tentacled creature lurking in the lake's dark waters. Elijah's ankle was attached to a bungee-style cord, then he was hitched up to a towering rig and jerked all over the place to simulate the monster's attack. Elijah loved it.

Meanwhile, Sean Astin hacked away at this invisible tentacle and Dominic Monaghan (Merry) and Billy Boyd held onto Elijah, screaming and yelling for Aragorn and Gandalf to help, who themselves were being battered by the monster's other limbs. As if this wasn't enough to take in, Peter was yelling out that arrows were flying over their heads, as Legolas (Orlando Bloom), off to the side, would later be filmed firing a volley of Elven missiles into the unseen beast. Then Astin, Monaghan and Boyd had to do the entire sequence again without Elijah, in case Peter decided that in the final movie they should just completely computer animate Frodo.

But, as I've said, I sensed more joy than frustration with this arduous shoot. At one point, Orlando Bloom approached me and said he wanted a Polaroid of us together, so we went over to a grassy knoll on one of the soundstages. 'I'm simply dazed by the fact that this shoot's coming to an end,' said the 24-year-old actor. 'We've spent so long here in this beautiful, impossibly remote part of New Zealand. It's going to be hard to leave.'

As another shot was completed, Peter shouted over to Bloom, 'Now this is epic filmmaking.' The look in Bloom's eyes as he remembered all the fantastic places he'd been during this massive cinematic undertaking was one of bittersweet sadness. Sure, he'd be back for pick-up shots, looping, publicity and all the rest, but the great adventure was coming to a close. 'I don't want to even talk about it,' he said quietly.

I've been a curious fly on the wall of *The Lord of the Rings* for what now seems like forever. I've been buzzing about the score by Howard Shore, the perfect Elvish language that's been created, the stunning make-up and what promises to be some great acting. And as the release date moves closer, the minutes seem longer and the days expand like some sort of cruel, taunting Alfred Hitchcock hallway.

But, just a week previous to the time of writing, Peter Jackson handed in the final print of *The Fellowship of the Ring* to New Line, and I spoke to someone close to the project who has seen the finished cut. 'I walked into this thinking there was no possible way it could live up to my expectations,' he told me. 'When I walked out, all I could think was that there's no way that *The Two Towers* and *Return of the King* can possibly live up to expectations. Because *The Fellowship of the Ring* is the benchmark by which those movies will be judged. It's perfect!'

The anticipation is killing me.

THE FELLOWSHIP OF THE RING
reviewed by Andrew O'Hehir

A village in the Shire, Middle-earth. After his uncle Bilbo vanishes on his 111th birthday, Hobbit Frodo Baggins inherits a magic ring that Bilbo found on a long-ago adventure. The Wizard Gandalf determines that this is the One Ring, forged centuries ago by Sauron, the Dark Lord of Mordor, and used to rule most of Middle-earth. Sauron now knows where the Ring is and has sent his nine sinister Black Riders after it; if he recovers it, the Free People of Middle-earth (Elves, Dwarves and Men, along with Hobbits) are doomed.

Gandalf entrusts Frodo to carry the Ring out of the Shire to the village of Bree, where he and his three Hobbit companions are attacked by the Black Riders but sheltered by a human named Strider. Strider leads the group onward; on a nearby hilltop they are again attacked by the Riders. Drawn by the power of the Ring, Frodo puts it on and is grievously wounded by one of the Riders. Strider, also known as Aragorn, enlists the aid of Arwen, an Elvish woman (and his betrothed) who carries the injured Frodo to the Elvish retreat of Rivendell. There he is reunited with Bilbo and Gandalf, who meanwhile has escaped the clutches of the Wizard Saruman, who has come under Sauron's power. At a conference, it is decided that the Ring must be carried into the land of Mordor and thrown into the Cracks of Doom where it was forged. Frodo volunteers for this desperate mission and is sent on his way with a fellowship of eight others: Hobbits Sam, Merry and Pippin; Legolas the Elf; Gimli the Dwarf; the Men Aragorn and Boromir, and Gandalf. The fellowship travels under the Misty Mountains through the Mines of Moria, where it is beset by armies of Sauron's Orcs. Gandalf is dragged into a chasm in a battle with the Balrog, an ancient evil spirit. The others escape and make it to the enchanted wood of Lórien, ruled by the Elvish queen Galadriel. From there they travel south by boat on the Great River. Boromir wants the Ring to help his own people fight Sauron and tries to take it from Frodo. Frodo slips on the Ring and escapes towards Mordor, followed by Sam. Merry and Pippin are seized by Orcs; the repentant Boromir dies trying to save them. Aragorn, Legolas and Gimli decide to follow the Orcs, allowing Frodo and Sam – and the Ring – to travel eastward on their own.

Perhaps the secret ingredient in Peter Jackson's extraordinary film interpretation of J. R. R. Tolkien's *The Lord of the Rings* is New Zealand itself. The director's temperate homeland, much of it still wild and little affected by industrial development, may be the best available substitute for the pre-modern landscapes of northern Europe so compellingly imagined in Tolkien's epic. By dragging his enormous assemblage of actors and technical staff to this remote location for a now-legendary eighteen-month shoot, Jackson transformed his film-making process into a real-life quest narrative, one nearly as foolhardy as Frodo Baggins' journey into Mordor. For all its models and computer animation – the most massive of the special-effects sequences is surely the battle in the Great Hall of Moria, a vaulted grand-opera set teeming with Orcs – *The Lord of the Rings: The Fellowship of the Ring* has an untamed human roughness, a feeling of damp ground and dirty clothing that it's difficult to

Elf Lord Elrond (Hugo Weaving) stirs his troops at the beginning of the trilogy. Throughout The Lord of the Rings, *Jackson displays a flair for battle sequences worthy of Kurosawa.*

imagine Spielberg or Lucas replicating at any price. When Frodo (played by the cherubic Elijah Wood, who darkens and seems to age appreciably as the story progresses) opens his hand to display the One Ring of Power, we see that his fingernails are filthy, the whorls of his palm caked with grime.

Jackson has made a grand, even visionary entertainment on his own terms, one meant to capture the spirit and the general narrative outline of Tolkien's epic trilogy. (For better or worse, the author's problematic little-Englander views of race, gender and politics have largely been submerged here.) Jackson's previous films – especially *Heavenly Creatures* and *Braindead* – certainly suggested that he had a flair for action, an eye for eccentric and decadent design, and a passion for storytelling. (That last crucial ingredient is what Tim Burton, for instance, lacks.) But he had never before worked on anything like this scale; it still seems amazing that he was entrusted with this gargantuan enterprise in the first place, and astonishing that he has succeeded to this extent.

Much of the film's design aesthetic is drawn from the ripe Victoriana of Tolkien's Jubilee-era childhood, and whether or not one entirely approves, it's a logical choice; Middle-earth is essentially medieval England imagined from the perspective of about 1903. Amid all the cascading ringlets and the pre-Raphaelite glow, Jackson is nonetheless capable of restraint. The enchanted wood of Lórien, which could so easily have been rendered as faeryland kitsch, is more suggested than seen, an Arts and Crafts backdrop for the beautiful but dangerous flame of Galadriel. Even the score by Howard Shore is a canny pastiche, reaching towards Celtic folk music and then towards the lush romanticism of Wagner and the pseudo-medieval modernism of Carl Orff.

If Wood's Frodo is the Alice in this Wonderland, and his coming of age is inescapably the central focus, Jackson's adroitly chosen cast provides other pleasures. As the Wizard Gandalf, who is both a kindly old geezer and a semi-angelic power, Ian McKellen serves to connect the film's two narrative spheres: the great mythopoetic narrative of Sauron and the Ring on one hand and the rustic comedy of the domestic-minded Hobbits confronting a wider world on the other. Jackson even locates a tragic hero whom Tolkien only half-notices in the conflicted figure of Boromir, played by Sean Bean as a man struggling against the corrosive power of the Ring. Bean's performance nearly overshadows that of Viggo Mortensen, who plays the saga's human hero, Aragorn, as a brooding Hamlet type.

It is already clear that Tolkien fundamentalists will have problems with this film, but the more they pick away at its particulars, the more they miss the point. Any reader of the books may be startled to see the Dark Lord Sauron himself – who never personally appears in Tolkien's book – show up inside the film's first five minutes, waddling across a crowded battlefield looking rather like a Gothic cathedral on stilts. Internet fan sites have fulminated for years over the news that Aragorn's lover Arwen (Liv Tyler) has been upgraded to a fully-fledged character, and that Tom Bombadil, a jolly nature spirit in Tolkien's book, has been dropped altogether. Both of those decisions, in fact, are dramatically sensible and could, especially in the Bombadil case, be viewed as improvements.

Indeed Jackson and his co-writers, Fran Walsh and Philippa Boyens, have significantly reordered and reshaped Tolkien's narrative, which widens its focus and quickens its pace gradually, requiring a hundred pages to get the Hobbits out of the Shire. But they have tremendous respect for the linguistic and mythic density of Tolkien's creation. (Tyler and Mortensen even play portions of two scenes in Quenya, the Finnish-like language of the High Elves.) Subsequent instalments of Jackson's trilogy should make clear how much of Tolkien's mournful, elegiac tone he captures. At the very least Jackson has translated the best-loved fantasy novel of our age into a commanding screen adventure, one with a sense of human terror and danger and grit under its nails, one that makes Harry Potter and Luke Skywalker look like the feeble wraiths they are.

IT IS A DARK TIME FOR THE REBELLION . . .
by Ian Nathan

Day One: Picture, if you will, a scene of such refinement and tranquility it was surely dreamed up under the porcelain gaze of Merchant and Ivory. As a prelude to luncheon, a string quartet gently evokes a touch of Bach in a minor key, tablecloths are being straightened and napkins folded, and from an adjoining room spills the aroma of food preparation. Order is everywhere, a hushed expectation of the meal to come. At a corner table, three Orcs are deep in conversation, their gnarled heads leaning close together; the ugliest of the trio (this is a thin distinction), whose nose seems to have been riveted several times, sucks idly from a carton of apple juice.

We may need to adjust the picture. The room is, to say the least, ramshackle; walls of crumbling brick decorated with 'Elf' vandalism reach inconclusively to the corrugated roof. Outside the rain is pouring like the end of the world. Then, as if some far-off bell has sounded, the room is suddenly engulfed with all manner of beings. More Orcs join their brethren, a small fellow with pointy ears and clown-sized feet wrapped in bin-liners has already got a plateful, and, as if it is the most normal thing in the world (which round here it is), Gandalf the White, Saruman the (formerly) Wise and King Théoden of Rohan saunter across to a table, waving casually to crew members.

Welcome to Catering, Middle-earth, Miramar Studios, Wellington, New Zealand. A place where anything goes, especially the chilli if you're not quick to the queue. 'Do you recommend it?' Saruman enquires of *Empire*, looking suspiciously at the dish of the day, obviously mistaking your intrepid journalist for one of the catering staff. 'Hmmm, better not,' he decides, patting his stomach. 'Have to be on set this afternoon.'

Despite the sudden tumult (and the Orcs have become quite unruly), the quartet – a weekly civility introduced by producer Barrie Osborne to salve weary brows – plays on regardless.

It's June 2002, and supplementary shooting – the process of ironing out the final wrinkles in the second film – is almost complete, leaving only the toil of post-production to continue apace until the December debut of *The Two Towers*. It was a hell of a kick-off, but it means nothing if this movie fails to match *Fellowship*'s giddy heights. So no-one is lapping up the successes of the recent past – the Oscars, the box office, or the critical acclaim. Every drop of sweat is devoted to getting the new film right.

'It was shot at the same time as *Fellowship*,' says Peter Jackson later – the sheer workload tending to keep him manacled to the sound stage. 'Obviously it has the same sensibilities working for it – the same writer, director, cast, DP; everything is a continuation. But it has a much different tone from *Fellowship*, and that's ultimately a healthy thing. In *The Two Towers*, the story centres more on the world of Men, which gives it a more realistic, historical feel – a little in the direction of *Braveheart*.'

There's also the arrival of CGI curios Gollum and Treebeard, and the cataclysmic hellfire of the Battle of Helm's Deep in a narrative splintered across storylines. This is the dark one, people mutter. While out in the real world, anticipation is boiling into a frenzy.

The confidence, though, is palpable. The unit publicist guiding us around takes on the breathy, enthused tone of a Disneyland host: nothing is off-limits; the paranoid secrecy of a Hollywood set doesn't translate into Kiwi. They've got nothing but pride in their accomplishments, and they just want to share it. Time to explore.

You can reach the Golden Hall of Edoras via the ruins of Osgiliath and the Dead Marshes. This may not exactly adhere to the copious maps that Tolkien personally provided for his books, but the publicist is keen to show off some of the backlot's exterior sets, and there's the opportunity for a toilet break. The journey goes via a 30-foot rock escarpment made of industrial polystyrene. 'They pride themselves on their rock,' she boasts. A bit like Deep Purple.

Tolkien warns that you stare into the Dead Marshes at your peril – the long-deceased spirits of slain soldiers are likely to stare right back at you. Yet, in the interests of journalistic integrity, *Empire* takes a peak into the small, purpose-built marshland complete with clumps of real sedge and moss. The water, bubbling out of a nearby pipe, is freezing, and the only sinister apparition to be found in its depths is an empty Coke can. Is this product placement? Sean Astin, Elijah Wood and Andy 'Gollum' Serkis were busily squabbling here only a week ago. Make your own deduction.

The fabulous, Nordic-flavoured carvings of the Golden Hall, royal palace of Rohan, lie on Sound Stage A, which is also currently occupied by an outcrop of Fangorn Forest (being dismantled) and some kind of torture chamber belonging to Christopher Lee. The economy of space is a marvel; the studio may seem cluttered, a kind of Middle-earthian junkyard ringed by the stalks of lighting rigs, but one glance into the monitor and there is Théoden's massive throne room, carved straight out of the pages of Tolkien's vast antiquity. The place is alive with activity, and dressed in scarlet leather, a cloak billowing behind him, Bernard Hill's noble Théoden wafts past.

Word has it that Gandalf is ready. Ushered quickly from the gold-leaf splendour of the echoing hall, we reassemble in Catering. Here, Sir Ian McKellen, back in a warm sweater and jeans, is sitting at a table with the comfortable air of a man entirely at home. 'It's a very nice atmosphere,' he says happily. 'It's almost like making a home movie. It just happens to be a home movie that the whole world likes!' Hold on a second, isn't he meant to be dead? The last time we saw Gandalf he was plummeting into the pits of Khazad-dûm, trailing a rather narked Balrog. The prognosis wasn't good. We've wept rivers of tears for the wizard . . . and he's alive?

'He's sent back to finish the job that he did not complete,' returns McKellen – as if a mere Balrog could put a crimp in Gandalf's staff. 'He is reborn, literally. He is now Gandalf the White, more energetic; he's a commander, a samurai. He's got a job to do and he's not going to be distracted this time.'

Indeed, Gandalf will now be resplendent in white robes, his hair and beard the colour of snow, and as McKellen puts it: 'much more manicured'. Acting as a military tactician, he will lead the charge against first Saruman's hordes and then the might of Sauron; the idea being to distract his enemies from the Ringbearer's quest. 'Unlike some action heroes,' he chuckles, tickled by the notion of being classified in the same bracket as Vin Diesel, 'we do see Gandalf off duty. He's still very humane.'

The first thing you notice about Viggo Mortensen is that he has no shoes on; he never wears anything on his feet if at all possible. It makes him feel, quite literally, more in touch with the world. He's also in a bit of a hurry as he fancies a bit of bareback horse-riding this afternoon, despite the fact the downpour now seems to be falling horizontally. Mortensen just shrugs – there's never a bad time to go riding. They weren't kidding when they said he actually *became* Aragorn.

'It really starts happening a lot in the second movie,' he says, frequently quoting from his rambling notes jotted down in a battered book, 'especially when we get to Rohan, which is a proud but isolated people. There's a value of working together, a commonality.'

This is how the Dane broaches subjects; not with a whip-crack soundbite, but the slow-burning philosophical angle. He is genetically incapable of trivia, but smiles easily, waxing lyrical about the higher messages contained in Tolkien's prose.

'It's a very complex story. The Ring is not evil in itself, any more than Mordor or Sauron themselves are. On the surface, the plan is to drop the Ring into Mount Doom, if possible. I believe the Ring is not one thing. The Ring comes from each of us. It resides in each of us as the potential for making selfish choices, as the potential for attempting to control the worlds of others. Aragorn and Gandalf are trying to find a way to get this job done, they have to find a way to unite people, to reject the impulse that is the Ring.' It's not the classical reading of the book, but he's willing to admit there's still plenty of action for the rugged hero in part two. 'He's much more of a soldier in this one, he is finally coming to terms with his destiny to be king.'

Talking of which, in what seems to have become a game of celebrity tag, Bernard Hill appears over Aragorn's shoulder and pulls a mock yawn. The guys have become good friends. 'Hey, it's his majesty,' sneers Mortensen good-naturedly as he gets up to go. Isn't it always the same? You don't see a king for ages then two arrive at once.

'Théoden and his kingdom are in serious decline when we see him at the start of film two,' begins the 57 year-old Hill, who has also returned to his civvies. 'His story is to do with the coming out of that, a rebirth, if you like.'

With his mind polluted by Saruman's lies, Théoden is drawn back to reality by Gandalf, finally facing up to the fact he has to go to war. 'It is an interesting dynamic, the idea that the world of man would be destroyed. You're talking about genocide. Théoden has to shake off the evil and become as pure as he can again. It's almost like he grows up. He comes from a birth, goes through the middle years and becomes old and wise by the end.'

Hill was well-versed in swordplay from his Shakespearean days. It's the horses he wasn't keen on, tricky given Théoden heads up an equine-orientated nation. Week upon week in the saddle were required to instil the requisite skill. That and a co-operative pony between his legs. 'Mine was called Depend,' he laughs, 'for "dependable". And nothing would rattle him. Viggo's bloody nag kept hitting reverse gear and murdering the shot.'

For Friday afternoon tea there's a raffle. And despite most of the cast and crew having worked on the films for nearly three years, the notion of winning a *Lord of the Rings* action card game, or set of die-cast, three-inch Hobbit figures, still fills them with delight. There is much whooping and hollering going on – the string quartet has finally given up the ghost. Our publicist, clutching a box full of names, stops by Bernard Hill to pick one and read it. With that an Orc fists the air in triumph and runs forward to collect his commemorative cap. Bet this didn't happen on *Titanic*.

Day Two: Scampering through the drizzle, we are guided to the interior of Orthanc where we are granted time to have a poke around. On closer inspection, Saruman's Gothic clutter starts to yield its secrets. Bottles of mysterious gloop contain the actual remnants of fossilised amphibians. 'Everything has to be authentic,' the publicist explains. 'There was a parchment written in Elvish which said something like, "Gary was here!"'

Christopher Lee as Saruman in The Two Towers, *with Grima Wormtongue. Saruman's fall was controversially omitted from* The Return of the King – *but restored for the DVD edition.*

Peter wasn't having it. There are people out there who know Elvish.' That said, upon opening one of the dented books, weathered to fit the scene, it turns out to be an anthology of the *New Zealand Gazette*. Saruman must get it on subscription.

'Sit on the throne,' the publicist implores, and *Empire* perches on the ornate seat and ponders for a second the oddity of the place. This may be simply a movie set made of fibreglass and wood, but it blurs around the edges where Middle-earth squeezes in. No-one calls it a set – they call it Orthanc. Mind you, the sixties-style, brown armchair, lodged behind a bank of flickering monitors, isn't very Tolkien. Even if it has been emblazoned with the White Tree of Gondor. And has Peter Jackson sitting in it. 'Oh, the props guys did this for me,' he says, pointing out the heraldic symbol for Minas Tirith. 'We got the chair for Harry Knowles when he visited.'

Jackson, on set, is in clover. The crew buzz around him as if responding to telepathic instructions. They've been at this so long, they can almost read his mind. 'We've got to get one more shot before lunch,' he explains, clutching a ragged piece of paper. 'It is helpful to have a line for an earlier scene shot years ago. The population of Edoras is fleeing to Helm's Deep, and I wrote a line to explain this with Wormtongue informing Saruman it is a good time to attack.' On the paper is a line of dialogue hastily scribbled in Biro. 'I'm in make-it-up mode,' he laughs.

With the sweep of a black cape, his face as ashen as nausea and distinctly short on eyebrows, in steps Brad Dourif, a.k.a. Grima Wormtongue, despicable right-hand man to Saruman. The poison in the heart of Rohan. His voice a whisper of evil, eloquent but starved of oxygen. Dourif, rumour has it, likes to stay in character. Spotting *Empire*, an oily smile turns his lips: 'So, you've come to see me fail?'

Not at all, but when Dourif, equipped with new jotted line, begins the scene direct to camera, he jerks and judders, frequently missing words as Jackson calmly asks him for another take. Then, like a key slotting into place, you can feel the line click and the insidious menace of Wormtongue swells onto the monitor.

'It's very easy, in a way, to be the bad guy,' admits the 52 year-old actor, famed for his array of slimeballs, dirt-diggers and out-and-out loonies. 'You are in control. Things don't happen to you – you do them to other people. If it wasn't for the devil there would be no story.'

Dourif has worked hard with the screenwriters on fleshing out Wormtongue's tortured backstory. Despite his obvious wickedness, including unhealthy designs on Miranda Otto's Éowyn, he is a tragic figure who has spent his entire life ugly and despised. 'He was a human who has turned evil,' he insists. 'He has totally come under the sway of Saruman and finally, of course, Sauron.' Given his sharp, duplicitous mind, Wormtongue has worked his way up to become advisor to Théoden. However, Wormtongue's double life is in for a rude awakening when Gandalf and the gang ride into Rohan.

Wormtongue's real boss, meanwhile, Christopher Lee, is keeping a dignified pose, despite the fact various people are fiddling with his skirts. They're trying to mike him up while he continues to make his point. 'It has been very satisfying coming back,' he says, his prosthetic nose wobbling at eye-level. Saruman, let's not forget, has the right arse in the second movie. His plan to grab the Ring has been foiled, so he decides to launch an army to wipe out mankind. Lee, in contrast, is feeling content. 'It's easy to feel confident,' he asserts as one of the chief clairvoyants of the triumphant debut, 'but I don't have fears as to whether it's going to do less business or whether it's not going to do as well. I think the anticipation is probably greater this time around. This movie is going to be better.'

Day Three: A short drive away, in another nondescript corner of Miramar, lies the Weta Workshop, the soul of the *Lord of the Rings* operation. Here is where dreams and nightmares are created, the contents of which could float on eBay and probably recoup the entire budget of the film. A Willy Wonka factory of props and models, the detail of which is mind-blowing. *Empire* grasps the shards of Narsil forged from sprung steel in the inhouse smelting works, the sword that severed the Ring from Sauron's pinkies. The publicist passes over Boromir's hefty blade: 'Careful, you could have someone's eye out with that,' she quips. Actually, you're more likely to have someone's head off.

There is a room devoted to every different Middle-earth locale: the Shire, Rohan, Gondor, Mordor . . . Hung up on a coat rack is this season's Orc couture in a variety of fittings. In all, 48,000 different items have been made over five departments: armour, weaponry, special make-up, miniatures and maquettes (the sculptures of creatures used as scanning guides for the computers). 'We've been doing this for five years,' chirps a Weta expert on cue, 'and we're still going strong.'

The industry and skill on show is staggering. Peter Jackson gives them copious notes, the artists conjure Tolkien's dreams onto paper and Weta turns them into three-dimensional reality. The net result, meanwhile, sits in a glass cabinet near the entrance, getting a quick buff from a cleaning lady.

'Coming home with the Oscar finally solidified for everyone that we could stand up and be proud,' asserts Richard Taylor, the mastermind in charge of Weta, whose vocal pitch is permanently on clarion call. 'It had been recognised that we weren't the poor cousins down in New Zealand.'

Taylor's twelve-inch statuette for Best Visual Effects was carried home in a Tesco bag. When he landed at Wellington airport, the innately modest genius, who has worked with Jackson since the humble beginnings of *Meet the Feebles* and *Braindead*, was startled to find the ground staff had laid out a red carpet and the entire arrival hall, along with all his co-workers, was cheering dementedly. 'I had managed to buy 100 miniature Oscars,' he recalls, 'and I had them in two big rubbish sacks. So I was able to hand out Oscars to everyone. It was a real scramble, then everyone drove out of the airport with them mounted on their roof-racks and bonnets. It was crazy.'

In the corner of a warehouse area, its back to the room like a scolded schoolboy, is what seems to be a large, vaguely humanoid tree. There is just enough room to squeeze in front and find the beard made out of vines; this leads you to a pair of eyes the shade of honey, with brows as thick as a forearm. This is Treebeard, the exotic companion for Merry and Pippin, who will prove a godsend to the good guys. As an Ent, he is also one of the potentially silliest additions to *The Two Towers*' creature culture. 'You have to find a way of creating something that isn't immediately risible,' says John Rhys-Davies, who will add the Ent's voice to his performance as Gimli. 'When you think about a walking tree, laughter is the response. You have to avoid that.'

Yet, as Jackson is at pains to point out, 'He's not a walking, talking tree, but rather a shep-herd of the trees. The trees have the ability to move and kill, but they have to be kept under control in the forests of Fangorn. The forests have shepherds who are supposed to look after them. That's what Treebeard is. His skin is like bark and moss, so he looks a bit like a tree.'

Born out of Tolkien's predilection for the woodlands around Oxford – and designed to echo his ecological concerns – Treebeard will mainly be a CGI creation; this animatronic version is used for the close-ups with Hobbit actors Billy Boyd and Dominic Monaghan. He is also the oldest creature alive, and has proved one slippery customer to nail.

'We plunged in and just experimented,' sighs Rhys-Davies, whose natural Welsh basso is as rich as malt whisky. 'You cannot do exactly as it is in the book because of his slow-ness – you can't afford that on film. I've had nightmares about this; it was both frighten-ing and very satisfying to find the Treebeard voice. I can't tell you that it actually works, all I can tell you is that Peter doesn't let go of things unless he is happy. I have only heard one finished line and it seemed to me pretty damn good.' His voice subtly takes on a deeper, mellower ring. Is that a hint of ancient bark and the soft rustle of leaves? The actor grins. 'I do know we created a moment in the Treebeard sequence that isn't actually in the book,' he adds enticingly. 'It will be one of the most astounding moments in the film. It should make your hair stand on end.'

In a smaller room, thick with the scent of rubber and sawdust, the maquettes are sculpt-ed. A large display case in the corner contains a detailed model of King Kong wrestling with a dinosaur. 'That was made when Peter considered the movie,' the publicist says of the project that was put into turnaround by Universal. 'I'm not sure he's going to do it anymore.'

A row of life-sized heads, each subtly different but quite revolting, adorn a bench. 'Oh, that's the change into Gollum,' says our guide, 'explaining that we will witness a time-lapsed transformation from the Hobbit Sméagol to Gollum the emaciated ghoul, cowed by the corruption of the Ring over 500 years.

'I personally think one of the scariest things in *The Two Towers* is the Frodo/Sam/Gollum relationship,' says Jackson of the monster who becomes a key player in film two. 'We took a lead from Tolkien, but have gone a bit further into the area of the psychological thriller.'

There are two things you need to know about Gollum. Firstly, he's a headcase: the former custodian of the Ring, addicted to its power and tormented by its absence. Secondly, he's played by British actor Andy Serkis, although Serkis won't, strictly speaking, be on screen.

'We are doing a CG character but having a human actor put his stamp on it,' continues Jackson, fully cognisant of the dangers of 'going Jar Jar'. This is different, he asserts; Serkis is acting the entire role in a motion capture studio, his every movement logged on a computer, and with the aid of 45 animators turned into the character. A process that has been evolving throughout the shoot.

'When I arrived there were vague notions of doing this thing called motion capture,' says Serkis, admitting he may have landed the part when they realised he bore a striking resemblance to their concept art of the creature. 'The whole ethos of the way Peter works is making it more truthful and not just a special effects movie. We pursued ways of making Gollum as fully integrated as possible.'

We've moved to the motion capture stage. In truth, another Miramar warehouse smelling like a school gym. Serkis is in a skin-tight Lycra get-up, doing exaggerated *Matrix* poses to make the crew laugh. Dotted across his catsuit like overgrown sequins are data reflectors 'capturing' his movements.

'He is an extraordinary character,' considers the 38-year-old star of *24 Hour Party People*. 'He is the audience's key into what the Ring does to you. He is a Ring junkie. He was a Hobbit, and I like to think he could have gone another way. Something very human.' Specifically, his frail psyche has fractured into two halves: the docile, subservient 'Sméagol', and the treacherous mental carapace of 'Gollum', who might yet betray Frodo in the desperate hope he can regain possession of the Ring, his *precioussss*!

Serkis can't resist giving a taster of the voice, his normal baritone strangled into an agonised wail, partly based on the sound his cats make when tormented by a fur-ball. 'It comes from where I think his pain is trapped. For him it was his throat. It's not always easy – I had to do a scene the other day eating a twelve-inch worm while doing the voice . . . It was jelly, not a real worm.' He takes on an announcer's prim tones: 'No worms were harmed in the making of this film!'

Day Four: We're in Lilliput, as in the miniatures studio. Everywhere you look are impossibly detailed models of the various towers, cityscapes, fortresses and palaces from the three films. *Empire* strokes the precision-built exterior of Barad-dûr at 1/66th scale and wonders how big the Airfix box would be. Smoked with dry ice and bathed in artificial sunlight, these bedroom-sized citadels take on the gigantic dimensions we witnessed in *Fellowship*. That's how Jackson wants it – none of this digital gloss, but real film in real cameras making their dynamic swoops for real. With a purpose-built, motion-controlled camera rig, today they have been skimming over the remnants of Osgiliath and circling the tower of Zirak-zigil, where Gandalf finally clobbers the Balrog.

Alex Funke, a jovial maestro of the technique, is trying to explain the process of melding shots of a four-foot Minas Morgul into a human-sized set-up. Spotting the envious expression on *Empire*'s mug, he emphasises he won't be selling Minas Tirith after the films are finished (no matter how well it might set off *Empire*'s living room), and that we really should come and look at Helm's Deep, because in *The Two Towers* this one is going to bring the house down.

Let's put this simply: Helm's Deep is a stone fortress where the population of Rohan have run for cover and which the massed ranks of Saruman's Uruk-hai army are endeavouring to smash to smithereens. Viggo Mortensen, Orlando Bloom, John Rhys-Davies and Bernard Hill spent months of night-shoots enacting its furious battle as hundreds of extras dressed as Orcs and soldiers gruffly laid into one another washed by the rain machine. It will have the gigantic heave of a David Lean spectacular, backed up by the digital creation of teeming Orcs spilling over the various models.

'It takes place mostly at night,' boasts Jackson, who was fed the growing miracle of the scene's effects on laptops while busy mustering the troops. 'It was so complex we filmed for about four months of nights. Aragorn, Legolas and Gimli have ended up there with about 300 soldiers, so it becomes them against 10,000.'

'Helm's Deep was an incredible challenge,' adds Richard Taylor of what is already being mooted as the new movie's *coup de cinema*. 'It was achieved using a number of different scales.'

There was the full-sized fortress built in a disused quarry outside of Wellington, a quarter scale miniature that filled a rugby field and a 30-foot scale miniature that occupies the sound stage here. Using a combination of these castles and some crafty compositing techniques, each version will be assailed by thousands of Orcs in front of our dazzled eyes. 'It takes three cents of ink and fourteen seconds to read the line: "The soldier glanced across the Plain and in front of them were tens of thousands,"' Taylor says soberly. 'To bring that to the screen is a five-year endeavour encompassing 1,000 people and millions and millions of dollars.'

He pauses and looks *Empire* straight in the eye. 'Helm's Deep will go down as one of the greatest epic triumphs of cinema history. It is a scene simply beyond comprehension.'

New York: On a blazing hot day in late September, thankfully within the air-conditioned confines of a polished hotel suite, Bernard Hill is pretending to be Peter Jackson, Brad Dourif is pretending to be Christopher Lee, and John Rhys-Davies is pretending to be a French female television host, Machiavelli's Prince and a whale. All are very good.

A host of *Two Towers* talent has gathered to further talk up the upcoming movie, and to a man/woman/Hobbit/Ent, they are getting into the swing of things. But, let's start with Elijah Wood, who is still trying to get his head around Gollum. He may have spent six months acting with him, but he hadn't seen him until this morning. There has been a fifteen-minute

Glimpsed only briefly in The Fellowship of the Ring's *prologue, Gollum becomes a central character in* The Two Towers. *His grotesque yet pitiful form was entirely created by CGI.*

preview of *The Two Towers* shown, including a five-minute scene of the finished Gollum wrestling with Sam and begging for mercy from Frodo: a sweaty, twitchy, fully-formed creature, oozing out of the screen. He ain't pretty, but set aside concerns – he really works.

'Wow, it was amazing,' says Wood with a shake of the head. 'I'd seen assembly stuff when I did the looping and they hadn't touched it up. It was really rough and Gollum was a wire stickman.' For Wood's alter ego Frodo, Gollum is where it's at. In fact, their relationship becomes the hub of the entire trilogy, each manipulating the other: Frodo using Gollum to get to Mordor, Gollum helping Frodo in order to get close to the Ring.

Wood nods in agreement. 'He pities him initially – he sees that underneath that wretched guise is a Hobbit that succumbed to the power of the Ring,' he explains. 'Frodo sees that there's still humanity in this wretched creature, but he also sees what he [Frodo] could become, which is much more interesting. If he holds on to the Ring for this length of time, he could become Gollum. And that's really frightening. So part of his mission in the second film is to prove that Gollum can come back from that evil place and extract the humanity out of him, because he knows that if he can get that out of Gollum, then he too can be saved.'

You may have already surmised that events for Frodo take a major turn for the grim from now on. He will spend the new movie with only Sam and Gollum for company, and their path will be beset by betrayal and disaster as Frodo sinks under the Ring's corruptive power and they close in on the perpetual gloom of Mordor.

'If you are doing scenes every day that are filled with despair, anguish, fatigue, cold, anxiety and obsession, all these extremes, it's an atmosphere you become, oddly enough, comfortable with,' he says, ever the pro. 'You don't actually take that home with you ... Although the fatigue I totally took home with me. I have never been so exhausted in my life.'

He pauses for a wistful, 'you had to be there to understand' kind of shrug then perks up again: 'It's weird, I had no concept of what everybody else's journeys were at that time, I could only see my journey, and so when I see this movie there is so much that I literally have no knowledge of.'

Meanwhile, Bernard Hill is discussing how Peter Jackson was always open to ideas presented by his cast. Eventually. 'Yeah, right, sounds great, he mimics in a soft, peevish, Kiwi accent that is a dead ringer for his boss not being overjoyed at being distracted by Hill's 'new idea'. Clearly, the nobility of his role was rubbing off: for a pre-battle team talk, he had the notion of passing along the massed ranks of his cavalry, touching each of their spears with his sword in a sign of fealty.

'It made it into the script and Pete did it,' he says proudly. 'But he did it the wrong way round, the silly fucker, because I'm left-handed and he made me do it with my right hand. But it's a very exciting moment. Pete was great like that, he was so open to stuff.'

Hill's eyes glaze over for a brief moment of reverie, his mind transported back to the tumbling plains of New Zealand; he returns to the Big Apple with a happy grin. 'This is going to be a better film,' he asserts as if it has just occurred to him. 'You're very quickly brought into human frailties, human failure, human emotions like loss, grief, jealousy, all those things that people identify with. And there is still the fantasy section – grand wizards and all that kind of stuff – but even more dynamic.'

An hour later, Brad Dourif is striding about the room, his nose to the ceiling and shaking his fist at the wall. He is explaining what it was like to work with Christopher Lee, for which you need to play the towering British thesp. There are just so many stories. Don't get him started, he implies, already off and running.

'Of course, he knew Tolkien, you know,' he intones in his tidiest, mock-posh English accent; it's not far off the great man. 'He really knew the names of everything. To be honest, he knows everything and everybody on the planet. I mean, you almost don't believe him, until you hear it is true.'

He plants himself down in his seat again, pulls what can only be described as a Brad Dourif kind of face – the eyeballs are an inch further forward than the rest – and reflects, 'You know what was weird about this film? Everybody was signing shit. Now, because of eBay, all this shit really has value. In this respect, it was the most unique thing I have ever done, the amount of shit I signed.'

John Rhys-Davies doesn't even need a question to get going. Ever the raconteur, he's up and running on a fresh anecdote before he reaches his seat. 'Do you know that French television host, Sophie?' he asks from somewhere left of leftfield. *Empire* shakes a baffled head. 'She is a gift sent down from heaven! Magnificent! You must meet her.'

It transpires that Rhys-Davies hasn't seen the exquisite Sophie since Cannes last year. She made a lasting impression.

'She was interviewing myself, Sean Bean and Viggo Mortensen, about the first film,' he continues in a dubious French falsetto. '"Ah, it was very exciting and spectacular, but what is there is very for the woman to enjoy?" And she looked at me and then she looked at Viggo and then she *looked* at Sean. "So tell me, *Sean*? How would you seduce me as a woman?" I love her! I love that girl! Sean, who is a sweet, lovely, gentle soul, was dumb-founded. We were like, "Go on. Sean! Go on! How would you seduce lovely Sophie?" Well, if you can't take the piss out of your fellow actors, what can you do?'

Welcome back to the bizarre, wonderful, alternative universe of John Rhys-Davies' head. And today he is on top form, although Treebeard is still a worry. 'How does a tree speak? It's such a risk, this one,' he wails. 'It's almost Machiavelli, isn't it? "The minds of men are timorous, they are voluble, dissemblers, anxious to avoid danger and covetous of gain . . ."'

Er, quite.

'. . . And sometimes you've got to risk a bit of artistic failure. If I fall on my face in this, then it's my fault.' He holds out his hands, as if waiting for the cuffs. 'You know, we even tried to add whale-like communication to his voice.' The Welsh actor sucks in a lungful of air before emitting an astonishing bellow: 'Wooooooammmmmmmerrrrrrrr!! [approximation only]. That kind of underpins the voice. I trust that P.J. has found the answer – I still haven't heard the finished thing.'

Not one to stay downcast for long, he puffs out his chest like a peacock and resumes his role as chief disseminator of hyperbole for the *Lord of the Rings* trilogy. 'This film is far more exciting, it is breathtaking. I would say it is almost of a different order than part one. This is the real meat of the story. We haven't seen a film on this scale in my lifetime.'

Day Five: Whatever the Hollywood gossips may prattle about over water-coolers and lukewarm lattes, what is evident here, back in luscious New Zealand, is not an issue of making a better film than *Fellowship*. That was never the point. The driving force for Jackson and his hungry troops is to make the best film possible, to make *The Two Towers* the best *Two Towers* possible. One that J.R.R. will look kindly upon from his Middle-earth in the sky. And the key to their realm of ingenuity, craft and extraordinary vision dubbed 'Wellywood' is a simple New Zealand tenet: 'Never say we can't do that.' Whatever the obstacle, Jackson and co. have found a way. Trees will walk and talk, CG characters will have substance and texture and not float around absurdly like they've been shaken out of *Toy Story*, and the mood will get darker, more disturbing and far more exciting.

The feeling pervades the whole of the country, the determination that these three films, each different but part of a whole, will be their cinematic legacy to the world. It is not just about the landscape, it is something innate in the people – they could not have been accomplished anywhere else.

Nowhere is this more apparent than at Roger's Tattooart. Located on the boho parade of Cuba Street in downtown Wellington, on the wall of this grungy parlour is a picture of Elijah Wood mugging away, having just got his Elvish tattoo. As is well known, the entire Fellowship got one (bar Rhys-Davies, who sent his double). They were then fol-lowed by Peter Jackson, executive producer Mark Ordesky and Bernard Hill.

According to Roger, who has his own set of facial rivets, Tolkien tattoos are all the rage. Here, and all over the world, *The Lord of the Rings* has made a lasting impression. Roger is even thinking of expanding his repertoire for *The Two Towers*, too. He smiles, stretching the shrapnel. 'After all,' he says. 'No-one ever asks for a *Star Wars* tattoo.'

CREATURE EFFECTS
FOR *THE TWO TOWERS*
Ray Harryhausen Visits Middle-Earth by Lawrence French

Although the giant spider Shelob's appearance was held until *The Return of the King,* Peter Jackson still managed to pepper *The Two Towers* with a smorgasbord of Ray Harryhausen-style creations. Among them are: the awesome Fell-beasts – the winged steeds that carry the Nazgûl in search of the Ring; the Wargs, wolf-like creatures the Orcs ride into battle; and the giant Mûmakil, mastodon-like creatures that the Haradrim will use to mount their assault on Minas Tirith.

'I'm a huge fan of Ray Harryhausen's films, like *The Seventh Voyage of Sinbad* and *Jason and the Argonauts,*' enthuses Jackson, 'and even earlier, of Willis O'Brien and *King Kong.* They are really why I'm making films today, because as a kid, I got so inspired by that kind of movie. In *The Two Towers* we have a real Harryhausen type of sequence with the Wargs. Today, stop-motion is regarded as an ancient art form, since computer animation came into vogue, but I was really determined that the creature sequences would feel less like computer animation, and more like a Ray Harryhausen sequence. In the first film, with the Cave Troll, I was able to do something Harryhausen was never able to do, which is to shoot with hand-held cameras, because his Dynamation technique was always very static. So I thought, "Wouldn't it be great to do a Harryhausen-style monster sequence, but make it feel much more like a documentary, by using hand-held cameras for coverage?" So it was a great joy for me, to finally be able to do homage to Ray's movies.'

To implement and oversee all the creature movements in a CGI style that would recall Harryhausen's work, Jackson hired a former stop-motion animator, Randall Cook, whose past work includes *Ghostbusters* and *Fright Night.* 'There was an interesting dynamic that occurred at Weta Digital,' notes producer Barrie Osborne, 'between those who wanted to go more towards key frame animation, and those who wanted to go with motion capture. It was a kind of tug-of-war, but Randy was the one actually calling all the shots on that, along with Peter, who gets extremely involved in the effects shots.'

As a result, a character like Gollum, who had to speak and move in a more human fashion, was created largely through motion capture, while the ferocious Wargs and Fell-beasts will be done entirely in key-frame animation. 'The Wargs are large wolf-like creatures ridden by the Orcs,' explains Richard Taylor, head of Weta Workshop. 'They're barely broken-in or controllable, and once they get their blood-lust up, they almost take it upon themselves to choose which way they will go, so when they rampage into the battle, the Orcs are barely able to hang on. We tried to create them as a hybrid of creatures from our own world, so they're totally believable and acceptable to audiences. We wanted to create a physical reality for all the different creatures. Even a character like the Cave Troll, as bizarre as it is, is still based very strongly within the confines of a bi-pedal humanoid creature. Likewise, in *The Two Towers* we have tried very hard to rationalise all the creatures. We wanted audi-

Gollum confronted by Samwise Gamgee (Sean Astin). From The Two Towers *onwards, the schizoid, sub-Hobbit Ring-junkie is the most affecting character of the trilogy.*

ences to believe that these creatures exist, as if they were an integrated part of this world.'

The Fell-beasts are saurian-like flying serpents that the nine Nazgûl ride in search of the Ring, after their horses have been drowned in the Mitheithel river. The job of creating them began with John Howe's illustrations. 'The concept drawings I did were turned into these astonishing sculptures,' says Howe. 'Every creature was designed by many different hands, so I can't claim paternity for them 100 per cent, because there were so many other people involved. The general outline was mine, but the sculptors and the animators took them so much further than I could have gone. I can't wait to see the Fell-beasts actually flying around onscreen. They were such a pain to draw properly, I'm very excited about finally seeing them fully animated in full 3-D.'

In sculpting the Fell-beast maquettes, artist Jamie Beswarick had to analyse the physical realities of the creature's design, making sure it would appear realistic. 'The Fell-beast has to have wings that could actually lift its body weight,' says Taylor. 'In a more fantastical film, like *Dragonheart*, the dragon's wings could be smaller, even though it would be a logistic impossibility for the wings to lift its body weight. In contrast to that, the Fell-beast needed wings the size of a jumbo jet, because that's the size the wings would need to be, to get its body off the ground. It was the same for the physical structure of the lower leg joints, when the Fell-beast is trying to land. That had to be analysed and fig-ured out, so people will accept it as a believable creature in this world.'

This was a lesson Ray Harryhausen first learned, back in 1940, when he visited Willis O'Brien at MGM, where the creator of the original *King Kong* was preparing his own flying beasts for *War Eagles*, a movie that was never made. Harryhausen showed O'Brien his dinosaur drawings and O'bie pointed out that the skinny legs Harryhausen had drawn wouldn't support the weight of a stegosaurus. 60 years later, Harryhausen was invited down to New Zealand, to offer his advice, and observe the workings of the Weta crea-ture shop. He was duly impressed. 'It's quite remarkable,' said Harryhausen, commenting on Weta's work. 'They are now able to use the computer to do lip-sync on the faces of their animated characters.' Of course, Harryhausen never attempted to lip-sync any of his own creations. In *Clash of the Titans*, for instance, he created Calibos in stop-motion, but to give him dialogue, he resorted to using an actor in make-up. 'No matter how careful-ly you animate a creature like that,' explains Harryhausen, 'if you attempt to use dialogue, you're really trying to play God, and that's not my mission in life. We started out with Calibos as a bestial character, with one cloven hoof and a tail, and naturally, you can't find an actor with a cloven hoof and a tail, so originally, he was just going to grunt and groan, *a la One Million Years BC.* Then, we decided that we needed some exposition and dia-logue from him, so we used an actor.'

Since Peter Jackson, Richard Taylor and Randall Cook are all big fans of Harryhausen's work, they were delighted to have the master animator visit Weta Workshop. 'We got to know Ray Harryhausen very well,' says Taylor, 'so don't think for a moment that we didn't borrow every page we possibly could from his book. He'd tell us about his work, and then we'd show him what we were up to. We tried to build on his design philosophy, and while he was here, he gave us some aesthetic advice, which we incorporated in our work. Ray loves to create fantastical worlds, and he based a great deal of his work on Gustave Doré's illustrations. Likewise, *The Lord of the Rings* is strongly based on a Gustave Doré design aesthetic. It was very interesting to have Ray appreciate the way we both had been influenced by Doré.'

Gustave Doré was also a strong inspiration for Willis O'Brien's work on *King Kong*, which Jackson and Taylor duly noted when they began designing their initial version of *Kong* for Universal. Of course, after the gigantic success of the *Lord of the Rings* movies, Universal quickly moved to rekindle the fires underneath the *King Kong* project. 'When we first began preparing *King Kong*,' says Taylor, 'we hired Bernie Wrightson to do some design work. The black and white illustrations he did for *The Frankenstein Chronicles* are a modern pop interpretation of Gustave Doré's classics. But in turn, Bernie created his own classic, his own beautifully lit, filmic images. So Doré was always a strong inspira-tion, even on Peter's first movies. We had already discovered Doré's work with light and darkness, which, of course, was many years before film was even invented.'

Indeed, Harryhausen notes that he often thinks of Gustave Doré as the first art direc-tor of motion pictures. 'When I started out,' says Harryhausen, 'I began doing big draw-ings in black and white, based on Doré's technique, because his drawings were perfectly set-up, with a dark foreground, a medium middle ground and a hazy-light background, which gave you a wonderful sense of depth.'

In *The Return of the King*, the city of Minas Tirith comes under attack from the Haradrim in the south, who use hulking 45-foot tall, elephant-like creatures during the battle of Pelennor Fields, but before then, the Oliphaunts (or Mûmakil) are briefly glimpsed in *The Two Towers*, making their way to Mordor. 'They were created both digitally and in full-scale versions,' says Taylor. 'And they were the biggest thing we've made. They are amazing creatures that carry the Haradrim into battle on these huge battle platforms on their backs. There are 50 or 60 soldiers on the upper battlements of these platforms. They were designed in the workshop, then maquettes were made of them, and we scanned and replicated them as digital creatures. The full size version of the Mûmakil we made was massive. It took eighteen house-removal tracks to get them to our location.'

The Trolls and the Balrog seen in the first film also return, albeit, for brief appearances. Two immense Mountain Trolls are seen pushing open the gigantic black gates of Mordor, and we see the Balrog continuing his titanic struggle with Gandalf, after falling off the bridge at Khazad-dûm. 'You see them battling in mid-air,' says Jim Rygiel, 'as they're actually falling, where before you saw them stationary, on the ground. Then, it ends up with them emerging from the depths of Moria, on top of the snow-capped peak of Zirak-zigil.'

Taylor concluded, 'The creatures of *The Two Towers* become more fantastical, more visceral and more real and gritty, as we move closer to Mordor, and they take on the mantle of Sauron's world.'

THE TWO TOWERS
reviewed by Kim Newman

Middle-earth. After the death of Prince Boromir of Gondor and the disappearance of the wizard Gandalf, the Fellowship of the Ring – a group of nine convened to bring about the destruction of an evil 'Ring of Power' created by Sauron, the Dark Lord of Mordor – has split up. The Hobbit Frodo Baggins, intent on taking the ring to Mordor to be destroyed, travels towards Sauron's realm with his loyal companion Sam, guided by Gollum, a creature who once possessed the Ring and is now obsessed with getting it back. The human Aragorn, the Elf Legolas and the Dwarf Gimli enter the Kingdom of Rohan, searching for Hobbits Merry and Pippin, who have been captured by the Uruk-hai, soldiers in the Orc armies amassed by the turncoat Wizard Saruman in the service of his alliance with Sauron.

King Théoden of Rohan, possessed by Saruman and badly advised by Saruman's ally Wormtongue, is in no position to resist Saruman's hordes, and Wormtongue ensures the death of Théoden's son and heir Théodred and the banishment of his nephew Eomer. Sam distrusts Gollum, but Frodo has sympathy with the former Ringbearer. Aragorn's party encounters Eomer, who has slaughtered the Uruk-hai party who took Merry and Pippin, but the Hobbits have escaped into the Forest of Fangorn, where they encounter Treebeard, an Ent (giant sentient tree), who resists getting involved in the coming war. Gandalf reappears, transformed into the equal of Saruman, and exorcises Théoden, who decrees that his people should retreat to the keep of Helm's Deep to take a stand against the armies of Saruman. Though Aragorn disagrees with Théoden's tactics, he pledges himself to the cause of Rohan, surviving a battle in which he is feared dead; he is also torn between the love he feels for the Elf Arwen and his attraction to Théoden's niece Éowyn. Frodo and Sam are captured by Faramir, brother of Boromir, who forces Frodo to lure Gollum into a trap, which embitters the former Ringbearer against the Hobbit, and decides to take Ringbearer and Ring to Gondor. Though an Elven army joins with the forces of Rohan to defend Helm's Deep, the Uruk-hai lay siege and are only defeated when a human army, gathered by Gandalf, come to their aid. After an attack on Gondor by the Nazgûl, a dragon in the service of Sauron, Faramir lets Frodo and the Ring go to Mordor. As Frodo and Sam walk on, Gollum plots to betray the Hobbits and take back his 'precious'.

Just as J. R. R. Tolkien's *Lord of the Rings* was initially published as three separate novels with nearly-year-long intervals between volumes but is now generally seen as a single continuous narrative, the ultimate form of Peter Jackson's trilogy-in-progress is liable to be marathon day-long sessions (or, more likely, DVD box sets) that run the three parts together into one very long film. To that end, *The Two Towers* – taken from the tricky, middle book, in which several sets of characters follow their own routes across Middle-earth to get to their starting places for the big finale – makes only a token attempt at getting newcomers up to speed. Generally speaking Jackson assumes you not only saw the first film but have total recall of it, picking up the pace a little for an episode that has few of the idyllic lulls of the establishing act. He has to cope with as many separate plot strands as vintage Altman, with the added handicap that they only come together in the next film.

Jackson and his collaborators continue their subtle work of adaptation, not so much updating Tolkien's characters as shifting emphasis to underplay his weaknesses. It's often remarked how few active female characters there are in the novel, but the film makes something of the implicit love triangle in which Viggo Mortensen's Aragorn is haunted by memories of his pact with Liv Tyler's Elf Arwen, but is drawn to Miranda Otto's determined princess Éowyn. Éowyn shows that she can wield a sword but is forced by duty not to be reinvented as a kick-ass warrior princess (she remains behind doors during the climactic battle at Helm's Deep).

The major alteration turns out to be felicitous: following a year overrun by giant mutant arachnids (*Eight Legged Freaks, Harry Potter and the Chamber of Secrets*, even *Spider-Man*), it makes sense to shift Shelob, the giant queen spider who threatens Frodo and Sam as they enter Mordor, to the first act of the next film. This allows for something close to a cliffhanger as Gollum, whose character arc is the spine of this segment, decides in the film's final moments that an unidentified 'she' should kill the two Hobbits. This reshuffling means that the need to cut between different sets of characters doesn't extend to Jackson's choice of climax – the battle of Helm's Deep. This is staged as a satisfying bit of spectacle including intricate medieval-style siege warfare and Gandalf showing up like the Seventh Cavalry at the end of *Stagecoach* (1939).

Grishnakh, one of the malevolent Orcs who besiege Helm's Deep. Some Tolkien fans blanched at the horror genre elements of The Two Towers, *but its darkness is inherent in the novel.*

Though Ian McKellen's Gandalf returns from the dead, *The Two Towers* relies less on the presence of great British acting talent than did *The Fellowship of the Ring*. Bernard Hill's King Théoden is a tentative replacement for Ian Holm's Bilbo, introduced as a fungus-covered zombie in the control of Brad Dourif's slimy traitor Wormtongue (not one of the subtler characterisations in book or film), and taking a view of the responsibilities of kingship different from the more adventurous princes of Gondor but just as disastrous. However, like Karl Urban's Eomer and David Wenham's Faramir, Théoden has to play catch-up to fit in with the mythic personalities established earlier, and the important politicking and warfare associated with these royal humans has less weight than the sometimes comic (sometimes camp) business between Aragorn, Orlando Bloom's Elf Legolas (who seems set up as yet another love interest for Aragorn in some scenes) and John Rhys-Davies' blustering Dwarf Gimli.

The debutant who steals the show is Gollum, barely glimpsed in the first film. A CGI creation, albeit with more than vocal input from British actor Andy Serkis, Gollum inhabits a live-action film as more than an equal of the unaugmented actors. He manages far better than Willem Dafoe in *Spider-Man* the trick of a schizoid talking to himself: the baser instincts of the cruel Gollum argue with the finer being he once was about the goodness of Frodo, until in a chilling culmination the two shattered halves of a personality agree with each other that further treachery is the best course. His non-human face has at least the expressive range of any other actor in the film, while the body seems to displace as much space as anyone who was actually on the set. Techies will gasp at the illusion when Gollum and the Hobbits are splashing in the same stream; others will just accept the perfect mimesis and not realise what has been achieved – another step towards the moment when CGI becomes so invisible it ceases to be recognised even subconsciously as effects trickery.

Considered as a work-in-progress, *The Lord of the Rings* so far stands among the best adaptations of a major work of fantasy ever managed by the cinema. But it remains an adaptation rather than an original, in the manner of a John Huston who could take perfect books like *The Maltese Falcon* and make great films by shooting what was on the page rather than that of a Howard Hawks who saw in novels like *The Big Sleep* a foundation for even greater films. Jackson's films are exciting cinema, with a knack of finding the spot of landscape or performance or artefact equivalent to the Middle-earth of the novel and a knowing deployment of the styles of past movie masters ranging from Ray Harryhausen to Kurosawa. Aside from some gruesome humour with Orcs reminiscent of *Bad Taste* and *Braindead*, Jackson's hitherto vital personality seems invisible here, as if the sacred task of filming *Lord of the Rings* involved channelling Tolkien rather than transforming the source material from one medium to another.

ALL HAIL *THE KING*
by Lawrence French

In December of 2003, the epic fantasy movie of our times arrived in theatres, bringing director Peter Jackson's magnum opus to fruition. At the time, Jackson promised he had saved the best for last. 'We've gone through two entire movies and six hours of exposition,' he explained, 'and now we get three hours of pay-off. I've come to realise that the third film is the reason why you make the first two. You want to get to this one. You want to finish it. Also, when film three is released you get this other dynamic: at that point it will probably become, in most people's minds, a nine-hour film.'

Producer Barrie M. Osborne concurred, saying, '*The Fellowship of the Ring* bore the brunt of the exposition of the story, explaining who the characters were and setting up the world. *The Two Towers* is the bridging movie between introducing the characters in the first, and the finale to this incredible journey in the third. So in *The Return of the King*, we're able to have a lot of fun, with very little set-up. Of course, all three have to be entertaining and well-made movies, but the third one has the resolution of all our characters' story arcs, which makes it a fun and more rewarding film, dramatically. And it's told against an even bigger tapestry than the first two.'

Jackson, who was busy adding and making changes to *Return of the King* under a month before its premiere, was looking forward to seeing the three completed films together. 'There's going to be a development in each film,' he said, 'as they become more and more intense. Each film becomes darker as Sauron's power grows, and they emotionally go places, which is very interesting. By the third film, the Ring is such a burden for Frodo, and he is starting to behave in such a strange way, I think the empathy of the audience will switch over to Sam. Frodo becomes so troubled by the Ring and the weight of his task that, in *The Return of the King*, we will be looking at the story through Sam's eyes, because the audience will identify with Sam's pain at witnessing Frodo's struggle. To a certain degree, Frodo is becoming like Gollum, so it's really a torturous journey he has to complete.'

The thrilling centerpiece of *Return of the King* is the battle of Pelennor Fields, where the Dark Lord Sauron has assembled an army of 200,000 Orcs, to strike the final death-blow against the free peoples of Middle-earth. 'At the end of *The Two Towers,* Gandalf exclaims, "The battle of Helm's Deep is over, the battle for Middle-earth is about to begin,"' observed Jackson. 'In a sense that does sum up *The Return of the King.* Helm's Deep was really just an opening skirmish. This is the real battle. It's the battle where the future of Middle-earth is decided. Are the Orcs and Sauron going to prevail? Or is Mankind going to prevail? It's in the balance.'

The actual battle was meticulously prepared with storyboards, animatic pre-visualisations, computer models and concept drawings. 'When you're planning a battle, the geography becomes quite important,' explained Jackson. 'We did this experimentation with lenses and we sort of built the landscapes in the computer, simply to try to get the geography down. The distances, the scale, the size of things, basing it on the description in Tolkien's books. You can't just invent the sequence, shot by shot, because there has to be continuity as the battle unfolds. So we are basically having to figure out the formations of Orcs: where they are, how quickly they close in around the walls of the city, when the siege towers go forward, when the catapults fire. The whole thing is actually like plotting a real battle, the night before, figuring out the campaign strategy.'

Of course, Jackson had a big advantage over a real general, in that he could control the troop movements on both opposing sides, just as he did as a little kid, playing with his toy soldiers. However, one big problem the filmmakers wanted to avoid was having the audience become confused by the vast movements of all the different forces who will be joining the battle. It's a problem that was cleverly solved by Akira Kurosawa in *Ran,* where the different armies, banners and uniforms were all colour-coded. 'In our film it's clear,' asserted Osborne, 'because the Rohirrim are on horseback, the Orcs are on foot, and the Gondorians are behind the walls of Minas Tirith. And the creatures in the battle, like the Mountain Trolls and the Oliphaunts, are so huge, they stand out from the soldiers. But there are many other challenges in doing a battle successfully. You want the audience to understand the strategy that is going on, how it's progressing, what's at stake and how's it's affecting the characters, so it gives it an emotional effect. A battle like this one, done on such a huge scale, is by its very nature impersonal, so we've tried hard to make it personal; otherwise it's just a big melee. We really needed to have it affect our characters, so the audience can have empathy with what's going on. To do that, the choreography of the battle has to be very clear. You have to understand where your key characters are, within this ongoing massive conflict.'

Indeed, as the battle progresses, numerous different episodes play out, as Jackson cuts between the Orcs attacking at the gates of Minas Tirith, using Grond, the awesome battering ram wielded by the Mountain Trolls, while inside the city walls, Gandalf and the Gondorians must stave off attacks from flying Fell-beasts and catapult fire. On the field itself, King Théoden leads a heroic charge of Rohan soldiers, along with Eomer, Merry and Éowyn in disguise as a soldier. Finally, Aragorn, Legolas and Gimli arrive on the scene, piloting ships up the Anduin river after their fearful encounter with the Army of the Dead. 'It's a multi-pronged battle that is taking place,' said Osborne, 'with different centres of activity that we are cutting between. You have all this spectacle going on, but you're telling a dramatic story, and you always want to keep that in mind, and keep it personal, otherwise you'll lose the audience.'

One of the key personal moments comes after King Théoden leads a heroic cavalry charge of his Rohan horse soldiers against the hordes of teaming Orcs that are surrounding Minas Tirith. At the height of the battle, the dreadful Witch-King of Angmar strikes down Théoden. Screenwriter Philippa Boyens said some of the best acting in the trilogy occurred during this battle. 'King Théoden has a great line in the battle when he rallies the Rohan troops,' revealed Boyens, 'which is, "Ride now, ride for ruin and the world's ending." And that's just what the whole battle feels like, it's the end of all things, it's so huge and phenomenal. So you have these great epic movie moments, like Éowyn's confrontation and slaying of the Witch-King, as well as some emotional moments, like the death of King Théoden. Both Bernard Hill as Théoden and Miranda Otto as Éowyn give beautiful performances. It's so rich it's really about shaping it and crafting it, so that it's not overwhelmingly rich. It's a part of the story that Peter has a huge hand in bringing together and making sure everything is just right. It really has been driven by Peter's eye. We just had to make sure all the characters had their moments, and that those moments were real. It's a sort of unleashing, where everyone knows that the end is now in sight, so we could just let go, and really let it rip.'

Before preparing to shoot the battle scenes, cinematographer Andrew Lesnie reviewed combat footage from such past spectaculars as *Ben-Hur*, *War and Peace*, *Braveheart* and *Spartacus*. 'Sometimes you just look at those references and pick things you like,' explained Lesnie, 'but everyone has personal preferences. What's also intriguing is not just the filmmaking, but the nature of the battle itself, and the nature of the movement of vast numbers of people. Just the perception of that vast movement is interesting. You hear people argue that once you have more than 6,000 people on a screen, there is no way of discerning any more numbers, because it just becomes an amorphous mass of grey. I don't know how true that is, but in the old classic films there were no digital effects, they actually had whole armies of extras to stage the battles. These days, we come at it from an entirely different direction. But when you go through what happens at Pelennor Fields, it's like a movie in itself that has its own chapters and sub-plots. It's an epic right from the very first moment that you see Pelennor Fields, when Gandalf rides up on the crest of a ridge and sees Minas Tirith. At the same time, you also see Faramir's troops evacuating from Osgiliath. From that point on, there are several stories that happen, so it's more than one battle. We spent many days out in front of the full-size Minas Tirith set filming assaults by the Nazgûl on their Fell-beasts and staging major battle sequences with the Mûmakils.'

Given the enormous size of the battle, production designer Grant Major selected a location that was about six football fields in size. 'The Pelennor Fields are so huge, we could never attempt to show the entire field, as well as Minas Tirith behind it,' said Major, 'so what we did was just make a setpiece for part of Minas Tirith. Then we staged the battle itself on the field with all our soldiers and horses. The battle is so much bigger than Helm's Deep it could only be done with computer-generated plates, adding on to what we couldn't build on location. And to set up the geography of the battle, we will be adding the Minas Tirith model on to it, and the Osgiliath model, as well. Then we'll add further extensions on top of that, like the Emyn Arnen hills that surround the battlefield. The actual location we found was big enough so you could stand in the middle of it and shoot the action sequences, surrounded by all our extras, without too much worry about seeing anything beyond it. Then we collaborated with Richard Taylor's crew and built a huge fallen Mûmakil body, that blocks off a part of the background, so you could shoot wide without expecting to see Mordor. Basically the rest of the backgrounds were covered with soldiers and Orcs.'

The fallen Mûmakil served another purpose in the battle, as Barrie Osborne explained: 'It was a very clever idea that Peter had, because we shot most of the Pelennor battle on the South Island, down at Twizel, but we wanted to do some pick-up shots for it closer to Wellington. So Peter said, "If we build a big Oliphaunt that's fallen over, that will become a key marker on the landscape that you can use to define the geography." So we staged the action around that, and it allows you to know where you are on the battlefield.'

To fill out the battlefield with soldiers, Jackson relied once again on the groundbreaking software developed by Stephen Regelous, known as Massive, which won a scientific achievement Academy Award in 2004. 'We have hundreds of thousands of soldiers at Pelennor,' exclaimed Osborne. 'King Theoden alone shows up with 6,000 Rohirrim, and you've got 2,000 Gondorians fighting against an overwhelming number of Orcs. But Massive is not a crowd replication system, it's a program where each individual soldier has a brain which can select between a range of motions that have been motion-captured by stunt-men on the motion capture stage. It's a very effective and realistic presentation for creating vast armies onscreen.'

With the Rohan horse-soldiers playing such a pivotal role in the battle, Jackson decided to adapt his motion capture system that was so successfully used to create Gollum, so it could replicate a horse's movement as well. 'Now, we're able to ride horses around and do things with them that are captured by the computer,' explained Jackson. 'We can do stunts that you could never do with real horses safely. It creates very exciting looking sequences, where, obviously, no animal is in danger. We also did a lot of the battle with real horses; we mustered together our own army of about 250 horses, which is a huge number of horses to see in one place.'

Pelennor Fields becomes the natural climax of the trilogy, since most of the members of the Fellowship are reunited there for the first time since the end of *The Fellowship of the Ring* – with the major exception of Frodo and Sam, who are still deep in the heart of Mordor, vainly attempting to destroy the Ring. Frodo's first stop in Mordor is the dark and forbidding lair of Shelob the Great, who according to Tolkien, 'has dwelt agelong

The Fellowship head the human armies to the Battle of Pelennor Fields, in The Return of the King *– the* tour de force *of Jackson's career to date.*

beneath the pass of Cirith Ungol, an evil thing in spider-form. Shelob was the last child of Ungoliant, who was there before Sauron, before the first stone of Barad-dur. She served none but herself, drinking the blood of Men and Elves. Sauron knew where she lurked and it pleased him that she should dwell there hungry but unabated in malice, a more sure watch upon that ancient path into his land than any other that his skill could have devised. Sometimes Sauron would send her prisoners that he had no better uses for: He would have them driven to her hole and report brought back to him of the play she made.'

Randall Cook, whose stop-motion talents have graced such films as *Ghostbusters* and *Caveman*, was responsible for bringing her ladyship to life, via CGI key-frame animation. 'Tolkien hedged his bets a little and basically said she's a spider-like thing,' noted Cook. 'So in designing Shelob, the New Zealand tunnel web spider was a heavy influence, but I think you'll find that the animators and designers at Weta have taken it a few steps beyond that, to make her more of an individual creature. My basic admonition to the animation crew was that Shelob should be equal parts Tolkien, fifties B-movie, Discovery Channel, and nightmare, with heavy emphasis on the nightmare. I think the result is not something that you'd confuse with a television documentary, but it certainly incorporates all the essences of spider-hood with a bit of a performance as well. I think she's quite frightening for the audience and a lot of fun for the animators.'

In animating Shelob, Cook was able to go far beyond the somewhat limited effects director Jack Arnold and effects cameraman Clifford Stine were able to achieve when using real tarantulas for their Universal classics, *The Incredible Shrinking Man* and *Tarantula*. 'On screen, you want a spider to do what a spider does in real life, during the most important moments,' explained Cook. 'In a film like *Tarantula* or *The Incredible Shrinking Man* you have these big tarantulas who are photographed with macro photography and slowed down. That's not a spider in its natural element, that's a spider being pushed around on a stage with air hoses, under hot lights, while a very noisy camera is grinding inches away. That tends to intensify whatever inhibitions a tarantula might have. As a result, you tend to get very slow, repetitive moves. Shelob, I think, will stack up quite successfully next to your eight-legged favourites. We tried to keep what's inherently frightening about that kind of creature and then intensified it.'

For actor Elijah Wood, working with Shelob was especially challenging, since there was nothing there to react to, not even a pole. 'It wasn't at all like Gollum,' said Wood, 'where we had Andy Serkis to act with. It was just blank space. There was nothing at all to react to, it was just Peter saying, "There's Shelob, you're scared, run." The only reference we had for Shelob was a large model foot, but that was it. The good thing was that, for all of the sequences where we were acting with creatures that we couldn't see on the set, we always had a reference that was readily available to us, whether it was a drawing, a model or a painting. So we always had an idea of what we were playing against. The only difficult thing was making that image up in your head. So I just had to try and imagine Shelob was actually there in front of me.'

Without any reference on the set, cameraman Andrew Lesnie also found photographing Shelob somewhat daunting. 'We all just had to use our imaginations,' said Lesnie. 'It wasn't only the actors, but in our framing of the shots, we had to imagine this huge spider coming at you from somewhere over there! I'd tell the camera operator to tilt up, because Shelob is coming closer, and of course, what they were tilting up to is nothing, just an arbitrary point.'

In the book, Tolkien describes Shelob's Lair as being pitch black, which, quite naturally, wouldn't work in a movie, so Lesnie used other subtle lighting techniques to suggest the absolute darkness of her cavernous home. 'Peter is always keen to make sure the audience can see the detail of what's going on,' said Lesnie, 'so I must say, it is pretty strongly lit. But if you want to achieve a sense of darkness, you can achieve that by either leaving parts of the image in darkness, or by exposing quite a lot of the scene, and then heavily underexposing the film. I've always felt that any night scene in a movie is a construct, unless you are going out and shooting with available light on the street. In reality, if you were shooting a scene between two people out in the countryside at night, it would have to be a radio play. So the moment you start introducing light, you are creating an artificial environment, which you are asking people to believe in. To me, there are other ways of achieving that feeling of darkness, that don't necessarily mean you have to plunge the screen into total black.'

Grant Major noted that while the set needed to be dark, they were able to introduce some light in the form of the glow emanating from the end of Shelob's stinger. 'We also had Galadriel's bottle of starlight, that Sam is carrying with him,' observed Major, 'so that gave the scene a certain amount of source-light. We had to electrically wire up those props, so actually the scene was very source-light driven.'

Peter Jackson quite wisely held off Shelob's appearance until *The Return of the King*, making it a fitting obstacle for Frodo's passage into Mordor. Had Shelob appeared in *The Two Towers*, as she does in the book, it would inevitably have been compared with the giant spider sequence in *Harry Potter and the Chamber of Secrets*. 'Early on, in writing the script,' said Jackson, 'Shelob was in the second film, but it all had to do with a feeling of shape and structure in the story. As we developed the script, we felt that Sam and Frodo's story was really about their journey towards Mordor with Gollum, and their meeting with Faramir. There were certain character dynamics happening between them. When they encounter Faramir, he is tested, to see whether he will take the ring from Frodo. So we felt this was really a story about Frodo, Gollum and Sam, a psychological drama that gets complicated when Faramir comes into the picture. It's told from the point of view of those characters, and we wanted to have a conclusion involving those three characters, and not just insert a climax with a giant spider that didn't really have anything to do with the character dynamics we had already set up.'

Although principal photography on *Lord of the Rings* ended nearly three years previously, most of the cast members were recalled to New Zealand to shoot additional scenes, a process Peter Jackson had always planned on. 'It's a great way to work,' said Jackson, 'because it allows you the chance to figure things out over time. In a sense, a film is never really finished. There's always room to go back and keep improving it, and I am continually doing that, looking at the movie over and over again, to see what is working, and what isn't. Maybe a scene I originally liked needs to be cut, or there are new ideas we've come up with since the original shooting ended.'

'I've been back to New Zealand many times,' noted Christopher Lee. 'I don't know if the new scenes I shot will be in the film or not. But they can't take any chances. Once they've started cutting the picture, if they feel an extra scene is needed, or bits of dialogue or action are needed, then they have to call us back. It's in our contracts. I think everybody, with the possible exception of Ian Holm and Cate Blanchett, went back at one time or another.'

The ending of *The Return of the King*, where Frodo departs Middle-earth from the Grey Havens, promised the kind of overwhelming emotional experience that would doubtless leave many viewers in tears. It would match the lyrical quality achieved by such classical film endings as those in Orson Welles' *Chimes at Midnight*, Francois Truffaut's *Fahrenheit 451*, Elia Kazan's *Splendor in the Grass* and Stanley Kubrick's *Spartacus*. 'I saw a rough cut of the sequence,' said Andrew Lesnie, 'with all the blue-screens in the shots, and it was still a staggeringly moving sequence – even though I wasn't looking at the finished images. You're cutting back and forth between the four Hobbits and Galadriel, and everyone is standing on the jetty next to the Elven boat that's going to sail away. Bilbo's gone and Gandalf says goodbye, and they summon Frodo, and then the other three Hobbits suddenly realise that Frodo is going as well. Even among the heads of all the departments, I don't think there was a dry eye in the house. It was extremely moving. Generally, you're having the screening to assess certain technical things, and it's very hard to make technical assessments when everyone is crying. One can only hope, in its finished form, the audience will be moved in the same way.'

The mood for such an elegiac conclusion was helped immensely by the settings and music. 'The Elves have been leaving for the West all through the three films,' explained Grant Major. 'Their time on Middle-earth is coming to a close and this Elvish migration through the Grey Havens gives the port a great resonance. It has an Elvish architectural style but there is also perhaps a bit of a Mediterranean feeling about it – a classical permanence. It has nuances of Arnold Bocklin's symbolist paintings [like *Isle of the Dead*]; the tall cypresses, the stonework, the views facing west and a certain emptiness. The Grey Havens don't open directly to the sea but are sheltered in the gulf of Lhun, so there are hills surrounding the wharf – it's not a big place but, being Elvish, it is very beautiful. As a set piece, we built only a small part of it in one of our moderate sized studios, essentially an entranceway. The wharf and part of the boat itself and the rest will be a computer-generated extension, using a series of collected scenery pieces and matte paintings. This is a really classic piece of Alan Lee's concept artwork.'

Unlike the phony sentimental endings dredged up in the typical Steven Spielberg movie, Jackson and his co-writers wanted to avoid that kind of forced quality, opting instead for a true, organic and emotional climax, which the filmmakers had certainly earned by the time *The Return of the King* came to its conclusion. 'We've got one of the great endings of all time,' said Philippa Boyens. 'In fact we may have too many endings. We worked very hard at trying to make the end of this film play. As Peter has said, "It is not the end of one film, it is the end of three." So during the pick-ups we added scenes to help drive the ending. If we deliver on what we attempted to do, then it will be an emotional experience for the audience. In the end, it is not just Sam, Merry and Pippin who must say goodbye to Frodo, it's the audience as well. If we can get to that point, I think we'll be able to touch audiences and really move them.'

For Jackson, the Grey Havens represent a culmination of the entire story, what it means to give, and to lose, and all the emotions tied to the opening line of the story, 'The world is changing.' 'The emotional story is where most of the power of *The Return of the King* really lies,' said Jackson. 'Every character that we know in the story, in some form or another, comes out of it different. It is an immensely affecting experience for them, and I hope for the audiences as well.'

With the completion of *The Return of the King*, Jackson took a short break and then plunged back into work on his next opus, *King Kong*, for release by Universal in December 2005. Strangely, Peter Jackson's own journey in making the trilogy might have become just as torturous as Frodo's, had New Line Cinema not stepped in and backed the project with such faith. Luckily for Tolkien fans worldwide, studio chief Robert Shaye recognised that Jackson's indomitable spirit would be a perfect match for the material and backed the Kiwi director to the hilt. As Christopher Lee, the only member of the production who actually met J. R. R. Tolkien, declared, 'These films are a modern miracle that will be remembered for a very long time. It is the soul of Tolkien on the screen. Professor Tokien had a vision for a very long period of time. Peter Jackson had a vision. And I have my own vision. I see Professor Tokien walking over to Peter Jackson, shaking his hand and saying, "Well done my boy, well done."'

Grateful thanks to Ross Plesset, who contributed to this story.

THE RETURN OF THE KING
reviewed by Kim Newman

Two Hobbits find a ring while fishing and are seized with an urge to own it; one, Sméagol, murders his friend and degenerates into the creature known as Gollum. Currently, Gollum is guiding Frodo Baggins, the Ringbearer, and his friend Sam into the dark land of Mordor (where Frodo intends to destroy the all-powerful Ring) but he is plotting to have the Hobbits killed and take back his 'precious'. In the aftermath of the battle of Helm's Deep and the defeat of the wizard Saruman, the remainder of the Fellowship of the Ring – Wizard Gandalf, human Aragorn (possible heir to the kingdom of Gondor), Elf Legolas, Hobbits Pippin and Merry and Dwarf Gimli – are allied with King Théoden of Rohan and his niece Éowyn. The Orcish armies of Saruman continue to wage war against mankind, now turning their attack from Rohan to Gondor.

Gandalf insists that Théoden aid Gondor in the war and sets out with Pippin to persuade Denethor, steward of Gondor, to mount a strong defence to keep the forces of evil occupied so that Frodo can get to Mount Doom, the only place where the Ring can be destroyed. Denethor, maddened by the death of his son Boromir, sends his less-loved son Faramir off in a futile battle. In Mordor, Gollum turns Frodo against Sam; the Ringbearer tries to send his friend back, only to be led by Gollum into the lair of Shelob, a giant spider who paralyses him and traps him in her web. Éowyn and Merry both resent being excluded from the armies sent to defend Gondor and join up anyway, while Aragorn seeks an alliance with an army of ghosts earthbound by an earlier betrayal. Sam finds Frodo and, thinking him dead, takes the Ring. Frodo later revives and is reunited with his friend, to press on to Mount Doom. The hordes of Sauron attack Gondor and the forces of good resist. In battle, the ghosts redeem themselves and pass on to another plane; Éowyn and Merry defeat Sauron's most fearsome lieutenant and the Orcish hordes are broken. In Mount Doom, Frodo hesitates to destroy the Ring and Gollum makes a last grab for it, dying in a vain attempt to preserve it from destruction. With the Ring melted, the power of Sauron is broken and an age of magic comes to an end. Aragorn is crowned King of Gondor and the Hobbits return to the Shire. With the age of Men upon Middle-earth, the Elves depart in a boat, taking Frodo and his uncle Bilbo, once a Ringbearer himself, with them.

As if realising that the third part of his *Lord of the Rings* triptych will be concerned with such momentous business that tiny felicities are liable to get squeezed, Peter Jackson opens *The Return of the King* with its smallest denizen, a wriggling worm destined to be impaled on a fish-hook by a beaming, puckish Hobbit. It's almost a joke at the expense of the remembering-who-everybody-is phase of the picture that the cheery Hobbit fisherman turns out not to be one of the four 'halflings' among the Fellowship but Andy Serkis as Sméagol, the previously unseen, pre-corruption incarnation of Gollum. The idyll – and for the pre-PC Tolkien, fishing, like smoking, boozing and leching after barmaids, is an archetypally innocent pastime – is darkened once the Ring is found at the bottom of the stream, and two mates out for a pleasure trip are turned into grasping

The Mûmakil carry the Haradrim warriors into Pelennor Fields. The seamless merging of realistic action and CGI creatures sets Jackson's fantasy triptych apart in modern cinema.

killers in a mini rerun of *The Treasure of the Sierra Madre* (1948). Sméagol's murder of his friend sets him on the path of transformation, vividly depicted in several stages, into the monstrous yet pathetic Gollum – who seems to be remembering this incident as we are dropped back into the narrative at the point where it was left at the end of *The Two Towers*.

The major challenge here is that the meat of the story and the emotional involvement are with Frodo, Gollum and Sam while all other business – far more conventionally spectacular – is essentially a side issue, a monumental feint orchestrated to keep the villains busy elsewhere while victory is won (though not easily) by throwing a trinket into a stream of molten lava. Whereas Tolkien had to interleave whole chapters on his various strands, Jackson can punctuate the central quest with snippet-like asides that keep us updated on what everone is doing. Occasionally, he tries shorthand – unwieldy in the dialogue that passes over what happened to Saruman, and more effective in the simple, ballad-scored précis of Faramir's doomed ride against Sauron's Orc armies (we stay with Pippin, forced to sing as the maddened Denethor picks at a meal after sending his surviving son to what turns out to be less than certain death). Nevertheles, all the cutting back and forth does undermine the general forward movement of the piece and sometimes gives the picture the air of a soap opera playing Dungeons & Dragons.

There is a great deal of bitty material to get through, as all the characters have to do *something* to justify their presence: Éowyn, configured by Miranda Otto as a post-Tolkien woman warrior, eclipses the giant spider Shelob – who would otherwise be the film's strongest female character – by besting a Dark Lord who has claimed no Man can defeat him with the cheeralong statement 'I am no man'; the Elf Legolas gets one sustained heroic sequence as he single-handedly boards and brings down a lumbering war-elephant (after the manner of the lone samurai who downs an attack helicopter in the Sonny Chiba movie *Time Slip: The Day of the Apocalypse*) before taking a well-earned bow. Jackson, confident in his effects team and post-production skills, puts on screen images that would have defeated any pre-CGI film-maker: vast chunks of masonry catapulted from the ramparts of a bisieged city to squash dozens of photo-realistic Orc goons, answered by equally devastating missiles from the attacking armies. Still, the most resonant moments are in the dark with the three 'small' characters: a giant spider attack scene guaranteed 75 per cent scarier than the one in *Harry Potter and the Chamber of Secrets*, and character business as Gollum cunningly makes a rift between Frodo and honest, lumpen Sam (like Sancho Panza, the *real* hero and identification figure).

A point comes when it's hard to tell whether praise or criticism is due to Jackson for his adaptation or Tolkien for his orginal text, which presents at least as many traps as opportunities. The side of the novel that seems twee and arch, epitomised by the songs and Hobbiton knees-ups, is kept in check until the epilogue, when it is unleashed along with the complex, very hard-to-dramatise bitter pill that the heroic triumph of the story which brings about the 'Age of Men' also means an end to the age of appealing magic that is the setting. As the Elves' boat sails off, Tolkien may have recalled the final chapter of *The House at Pooh Corner*, where Christopher Robin grows up and puts away childish things so that the Hundred Acre Wood survives only as a cherished memory; but he was also writing at the time of *The Searchers* (1956), in which John Wayne has to walk off into the desert as the door shuts on him (the last image here is another door shutting, this one sealing Sam inside his happy home). Also problematic is that all richness of character is on one side (Gollum, though ultimately corrupted, is *not* a minion of Sauron), and so we see how the forces of good are riven by personality conflicts, misjudgements and prejudices while the hordes of evil are monolithically rotten. History suggests that societies like Nazi Germany or Stalinist Russia collapse because it's impossible for self-seeking bad men to make common cause, but the armies of Mordor march as one.

Considered as a stand-alone film, *The Return of the King* plays least well of the three: it's three-quarters climax and one quarter straggling epilogue. The reintroduction of Ian Holm's Bilbo comes well after business has satisfyingly been concluded and demands a shift of attention when general audiences will be reaching for their coats. However, as the last act of a nine-hours-plus movie, it fits perfectly, the pay-off after the division of forces at the end of *The Fellowship of the Ring* – when Frodo reacts to seeing Gandalf again, you have to work hard to remember than he thought the Wizard died back in the first film. Now it's over, the production of *The Lord of the Rings* has to take its place in film history: certainly, it exposes the initial *Star Wars* trilogy as a mere rough draft (any objections to the resolution evaporate at recall of the dancing Ewoks in *Return of the Jedi*) and it stands as the most successful filming of a monumental bestseller since *Gone with the Wind* (1939). That it won't stand as substitute for the original in the way that the Selznick picture does for Margaret Mitchell's (now unreadable) book is down to the fact that Tolkien can't be processed into a film equivalent as comfortably, and that the novel has been around unfilmed for so long that it has displaced its own cultural water separate from any movie version. However, the sense of what is possible in mainstream cinema has been changed by Jackson's achievement in ways that will take a while to assimilate.

KINGDOM COME
by Graham Fuller

A century after Georges Méliés's *A Trip to the Moon*, Peter Jackson has completed the most ambitious fantasy film of them all. Promethean in girth and daring, Jackson's three–part adaptation of J. R. R. Tolkien's *The Lord of the Rings* comprises the first epochal main-stream movie event since the *Godfather* and *Star Wars* series began in the seventies.

Jackson's version of the novel was always likely to outflank its geek appeal, despite the absence of stars, and it's done so with a vengeance. Together, the first two instalments earned $653 million in North America alone. The recently released *The Return of the King* is favoured to win the Best Picture and Director Oscars, honours denied *The Fellowship of the Ring* (01) and *The Two Towers* (02).

Yet Jackson's endeavour has so far generated little in the way of serious analysis, as if a story involving Dwarves, Wizards, Trolls, immortal Elves, and the yokelish, hirsute Hobbit protagonists were somehow unworthy of film scholarship. It's the lingering stig-ma of the 'fairy story' infantilisation that Tolkien feared would taint any movie version of his heroic romance but that Jackson's has wholly avoided. Even so, not every discerning filmgoer has been prepared to take the leap of faith. 'It's just not my kind of thing,' a respected critic told me. 'I haven't seen any of them,' a top editor confided.

Are they right to be sceptical? Beyond its gripping pseudo-mythical tale, magisterial pictorialism, cataclysmic battles, and ravenous monsters, is *The Lord of the Rings* more than a superior action-adventure blockbuster? Does it improve on the book's skimpy psycho-logical realism or introduce themes, even unwillingly, outside Tolkien's purview? And what does the *mise-en-scéne* convey above and beyond information and style?

The Lord of the Rings was filmed - at a cost of $300 million over an eighteen-month production period in 1999-2001 in New Zealand – as a single narrative but has ubiqui-tously been described as a trilogy because, for obvious commercial reasons and practical necessity, it has been released in three segments. 'The book, of course, is not a "trilogy",' Tolkien wrote in 1955. 'That and the titles of the volumes was a fudge thought necessary for publication, owing to length and cost. There is no real division into three, nor is any one part intelligible alone.' The point is crucial since, as with the original, Jackson's sto-rytelling accrues its power from the tidal flow of incidents over the long haul.

Jackson's triptych – if you will – follows the terrifying odyssey undertaken by the Hobbit Frodo Baggins (Elijah Wood), who, though he gains wisdom, changes from a live-ly, unassuming youth into a grave-faced martyr. Traversing Middle-earth, an ancient realm

King Théoden (Bernard Hill, right) — described by critic Kim Newman as 'a fungus-covered zombie', his vital energy is drained by his treacherous adviser, Wormtongue (Brad Dourif).

of cruel topographical extremes and formidable Gothic fastnesses, he embarks on a reverse Grail quest: instead of searching for a supernatural talisman, he must destroy the Ring of Power, the key to omnipotence that is coveted by its maker, the necromancer Sauron, Dark Lord of Mordor and personification of absolute evil. Sauron's war to conquer and enslave Middle-earth's free peoples — Hobbits, Elves, Men, Dwarves — can be stopped only by melting the Ring in the volcanic furnace in Mordor's Mount Doom, where it was forged.

Initially, Frodo, the Ring-bearer, journeys with three of his hobbit friends, Sam (Sean Astin), Merry (Dominic Monaghan), and Pippin (Billy Boyd), narrowly escaping Sauron's chillingly-depicted nine Black Riders, or Ringwraiths, with the help of Aragorn (Viggo Mortensen), a human Ranger of the north, and the elf maiden Arwen (Liv Tyler), whom Aragorn loves. At the Elvish settlement of Rivendell, the Hobbits join in the Fellowship of the Ring - with Aragorn, actually the uncrowned King of Gondor; the corruptible Boromir (Sean Bean), eldest son of Gondor's steward; the Elf Legolas (Orlando Bloom); the Dwarf Gimli (John Rhys-Davies), and the avuncular Wizard Gandalf (Ian McKellen), who is Sauron's chief foe — to take the Ring to Mordor.

Jackson and his co-writers, Fran Walsh (his wife, who also directed some sequences) and Philippa Boyens, made some simple changes to the structure of the book. Their prologue ingeniously telescopes nearly 5,000 years of Middle-earth history into seven minutes: the Elf Lady Galadriel (Cate Blanchett) narrates the origins of the Rings of Power over a tableau sequence and then tells how Sauron, seen for the first and only time as a surreally armoured warlord, was vanquished at the battle of Dagorlad. As Sauron combusted, Aragorn's ancestor Isildur (Harry Sinclair) seized the Ring from his severed finger but was himself soon killed by Orcs (the expendable schlock-horror goblins who form Sauron's infantry). The Ring is next seen in the hands of the reptilian Gollum, who was corrupted by it and who after 500 years lost it to Frodo's uncle, Bilbo (Ian Holm) — we get a glimpse of Bilbo's adventure from Tolkien's earlier novel *The Hobbit*, which Jackson may yet direct. As the main narrative begins, Bilbo uses the Ring to make himself disappear at his lllth birthday party, only to be persuaded by Gandalf to relinquish it to Frodo. Sauron has risen again in the East, Gandalf warns, and is seeking the Ring.

The screenwriters further streamlined the story by cross-cutting between the splintered parties of the Fellowship in *The Two Towers* and the first half of *The Return of the King* instead of treating them in 'coherent sequence', as Tolkien put it. (He hoped any film version would keep these strands untangled.) The voracious spider Shelob, to whom Gollum serves up Frodo and Sam as prey, was moved from *The Two Towers* to *The Return of the King*, in which the tormented Gollum — fond of Frodo but fonder of the Ring — emerges as the pivotal character and Sam as the quest's saviour.

Jackson was obliged to omit characters and chapters inessential to the quest. The jolly nature spirit Tom Bombadil and his wife Goldberry, the ghoulish Barrow Wights, the Elf Glorfindel (whose rescue of Frodo is here performed by Arwen), and the Wild Men of the Woods all proved extraneous. The episode in which Aragorn heals the wounded shield maiden Éowyn (Miranda Otto) and Faramir (David Wenham), Boromir's brother, was cut from the release print of *The Return of the King* but will be included on the extended DVD.

Jackson had no interest in filming scenes from the book's penultimate chapter, 'The Scouring of the Shire', in which the four Hobbits return home to find their land laid waste by the evil Wizard Saruman (Christopher Lee) — it could have added twenty minutes or more to the conclusion. As it is, the film's 'falling action' shows the reuniting of the Fellowship, Aragorn's coronation and marriage to Arwen, the Hobbits' return to the untainted Shire (where they feel like strangers), the departure — lamented by Sam — of Frodo and the other Ring-bearers on a ship 'into the West', and, finally, Sam being welcomed home by his wife and children. Some audiences have become restless during this long ending but it is warranted after ten hours of film — it would not have been feasible to say goodbye to Frodo and Sam marooned on a rock in the boiling lava of Mount Doom after the Ring was destroyed.

Jackson deploys flashbacks throughout, often expanding on sequences we have already seen. Isildur's tragic role as a Ring-bearer, introduced in the prologue, is elaborated later on in *The Fellowship of the Ring*, for example, when the Elf Lord Elrond (Hugo Weaving) acidly recalls how he was there '3,000 years ago on the day the strength of Men failed', when Isildur refused to throw the Ring into the Cracks of Doom. Instead of showing the capitulation of Saruman — which in a contentious decision was deleted from the final cut of the release print — *The Return of the King* begins with Gollum's backstory: as the Hobbit-kind Sméagol (Andy Serkis), he is seduced by the Ring into murdering his angler friend for possession of it and evolves into the wretched creature that was seen, in the prologue, squatting on a rock and gazing at his 'Precious', deep under the Misty Mountains.

Some critics have complained that they didn't need to be 'kept up to speed' by such flashbacks, but, like threads being woven into a tapestry, they are integral to the onscreen myth-making process. The ebb and flow of past and present also replicates the way memories crop up like rocks in our streams of consciousness.

This notion of 'interior' movement coalesces with the eastward trajectory of Frodo and his companions. In *The Fellowship of the Ring,* Andrew Lesnie's camera whirls around them from on high as they pick their way across hostile terrain. We're also treated to computer-generated movement: a vertiginous plunge from the top of Saruman's tower into the subterranean industrial dystopia where disinterred Orcs wake blinking in the slime; a crane up the wedding-cake tiers of Minas Tirith as a series of cuts brings Gandalf and his white mount to a sky-level pow-wow with the steward Denethor (John Noble); and, most perilous of all, a swoop down on the sleeping Frodo and Sam on the edge of the precipice above Minas Morgul where Gollum, their guide, prepares to betray them.

These consciously bravura shots suggest that someone else – other than the audience, other than Sauron – is watching, the same feeling one gets watching the fairies of *A Midsummer Night's Dream* watching Theseus's court watching the Athenian workmen performing their play – an ever-increasing spiral of audiences. Implicating us in the act of feasting our eyes on its beauty, Jackson's films are as much about spectatorship as they are about the enjoyment of the spectacle.

Interspersed throughout are smash cuts to Sauron's disembodied eye – the vortex at the centre of the storm – as he tries to locate Frodo. This eye was printed horizontally on the cover of the 1954–55 British first edition, but the eye in the movies is vertical – resembling a pulsating vagina. This malicious gynecentrism, intended or not, is reiterated in the images of hapless males imperilling themselves by entering clefts, crevices, caves, and narrow doorways time and time again: the portals to Moria, the Paths of the Dead, Shelob's Lair – where the bloated female spider devours flesh – the scalding Cracks of Doom. Much of this symbolism originated unconsciously with Tolkien, who, though a realist about sex, revealed a distaste for 'flighty' or 'plain wanton women', in a letter to his son Michael in 1941 that indicates a fear of female sexuality

The films are pleasingly true to the Anglo-Celtic ambience of much of the novel. Tolkien sought to instill a tone that was 'somewhat cool and clear and, while possessing (if I could achieve it) the fair elusive beauty that some call Celtic, should be "high", purged of the gross, and fit for the more adult mind of a land now long steeped in poetry.' This tone is most evocatively rendered in the image of the effulgent but unloved Éowyn – 'fair and cold, like a morning of pale spring' – looking out across the plains of Rohan in the lee of the White Mountains, her golden hair streaming in the wind like the pennants on the battlements. Seeking her kinsmen, harbouring unrequited love for Aragorn, Éowyn is a Pre-Raphaelite equivalent of John Ford's waiting women.

The decision to have Enya and Annie Lennox sing on the soundtrack seems like a sop to a more commercial variety of Celtic mysticism, and it sits uneasily beside composer Howard Shore's plangent main theme and Wagnerian chords. Otherwise, Jackson mostly eschews the New Agey stylisation of many Arthurian movies and miniseries. He sustains long passages of melancholy, epitomised by Éowyn and Frodo, and a sense of unreality that afflicts even the self-sufficient Aragorn.

'I thought I had strayed into a dream,' Aragorn says in *The Fellowship of the Rings*, reminiscing with Arwen about their first meeting 67 years before. He is talking about being transported by love into a state of enchantment rather than an oneiric experience. A romantic idyll that looks as if it were art-directed by Maxfield Parrish, the scene in which he makes this disclosure – like the Fellowship's hourless sojourn with Galadriel in the Elven woods of Lothlorien – provides ethereal respite from the films' thunderous blasts of warfare and the jaw-dropping phantasmagorical interludes.

But during the evacuation of King Théoden's people in *The Two Towers*, Arwen does appear in Aragorn's dreams, reaffirming her love for him and further beguiling him – like a benign version of the siren in J. W. Waterhouse's painting *La Belle Dame Sans Merci* – at the moment he becomes aware that Éowyn, the king's niece, has set her cap at him. (Arwen also uses her remarkable powers of telepathy to rescue him when he's driven over a cliff by Orcs, in one of the scenes expanding Liv Tyler's role that have angered Tolkien fans – and that indeed takes liberties with the text.) Like Frodo – shown in the act of waking several times – Aragorn, though a saturnine man of action, is a dreamer within a dream. The hesitancy he and Frodo feel about their assigned roles make them the male characters with whom it is easiest to identify, even more so than the doughty, resolutely rustic Sam. (Éowyn is the only empathic woman.)

The films are less dreamlike in their narrative logic, however, than they are suggestive of an alternative universe long since disappeared and for which we mourn, even as it eternally returns through the wizardry of the extended DVDs, with their Tolkienesque appendices, their 'making of' lore, their disembodied commentaries by the actors. All help add to the notion of Jackson's triptych as a dream of cinema – as fey and death-laden as it is numinously elegiac, as empyreal as it is grounded in landscape (mountains, tunnels, ridges, forests, plains, swamps, rivers), architecture (obelisks, fortresses, walls, causeways, bridges, mines) and technology and marketing (the DVDs as artefacts that enable us to 'own' the dream). Not the least of Jackson's triumphs has been his harnessing of computer-generated imagery – enabling Armageddon-like battles and begetting the Balrog fire demon, Treebeard (the humongous bark-skinned shepherd of trees), Shelob, and the slinking Gollum – to bring verisimilitude to the more grotesque aspects of Tolkien's humanistic tale. Miraculously, the films seem more painterly than digitized. To see the great armoured hosts clashing at Helm's Deep in *The Two Towers* and at the Pelennor Fields in *The Return of the King* is to see Albrecht Altdorfer's *The Battle of Issus* (1528-29) come tumultuously to life.

Gollum's scaling of rock faces echoes the lonely figure clambering up the gigantic red edifice of John Martin's *Sadak in Search of the Waters of Oblivion* (1812), of which Mount Doom's sulphurous implosion is also redolent. The flight of Frodo and his companions over the bridge of Khazad-dûm in *The Fellowship of the Ring* and the destruction of Sauron's tower of Barad-dûr respectively suggest Martin's mezzotint *The Bridge over Chaos* (1824) and *The Great Day of His Wrath* (1852). Though Jackson told me in 2001 he was unfamiliar with Martin, he is the first director in modern times to channel that English Romantic painter's apocalyptic vision.

Tolkien began writing *The Lord of the Rings* in December 1937 and completed it in the autumn of 1949. WWII had intervened between conception and completion, and the author was hard-pressed to deny the book was an allegory of the war against Nazism. He wrote in the foreword, 'One has indeed personally to come under the shadow of war to feel fully its oppression; but as the years go by it seems now often forgotten that to be caught in youth by 1914 was no less hideous an experience than to be involved in 1939 and the following years. By 1918 all but one of my close friends were dead.'

In *Tolkien and the Great War*, John Garth reveals how Tolkien's experiences as a signaller in the Lancashire Fusiliers at the Battle of the Somme in 1916 – and specifically the deaths of two comrades – shaped his future fiction. Although Tolkien's statements about the influence of WWI were 'few and wary', Garth writes, he admitted that the Dead Marshes and the approaches to the Morannon – the gateway to Mordor – 'owe something to Northern France after the Battle of the Somme'.

Jackson indeed conjures the Western Front with eldritch lyricism in the Dead Marshes, where fires blaze and the faces of slain warriors peer out of the muddy pools at the mesmerised Frodo and Sam and the hungry Gollum. The ruins of Osgiliath resemble those of Arras, Ypres, Lille. The highlighting of the camaraderie, affection, and humour between the two pairs of Hobbits and the sharing of food and tobacco as they hide in craters and 'foxholes' gives a visceral sense of the misery and privations soldiers of the Great War endured in the trenches. The Hobbits' reunion in a deeply moving scene at the end of the film spiritually fulfils the wish Tolkien surely entertained about his lost brothers-in-arms.

But Jackson's *Rings* suggests other movies and other wars, too. As Frodo sinks to his lowest, he recalls Lew Ayres's trench-bound German soldier shortly before he is shot in *All Quiet on the Western Front*. When Aragorn, Legolas, and Gimli approach the skull-encrusted entrance to the Paths of the Dead and Orcs pelt the defenders of Minas Tirith with the heads of its slain soldiers, Kurtz's compound and the atrocities committed by his Montagnards in *Apocalypse Now* come fleetingly to mind. Théoden's and Aragorn's rallying of their cavalry pallidly mimics the St. Crispin's Day speech before Agincourt in *Henry V*.

And when the burning body of the suicidal Denethor is seen plummeting from the great tower of Minas Tirith in long shot in *The Return of the King*, it is the death leaps from the World Trade Centre on September 11, 2001, that we think of, no matter that principal photography was finished before the terrorist attack.

The PG-13-rated *Lord of the Rings* is suffused with morbidity, in keeping with Tolkien's avowal that 'the tale is . . . about Death and the desire for deathlessness'. If not graphically bloody, the films depict unquantifiable carnage – and several resurrections (Sauron, Gandalf, and Frodo thrice). Still, it is the state of being undead and Arwen's choice to become mortal that carry more metaphysical weight.

The Ringwraiths, once-human Ring-bearers who became Sauron's fell emissaries, and the spectral Shadow Host of dead malefactors, summoned by Aragorn, that swarms like a plague of locusts to overwhelm Sauron's forces, are souls in purgatory. According to Roman Catholic doctrine, of which Tolkien was a devout practitioner, the souls of those who die in God's name have to atone for past sins to enter heaven. After enabling Théoden's Rohirrim to prevail in the monumental final battle, Aragorn releases the Dead from their bond – their king responds with a demystifying smile – and they evaporate into the ether.

Mirroring some of Tolkien's most florid writing, these sequences are awe-inspiring but

Gollum and the Hobbits reach their destiny at Mount Doom. Andy Serkis, whose remarkable offscreen performance incarnated the CGI character, performs a similar role in King Kong.

literally incredible: there is a Book of Revelations hyperbole about them. (Jackson has said that having invincible ghosts turn the Battle of the Pelennor Fields against Sauron drained it of tension.) Subtler dabs of Catholic imagery – the Madonna-like statue of Aragorn's late mother at Rivendell, Arwen's blue cowl, Gimli's devotion to the Lady Galadriel – as well as a closeup of Frodo's Christ-like agony at his moment of deliverance above the Cracks of Doom – invite a theological deconstruction of the films.

A psychoanalytical reading would also stand up given the number of dysfunctional relationships, more explicit in the movies than the books. Denethor, grief-stricken by the death of Boromir, sends Faramir to fight a hopeless battle and then almost cremates his apparently lifeless son on a funeral pyre. Arwen's decision to forsake her immortality by marrying Aragorn requires her to turn her back on her father, Elrond (Hugo Weaving), who will join the Elves' exodus from Middle Earth to an earthly paradise over the sea. In the films, Elrond's anger at Arwen's choice implies a sublimated sexual jealousy, especially since she will be marrying the future king – newly endowed with the reforged sword that 'slew' Sauron at Dagorlad.

This phallic byplay is not insignificant: Aragorn's huge weapon is wittily compared with the much smaller one wielded by Merry, who is taught how to use it by the highly amused Éowyn. Both are frustrated at being told by Théoden (Bernard Hill) to stay behind as he leads the Rohirrim to war. Éowyn, whose father was slain when she was a child and who had been neglected by Théoden, has sought the love of another man she cannot have, Aragorn, and her pursuit of him – made more of in the films – is charged with Oedipal despair and a hint of penis envy. She has earlier tried to show her mettle by fencing with Aragorn; in *The Fellowship of the Rings*, her rival, Arwen, places her blade against the unsuspecting Aragorn's throat on her first appearance. Each woman manifests her desire for the passive male love object in these scenes by assuming the role of sexual aggressor, though each also embraces him (and Arwen kisses him passionately).

Nursing a death wish because of her romantic disappointment, Éowyn girds up as one of the male riders of Rohan and whisks Merry off to battle. His small sword proves potent enough when he stabs the Witch-King of Angmar, Sauron's captain, before Éowyn extinguishes him with a single thrust of her own sword. Some feminist critics of the novel have suggested Éowyn's proclaiming her gender before this feat of arms trivialises it. Transcending sexual politics onscreen, it is the greatest act of self-realisation by a human character in the entire saga – and one of the most spine-tingling moments.

Though not without flaws, these films afford many such moments – and as many again that are serene, frightening, and bewildering. In Peter Ackroyd's *Albion: The Origins of the English Imagination*, he cites Tolkien's recollection of the moment he discovered a line – 'Hail Earendel, most bright angel' – by the eighth- or ninth-century clerical poet Cynewulf: 'I felt an unconscious thrill, as if something had stirred me, half-weakened from sleep. There was something very remote and strange and beautiful behind those words, if I could grasp it, far beyond Ancient English.' Watching Jackson's triptych, we may feel something of the same.

THE LORD OF THE OSCARS
by Russell Baillie

Peter Jackson was crowned king of the movie world yesterday [1 March 2004] when he and the New Zealand team behind *The Lord of the Rings* triumphed in a clean sweep of the Academy Awards.

In what will endure as the proudest moment in New Zealand film history, Jackson's *The Lord of the Rings: The Return of the King* won all eleven awards for which it was nominated.

The sheer size of the film's Oscar haul was the surprise in a night short on upsets.

Jackson took away three Oscars – for best director, best motion picture with partner and co-writer Fran Walsh and co-producer Barrie Osborne, and best adapted screenplay with Walsh and Philippa Boyens.

Afterwards a dishevelled, tie-askew and overjoyed Jackson told the *Herald* he had been incredibly nervous all day.

'Your guts are all churned up and you've got butterflies the size of jumbo jets. You have to look cool but . . .'

The Urak-hai, raised from embryonic sacs in the earth, are the Rings *trilogy's most fearsome creatures. For all his success, Jackson remains a monster-movie maker at heart.*

He was stunned that the film won all eleven categories in which it was nominated.

'All eleven was amazing to me. It just showed there was incredible goodwill from the industry towards the films that we had made and that was really touching – that people wanted to vote for these movies and showed their appreciation with their votes.'

Jackson becomes the fourth film-maker to take the triple crown of writer-producer-director in one night, after Billy Wilder (1960), Francis Ford Coppola (1974) and James L. Brooks (1983).

The Return of the King joins *Ben-Hur* and *Titanic* as the films with the most Oscars in one sweep.

But *Rings* is the first to win every category in which it was nominated.

Earlier, Jackson said the history behind the Oscars made the awards 'so much more special than anything else'.

And he had a message to the fans back home: 'I hope they're all having a hell of a good time because they deserve it.'

Accepting the best picture award, Jackson paid tribute to New Zealand's support of the trilogy.

'I just want to say a very few quick words, especially to the people of New Zealand, to the Government of New Zealand, the city councils and everyone who has supported

Oscar-winners at work: Peter Jackson checks out Howard Shore's score for The Fellowship of the Ring. *Shore has rejoined the Jackson team for the much-anticipated* King Kong.

us the length and breadth of the country.'

Making reference to host Billy Crystal's running gag about New Zealand taking over the Oscars, he said: 'Billy Crystal is welcome to come and make a film in the country any time he wants.'

Jackson said he was 'so honoured, touched and relieved that the academy and the members of the academy that have supported us have seen past the Trolls and the Wizards and the Hobbits and recognised fantasy this year.'

The Return of the King is the first fantasy or science fiction film to win a best film Oscar.

Jackson's *Rings* trilogy is a nine-and-a-half-hour saga that blends live action and computer animation, putting real actors alongside the mystical creatures of J. R. R. Tolkien's imagination.

The first two films in the trilogy won six Oscars in technical categories, and were nominated for best picture.

By the time *The Return of the King* had picked up Oscars for art direction, costume design, visual effects, make-up, sound mixing, musical score, editing, song, and best adapted screenplay in quick succession, an across-the-board sweep seemed likely.

Again and again, the New Zealand accent was heard around the world, thanking co-workers at home.

Weta Workshop's Richard Taylor, a double winner for the first film, *The Fellowship of the Ring*, again took away two Oscars.

As well as winning best make-up with Peter King, he was a winner for best costume design with Ngila Dickson, who was also nominated for her work on the New Zealand-shot movie *The Last Samurai*.

As Crystal noted early in the evening, 'it's official, there is nobody in New Zealand left to thank.'

The Return of the King overshadowed almost every other nominated film.

The nearest to it was *Mystic River* with two acting Oscars – best actor Sean Penn and best supporting actor Tim Robbins.

Master and Commander won in two categories for which *The Return of the King* was not nominated.

Jackson's three Oscars cap a career marked by leaps in style and scale.

His first feature was the DIY alien zombie movie *Bad Taste*, made in the hills of his childhood home north of Wellington.

It appeared his early career was destined for cultdom with the splatter-fests *Meet the Feebles* and *Braindead*.

On the Oscar stage, thanking friends who had stuck by him from his early film-making days, Jackson joked that these films were 'wisely overlooked by the academy'.

Jackson, with co-writer Walsh, served notice of better talent on *Heavenly Creatures*, which was nominated for a best-adapted-screenplay Oscar.

Jackson further honed his special effects skills on the Hollywood ghost story *The Frighteners*.

He then pulled off the movie deal of the decade, convincing the New Line movie studio to back a US$300 million (NZ$434 million) three-movie New Zealand-filmed adaptation of *The Lord of the Rings*.

Jackson said New Line had done 'the most risky thing I think anyone has ever done in this industry' in backing him.

The three movies are all now among the top ten grossing movies, generating more than US$1 billion (NZ$1.47 billion) at the box office.

Receiving the award for best adapted screenplay, Jackson said 'hi' to children Billy and Katie 'for putting up with their mum and dad working on this film all their lives, because they are only seven and eight years old.' And he acknowledged his late parents, Bill and Joan.

'They supported me all the way through the years. I paid tribute tonight because my dad died during the pre-production on *Lord of the Rings* and my mother passed away three days before *Fellowship of the Ring* was finished. She was hanging on to try and see it and she didn't quite make it.'

On his lapel, Jackson wore a pin by US jeweller Paul Badali, who had previously created 'good luck' pins for cast and crew of the three films.

Additional reporting: NZPA

KONG COMETH!

PETER JACKSON DIRECTS
KING KONG
by Lawrence French

On September 6th 2004, Peter Jackson began principal photography to bring his version of 'the eight wonder of the world' to the screen – his long-cherished re-make of the 1933 RKO classic, *King Kong*. Executives at Universal were easily able to persuade Jackson to make *Kong* his next project, once he finished working on his monumental *Lord of the Rings* trilogy. Weta Workshop had already done over six months of pre-production work on *King Kong* back in 1996 – before Universal decided to pull the plug, due partly to the enormous costs such a undertaking would entail, and also because, at the time, Jackson had no track record with big-budget effects films. Luckily, when *Kong* was cancelled Jackson was able to quickly switch gears, and begin making *The Lord of the Rings*. Ironically, it was the enormous success of the first two instalments of *The Lord of the Rings* that gave Universal the incentive to come back and offer Jackson and his writing partners a $20 million deal to re-make *Kong*. The film's ultimate budget is now expected to reach $200 million.

'No film has captivated my imagination more than *King Kong*,' Jackson said. 'That's really the reason I'm making movies today, because I saw *King Kong* one Friday night when I was nine years old. The film literally changed my life. It made me want to become a filmmaker and got me thrilled about the magic of movies, their escapism and special effects. It has been my sustained dream to reinterpret this classic story for a new age. The story of *Kong* offers everything that any storyteller could hope for: an archetypal narrative, thrilling action, resonating emotion and memorable characters. It has endured for precisely these reasons and I am honored to be a part of its continuing legacy.'

While Jackson's new version of *King Kong* promises to be far more faithful, in both plot and tone, to the original 1933 movie than Dino De Laurentiis's lamentable 1976 re-make, it will also be subject to heavy fan scrutiny, since the original has become such a beloved cinematic icon. Jackson plans to expand on many aspects of the original film, especially when it comes to the area of CGI animation that will be used to create the giant ape and his encounters with the dinosaurs that populate Skull Island. Actor Andy Serkis, who provided the artists at Weta digital with the movements for Gollum, will return to be the acting model on which Kong's movements will be based.

In order to make Jackson's story 'about love' seem believable, the director plans to make his Skull Island settings as realistic as possible. And like Gollum's interaction with Sam and Frodo in *The Lord of the Rings,* Jackson will make Kong's relationship with Ann Darrow very much a psychological one. 'Kong is a very old and brutal gorilla,' says Jackson, 'and he's never before felt a single bit of empathy for another living creature. For

This pre-release ad for King Kong *(1933) features a Kong barely twice the size of leading lady Fay Wray. Jackson invited Ms Wray to appear in his remake shortly before her death.*

the first time in his life, he feels empathy when he meets Ann Darrow. Initially he thinks he's going to kill her and then he slowly moves away from that.'

A first draft script written by Jackson and his partner Fran Walsh in 1996, was based on the original *King Kong* screenplay by James Creelman and Ruth Rose. It subsequently appeared on the internet and has been completely revamped with the help of Philippa Boyens, who collaborated with Jackson and Walsh on all three *Lord of the Rings* screenplays. Commenting on the first *King Kong* script, Boyens said, 'That was actually just Fran and Peter very hurriedly getting something down on paper. You wouldn't even call it a concept drawing. It was more one of many possible ways the story could go. Now, Peter's mad genius is going to be truly unleashed. I have a feeling that *Return of the King* will look relatively restrained next to *King Kong*. I think it will be quite fantastic.'

Elaborating on his new screenplay, Jackson said, 'When Philippa joined us, it gave us the chance for a fresh start. We're better writers now than we were in 1996. And our new script is based on the 1933 movie, not on the 1996 script. In hindsight, fate has been kind to us, because this movie will be so much better than the 1996 film would have been.' One exciting change will see most of the movie take place on Skull Island, with its huge population of dinosaurs. Only the final third of the picture will be set among the skyscrapers of Manhattan.

Among the dinosaurs featured in Jackson's original 1996 treatment of the story were a pack of fifteen carnotaurs (slightly smaller versions of a t-rex) who pursue a stampeding herd of brontosaurs before turning their attention to Carl Denham and his hapless crew of sailors. There is also a family of triceratops that threatens the crew of the Venture on an inland beach of Skull Island. In a nod to both Willis O' Brien and Ray Harryhausen, who both favored animating allosauruses over t-rexes (O'Brien in *The Lost World*, Harryhausen in *The Valley of Gwangi*), Jackson has included a titanic battle between Kong and no less than three allosauruses. The famed log scene from the original *King Kong* has also been retained, and when Jack Driscoll and his companions fall into the gaping ravine, they are attacked by an assortment of huge insect-like creatures, which are described as 'combinations of Spiders, Crabs, Mantises and Centipedes'. Also appearing will be a group of giant spiders with seven-foot leg spans. In the original *King Kong*, the giant spider sequence was famously cut from the finished film. Other highlights will show Kong defending his beloved Ann Darrow from the many dangers on Skull Island, including a flock of sinister bat-like creatures with eight-foot wingspans and taloned claws.

To realise the many animated creatures and effects shots, Weta workshop and Weta Digital will utilise the expert staff they've assembled to make the three *Lord of the Rings* movies. Jackson obviously wanted to keep all his talented effects people in place, and by making another effects extravaganza on the heels of *Lord of the Rings*, he will now have the means to keep them all duly employed.

Postulating on why Universal got cold feet on doing the re-make of *King Kong* back in 1997, Jackson noted that studios often have been somewhat mystified and ambivalent over fantasy scripts. 'Fantasy is a strange genre that has usually been treated with suspicion and contempt by Hollywood,' explains the director. 'Certainly they have lacked confidence with fantasy subjects, and because they lack confidence they tend to make them a little campy, or a little over the top. They also get over-designed, so it all becomes about production design and not about the story and the characters. As a result, the characters usually end up being very clichéd.'

Besides the 1976 *Kong* re-make, Hammer Films had once looked into re-making *King Kong*, after working with Ray Harryhausen on *One Million Years BC*. 'But they couldn't get the rights,' recalled Harryhausen. 'I was interested up to the point of what direction the script would have taken, because so many companies like to make send-ups of classics like that. I've always been against send-ups. To me, they are an apology for not knowing what to do with the original material.' Harryhausen was also approached about working on the De Laurentiis re-make of *King Kong*. 'Two weeks before they were going to start shooting, I got a call from them,' he revealed. 'But it takes us a year of pre-production on our pictures, so I couldn't see me getting involved with *that*. I don't think you can take a classic like *King Kong*, unless you do it almost scene for scene, and use Max Steiner's score. I mean Rick Baker made a marvelous gorilla suit, but because the hair didn't shift, it wasn't Kong, it was just a big gorilla. It didn't have the fantasy elements that the first *Kong* had, and I think that's why people expected more from it than they got. It was really just a product of publicity.'

Harryhausen thinks that if anyone can do a good job at re-making *King Kong*, it is Peter Jackson. 'I think *King Kong* was the greatest fantasy film ever to be put on the screen,' declares Harryhausen, 'but Peter loves *King Kong* as much as I do and he has taste, so I think he'll do an interesting job with the subject. But it won't be quite the same as the original, because Peter has his own style. I've seen sketches for some of the action sequences with the dinosaurs and the animation – which will all be done with CGI – and they're all very impressive. I'm sure he'll do something that will make billions of dollars.'

Jackson is shooting the film on locations entirely in New Zealand, which will stand-in for the primeval jungles of Skull Island. The film's famous finale on top of New York's Empire State building will also be filmed in New Zealand. 'We will play on the similarities between the jungle of the New York skyscrapers and the jungle where King Kong lives,' explained Jackson.

Jackson cast Naomi Watts as Ann Darrow, whose beauty manages to tame the savage beast, while the famed movie director Carl Denham will be played by Jack Black. Adrien Brody rounds out the cast as Jack Driscoll, the adventurous screenwriter who is penning Denham's planned movie epic. Sadly, although Jackson met the 96-year-old Fay Wray at her New York home five months before she passed away, she apparently rebuffed all attempts to appear in a cameo role at the end of the picture. The original plan was to have Miss Wray deliver *Kong*'s famous last lines: 'It wasn't the airplanes – it was beauty killed the beast.'

KONG COMETH!
by Paul A. Woods

So much for a return to small-scale movies on a low budget. As the 2003 postproduction on *The Lord of the Rings: The Return of the King* drew to an end, Universal Pictures announced that the next project for Peter Jackson, and his by-now regular team, would be their near-aborted remake of *King Kong*.

'We just felt that having to scale down and lose a lot of our crew to do a small film, then have to get them back again in a few years to do *Kong*, didn't seem like a very good idea,' rationalised the little guy now recognised as the Big Kiwi. 'We realised that the most sensible way to do *Kong* would be to roll the *Lord of the Rings* crew into another big film, which is what we've done.'

While lacking the scope of the Tolkien saga, *King Kong* will, if justice is done to the original 1933 monochrome screen dream, lose none of the scale. Once again, the movie screen's greatest mythic dreams are to be realised in a tiny Antipodean nation of four million, on a budget of a reported $200 million. From this, Peter Jackson is believed to be receiving a record fee of $32 million. The former low-budget, state-assisted New Zealand splatter moviemaker has now become the highest paid director of all time.

'It's already happening now,' Jackson confirmed at the time of the announcement. '*Kong* is in production, because in the last couple of months, as Weta computer artists and Richard Taylor's guys have been finishing work on *Rings*, they've just gone straight into *Kong*, and we've ended up with a big team of people working on it now. We have CG models being built, and maquettes of different characters and dinosaurs that we're using, and some of them have been scanned. We've got Manhattan circa 1933 that we're currently building in the computer.'

Unsurprisingly, after the *LOTR* cycle's miracle meshing of live action and CGI, Kong and all his dinosaur compatriots will be entirely computer generated. 'Production will be based in Miramar, Wellington, at Stone Street Studios, which is having a new huge soundstage built to accommodate our needs. All postproduction will occur at Weta Digital for CGI and Park Road Post for the sound mix and lab work – both in Miramar also. There will be some, but not much, location shooting elsewhere in New Zealand, but we're not sure where yet.

'I'm interested in *Kong* being quite stylised and the jungles of Skull Island I want to be very over-the-top, like a jungle from hell. I imagine we are going to be much more successful pulling that off in the studio or in a back lot than we are trying to find a beech forest in the South Island.'

Indeed, remembering the fogged oneiric swamps of the 1933 original (for which movie buff Danny Peary made a good case as the realisation of documentary showman/Third World exploiter Carl Denham's subconscious, in his *Cult Movies*), it can be argued that Jackson and his Weta pals have a much harder task in hand. They have to remain true to the vision that bowled over Depression-era audiences and a quiet nine-year-old Wellington schoolboy alike.

Skull Island is never referred to as such in the original film – it's Skull *Mountain* that is Kong's island home. Nevertheless, the name has stuck, to the extent that Jackson paid tribute when the rat monkey that originates the zombie plague in *Braindead* hails from the Sumatran 'Skull Island'. It's also been suggested, viz Peary, that the location is really the inside of Denham's skull, where the sexually-repressed 'hardboiled egg', who refuses to 'go sappy' over a pretty face, faces all the most primal, irrational elements of his mind: steaming fauna and deadly giant lizards; treacherous dark waters and a rampant but frustrated great ape.

Whether we accept the metaphorical interpretation or merely suspend disbelief in the grand tradition of sci-fi fantasy, Kong's environment has to have a feral grandeur that surpasses realism. At least one part

The original King Kong *towers, hundreds of feet tall, over the skyscapers that his onscreen counterpart will climb. The archetypal great ape is both a primal and a primeval force.*

of Jackson has grown up in that imaginative territory, and it's to be hoped that he returns from his travelogue with as good an audio-visual record as that suggested by his 1996 screenplay:

The vegetation is THICK, the JUNGLE DARK. ANCIENT GNARLED TREES twist out of the ground, thick LICHEN and long MOSSES hang from branches and TANGLED VINES. STEAM RISES from festering SWAMPS . . . DEEPER into the island, the steam is VOLCANIC – hissing out of FISSURES and BUBBLING MUD POOLS. The way light and contrast play on the landscape is reminiscent of the etchings of 19th century artist Gustave Doré.

This is, as Walsh and Jackson write, their 'Jurassic Park from Hell'.

The archetype of the original *Kong*, for a long time cheapened by camp pastiche, is that of the savage beast who inhabits the form of a cuddly toy. (Even the 1933 *Variety* review stressed that suspension of disbelief was required to accept the great ape model blown up to scale, challenging assumptions about the early talkies audience's lack of sophistication.) But it also contains an animalistic force of rage most of us recognise as one of the essences of both human and animal life. It's this dualism, the chest-beating cuddly toy and the ravening beast, that makes the original Kong so effective. Kong is Freud's innocent baby that would destroy the world if only it had the power, so much more sympathetic than his many nameless human victims that we hardly care about.

For Jackson, a lifelong obsession grew from the original film. Recalling how he 'cried when King Kong fell off the Empire State Building . . . [and was] thrilled by the dinosaurs earlier in the story . . . that wonderful combination of spectacle and intimate story,' his obsession has manifested on an ever larger scale throughout his life.

'When I was a teenager, I tried to do a remake of *King Kong*. With a rubber gorilla and stop motion. And I made the top of the Empire State Building out of cardboard and tried to do this little animated version of *King Kong* when I was about fourteen or fifteen.' (Photos of Jackson and his pals in later adolescence, modelling early attempts at ape make-up, can currently be seen on *The Bastards Have Landed* fansite.)

When Jackson's remake of *King Kong* was first mooted for production in the mid-1990s, Fay Wray, the 1930s scream queen who first took the role of Kong's unrequited love interest, the put-upon blonde Ann Darrow, was reputedly asked to give a one-line cameo at the end of the film. As the great ape lies tragically fallen, brought down by those pesky human mosquitoes and their aeronautics, she was to utter Denham's final portentous line: 'It was beauty killed the beast.'

But the long-retired Ms. Wray, then well into her nineties, declined the offer. 'Kong was always an independent kind of guy and I think he should stay that way,' she would joke in 2003, just over a year before her August 2004 death at the age of 96. (By a sad irony, at the same time as the Jackson team were finally about to start shooting *Kong*.) 'I think it is excellent and honourable that Peter Jackson wants to be true to the original.'

But, at the time that Jackson and Fran Walsh wrote their 1996 screenplay, they weren't toeing the line quite so respectfully. As the director now observes, 'Our first script was sort of *Indiana Jones*-ish and rather flippant. It was what I regard as a very Hollywood script, but now, what we've come to like with *Lord of the Rings* is the approach of making the situations feel very real, even though we're dealing with extraordinary situations and weird characters like Elves, Hobbits, Trolls, Orcs and the like. We didn't let the fantastic nature of the story dictate the tone . . . We decided that that was the approach we wanted to take with *Kong* as well.'

Indeed, in the largely abandoned 1996 blueprint, the tone is one of affectionate pastiche – not so far from that of the screenplay for Universal's 1976 remake by Lorenzo Semple, Jr., whose knowingly satiric approach, despised by Peter Jackson, was no more the definitive *King Kong* than his scripts for the campy mid-1960s TV series were the definitive *Batman*.

'We looked at other Hollywood blockbusters that were out – like *The Mummy* and the *Indiana Jones* films and *Jurassic Park* to some degree – and we just thought that was what we *should* be writing,' confesses Jackson, with a small touch of undue modesty.

There is certainly a jokey *Jurassic Park* reference – 'Hey! I gotta great idea!' announces Denham, 'We could turn this place into a huge amusement park sorta like Coney Island with dinosaurs!' – and there is more regular dinosaur action than in the original film, where the prehistoric reptiles appeared mainly as adversaries for Kong. It's also true that an *Indiana Jones*-style pretext – reinventing heroine Ann Darrow as a British archaeologist on the isle of Sumatra and hero Jack Driscoll as a disillusioned airman-turned-timber-merchant – supplants the original story of Denham offering starving Ann the chance to be a starlet in the Depression era, and provides a personality clash between a much more sophisticated Ann and a much coarser Jack. Both are akin to the hero/heroine that would appear in Universal's *The Mummy* (1999) – the hit that recreated Karl Freund's slow-moving 1932 drama of love after death as a CGI-infused action movie in the *Indiana Jones*-style. As it appeared three years *after* Walsh and Jackson had completed their *King Kong* screenplay, there's every chance that their script had been passed around the studio and had exerted its own indirect influence.

The original screenplay also matches much unsophisticated Jacksonian humour – profane British-style exclamations, an imbecilic seaman who can speak Indonesian fluently and also loves classical music – with ironic anachronisms. ('The sooner we clear this rainforest the better,' exclaims disillusioned hero Driscoll.) There is also a strand of the more knowing cinebuff humour exhibited in *Forgotten Silver*. (Denham refers to his latest film, *Indonesia . . . Hell Hole of the World*, to be narrated by 'Ernie' Hemingway.)

It would be nearly three decades on from his first viewing of the original that Jackson's oft-mooted project to remake *Kong* – which eluded him while the more unlikely *Rings* trilogy got the green light – would finally be an actuality. The monster fanboy director has since altered his plans, claiming, 'I don't want to change what I loved about it. I don't want to reinvent it because it doesn't need reinventing,' perhaps as a sideswipe against Tim Burton's disappointing 're-imagining' of *Planet of the Apes* (2001).

(Jackson was once mooted as a likely director for the *POTA* remake, which may have rankled, given that the original was his other favourite great ape-monster movie as a child. There is a jokey reference to the film in the 1996 *Kong* screenplay, where Ann tries to protect Kong by shouting at Denham, 'Take your filthy paws off him – you ignorant pig!' But it's unlikely Jackson could have been much more successful than the usually inspiring Burton, if saddled with the same leadenly literal *POTA* screenplay.)

As Fran Walsh confirms, 'The 1933 version is the one that Peter fell in love with and that will be our template for the film we make.' Philippa Boyens, the Jackson-Walsh partnership's friend and co-screenwriter on *The Lord of the Rings*, is also on board to help rewrite the script from scratch. She confirms that the period setting and look of the film will be 'definitely 1930s, which is a fascinating era in human history. Pete was inspired by the original, so . . . the landmarks of that story are going to hold true. [Kong is] going to New York. He's going to climb the Empire State Building.'

Due for delivery in February 2004, writing the new screenplay allowed for another full six months of pre-production before cameras would roll in August. Jackson now decried 'the flip, smart-arsed tone of our old script.'

In fact, the '96 screenplay has a number of intentional echoes that pay tribute to the original film: Captain Englehorn, the skipper of the Venture, tells of the captain of a Norwegian barque he picked up as a castaway, his mind destroyed by his experience as the only survivor of a chance expedition to Skull Island, and an encounter with 'the Beast' that lives there; an elderly woman patron and an usher at the show where Denham presents Kong on Broadway quote the original dialogue word for word – 'Is this one of

Mr. Denham's cute little animal pictures?' 'This is not a motion picture, Madam. It's more in the nature of a personal appearance.' – as does Denham's introduction to the great ape: 'One who was a King and a God in the world he knew, but who now comes to civilisation as a captive . . . Look upon Kong – the Eighth Wonder of the World!!!' And, of course, there was Fay Wray's intended cameo-cum-in-joke at the end.

Instead of pastiching the original, however, Jackson now cites a more noble pretext for his obsession with remaking *Kong*: 'There is a generation of kids today that don't watch black and white films anymore . . . I love old films and I saw them all the way through my childhood and wasn't concerned at all. But your average teenage kid today just isn't interested in black and white films . . . They won't watch them . . . I just thought it's a good time to give kids a realistic looking Kong because that's what they're going to respond to.' Certainly, given the demonstration of the power of CGI in such recent Hollywood franchises as *The Mummy, Star Wars Episodes I-III* and, not least, *The Lord of the Rings*, there's little doubt that Jackson's technological tools will be the equal of his imagination.

For all the high-tech spectacle, however, Jackson stresses that he's seeking to recreate the original's emotional charge. 'OK, lets say there *is* a gorilla on this island and he *does* kidnap the girl and he *does* think he's going to kill her but then he decides not to because it's the first time in his existence that he's ever connected with another human being [sic] . . . You know, to actually tell that story with real heart and a sense that you can believe it and buy into it and don't get overwhelmed by the fantastic elements of it. That's what we're going to try to do.'

In fact, in Walsh and Jackson's earlier screenplay, their Ann Darrow, contrary to the character who constantly screams at the sight and touch of Kong in the 1933 film, almost colludes in his strange obsession with her in order to save her life – at one point singing him Brahms' 'Lullaby'. She repeats this at his tragic death scene atop the Empire State Building, whereas Ms Wray remained screaming up until the point where he put her down in a safe place before expiring. Questioned as to whether Ann would need the scream-queen potential of a Fay Wray (who also shrieked to the rooftops in *The Most Dangerous Game, Doctor X, The Mystery of the Wax Museum* and *The Vampire Bat*, all in the same early thirties period as *Kong*), Jackson reflected, 'That will be part of the auditions, I guess, asking them to scream. We'll have to do it in a sound-proofed room.'

The blonde beauty who won the day is Naomi Watts, the 35-year-old Australian who first came to prominence in David Lynch's characteristically hypnotic *Mulholland Drive* (2001) and scored a success in *The Ring* (2003), the Hollywood remake of Hideo Kanata's seminal Japanese horror movie. 'Naomi's the only person that we've really approached because she's becoming so eagerly sought after by everybody,' Jackson confessed of the not-so-wide-ranging search. Reports that the director wanted top-drawer names Robert De Niro as Carl Denham, the filmmaker/showman who brings Kong back to civilisation, and George Clooney as Jack Driscoll, the ship's first mate and love interest of Ann Darrow, were accurate but outdated.

Both referred to Jackson's high hopes back in the mid-nineties, when he was awaiting the green light that never came, and a World War One subplot was added to the initial story to make Jack into a former fighter pilot who would – in the spirit that regards the death of the great ape as the only truly tragic demise amidst all the fatalities in *King Kong* – actually try to defend Kong at his last stand. Denham, meanwhile, would be less the sympathetic opportunist that he was in the original film and more of a comic villain – as already exemplified in the 1996 screenplay, where, as a cartoon Hollywood philistine boor, he glosses over the fact that his cameraman lost a limb while filming mating bears with the line, 'Pain is temporary, Film is forever.' (Needless to say, in this version Denham meets a well-deserved end beneath Kong's foot.)

As pre-production finally began in the new millennium, however, Jackson would cast US comedian-actor Jack Black and character actor Adrien Brody – now recognisable as Corporal Fife in *The Thin Red Line* (1998) and the title role in Polanski's Holocaust drama *The Pianist* (2002) – as Denham and Driscoll.

Reports have stressed that *LOTR* veterans from Ian McKellen to Elijah Wood were also hoping for parts, with McKellen enticed by the suggestion of a supporting role from their former Kiwi captain. 'I don't blame them,' says *School of Rock* star Jack Black. 'You know, all my friends are telling me the same thing, too: "Get me in *King Kong*, man, you're tight with Jackson!"'

One walk-on cameo is rumoured to be by the amateur thespian who made semi-history as Derek in *Bad Taste* and as the stroll-by street tramp in *Heavenly Creatures*. The latest Hitchcockian walk-on by Peter Jackson may be, according to New Zealand's *Sunday Star-Times*, as 'the pilot who shoots down King Kong in the film's climax', giving the Kiwi kingpin a chance to indulge his WWI biplane fetish on a large scale (itself probably fuelled in the first place by the climax of the original *Kong*).

By far the biggest part in *Kong*, however, will go to the *Rings* stalwart who dominated the last two films yet never fully appeared on camera. As Jackson has been widely quoted as saying early in the pre-production phase, 'Creating a strong emotional presence of Kong himself will be a challenge since he obviously won't be joining us on set.'

This has all changed, however. Thanks to Brit character actor Andy Serkis, who made the similarly CGI-animated Gollum into a slimily debased character you can almost smell, the great ape will not merely be the son of a computer. As Jackson acknowledges, 'There's not even any need today to build a giant robot hand, like the first version or the Dino [De Laurentiis-produced remake] film in the seventies. With technology the way it is now, we can put the actress [playing Ann Darrow] in some sort of harness and add the hands and fingers later.'

As Naomi Watts confirms of her director's intentions, however, her tall, dark and hairy leading man 'won't be nothing [onset]. That's one of the things he told me in our initial meeting, because I would be very worried about that. Andy Serkis is going to be not only a character in the film, but he's going to be a pair of eyes for me to look at.'

As a logical extension of their success in making Gollum almost human, Serkis has this time been recruited to provide appropriately simian movement and anthropoid expressiveness – both on stage/unseen as the cameras roll, and as the guiding physical force behind the CGI monster onscreen.

Serkis will also take the more humanoid role of Lumpy, the cook for the crew of the Venture, the old steamer that sails to Skull Island (after the Chinaman Charley, in the original film). 'I expect this time round will be a very different experience for both Andy and

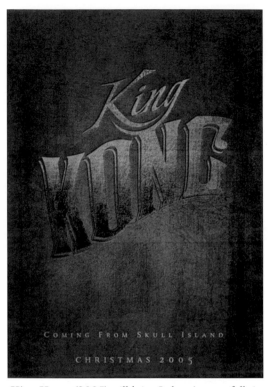

King Kong (2005) will bring Jackson's career full circle: 'the reason I'm making movies today [is] because I saw King Kong *[1933] one Friday night when I was nine years old.'*

myself as we'll actually get to shoot extended drama sequences together,' Jackson has told *The Hollywood Reporter*. 'It will be a little weird seeing Andy out of his Gollum gimp suit ...'

Jackson is also aiming to standardise Kong's height (the '96 screenplay has Driscoll refer to 'a 25-foot gorilla on the loose') – though his constantly changing proportions are, for this writer, part of what makes him such a potent archetype of primal destructiveness. It remains to be seen whether Kong will be visually represented as the authentically simian creature described in the '96 screenplay:

```
. . . a 25 foot SILVER-BACK
GORILLA. His fur is MATTED,
ANCIENT SCARS mark his body –
evidence of life and death
struggles with unknown
beasts. His face is AGED –
SILVER HAIR predominant. He
is resting on his KNUCKLES .
. .
KONG BOUNDS AFTER THE CAB,
running on FOURS with incred-
ible speed.
```

Peter Jackson's fourth (near-consecutive) Christmas present to the world has much to live up to, and much to deliver, when it takes the screen in December 2005. 'King Kong is going to be scary as hell, dude,' says Jack Black. 'He's not gonna be sweet and cuddly. It's not gonna the cute kind. He's a fucking carnivore, as in, *eats flesh!*'

But then, those of us who always loved Kong, mankind's primal shadow, always knew that. Before the Japanese turned him into a man in a monkey suit to fight Godzilla and a giant robot, before 1960s US kids' TV turned made him a friendly cartoon character, or Dino De Laurentiis fell short of the Japs by putting Rick Baker in an ape costume atop the Twin Towers, there was the *real* Kong. The Kong who punches through a subway train in the original 1933 film. The Kong who decimates the Skull Island natives and who can be seen, in the restored 1990s print, masticating on the villagers in close-up.

As Jackson confirms, 'While Andy [Serkis] will provide very valuable onset reference, this doesn't mean we will be softening Kong by attempting to humanise him. The power of the story lies in the fact that this is a savage beast from a hostile environment and we don't intend to compromise that.'

This is the conception of *King Kong* as originated by director/producer Merian C. Cooper and writer Edgar Wallace (who never lived to see the film completed). It is the Kong who's dear to the heart of Peter Jackson. It is the miniature figure that raises bloody havoc. The childlike fantasy born of the universal appeal of wanton destructiveness and obsessive love.

It's also the Kong who was signified, in tongue-in-cheek style, by three vital scenes of Walsh and Jackson's 1996 screenplay:

```
A NATIVE loses his balance and topples off! He THUDS INTO THE
GROUND at KONG'S FEET . . . KONG quickly scoops him up and BITES
HIS HEAD OFF in a PG 13 kinda way!
    A HUMAN RIB-CAGE juts out of the MUDDY GROUND. ANN sobs as she
SEES ALL AROUND HUMAN BONES, some still encased in the remnants
of BRIDAL DRESS and HEAD-WEAR . . .
```

```
The SURVIVING NATIVES scatter! KONG rampages after them, STOMP-
ING ON THEM and BITING THEIR HEADS OFF . . . in a scene that not
only gets a PG 13, but is PRAISED by the MPAA for its sensitivity!
```

Characteristically, Jackson also intends to pay tribute to a scene notorious for *not* appearing in prints of the original film. In the celebrated scene where Kong shakes the surviving sailors pursuing Ann and himself from a log into the ravine, it was originally the intention of directors Merian Cooper and Ernest B. Schoedsack to feature giant spiders emerging from the rock to devour their bodies. This was cut from the original release print, and remains known to *Kong* obsessives only via a rare still that appeared in *Famous Monsters of Filmland*. Jackson, the epitome of the grown-up *Famous Monsters* reader, intends to both include this scene and elaborate upon it.

As Naomi Watts affirms, 'Peter Jackson is a genius. He will make it his own and do something completely different and modernise it, even though it's set in the thirties.' (1933, to be exact – in February of which year, the original *King Kong* first became a big hit in the Manhattan that he physically assaults onscreen.)

'We're going to make it very dramatic and feel very true. We're not going to go for too much tongue-in-cheek stuff or humour,' claims Jackson himself, recognising the pastiche elements that undermined his first screenplay. If Peter Jackson stays true to his intentions, then his *King Kong* will, indeed, be the darkest fantasy ever rated PG-13. One can only hope that his bite is as bad as his roar.

FILMOGRAPHY

THE DWARF PATROL
Soldiers: Peter Jackson and friends
Special Effects, Photography and
Direction by Peter Jackson
Super 8 short, 1971

WORLD WAR TWO
Soldiers: Peter Jackson and friends
Special Effects, Photography and
Direction by Peter Jackson
Super 8 short, 1973

THE VALLEY
Sailors/Adventurers:Peter Jackson, Ken
Hammon, Pete O'Herne
Special Effects, Photography and
Direction by Peter Jackson
Super 8, 20 mins, 1978

COLDFINGER (aka **JAMES BOND**)
James Bond: Peter Jackson
Villains: Ken Hammon, Pete O'Herne
Special Effects, Photography and
Direction by Peter Jackson
Super 8 short, 1979

**THE CURSE OF THE GRAVE-
WALKER**
Captain Eumig: Peter Jackson
Murnau: Pete O'Herne
Vampires: Ken Hammon
Special Effects, Photography and
Direction by Peter Jackson
Super 8 short, uncompleted, 1981

BAD TASTE
Cast
Ozzy/Third Class Alien:Terry Potter
Barry/Third Class Alien: Pete O'Herne
Giles/Third Class Alien: Craig Smith
Frank/Third Class Alien: Mike Minett
Derek/Robert: Peter Jackson
Alien Leader: Doug Wren
Alien Leader's Voice: Peter Vere-Jones
Third Class Aliens: Dean Lawrie, Ken
Hammon, Robin Griggs, Michael
Gooch, Peter Gooch, Laurie Yarrall,
Shane Yarrall, Philip Lamey, Costa Botes,
Graham Butcher
Crew
Crew: Ken Hammon, Philip Lamey,
Dean Lawrie, Mike Minett, Pete
O'Herne, Terry Potter
Music: Michelle Scullion
Art Department: Caroline Girdlestone
Car Explosion Effects: Grant Campbell
Titles: Arie Ketel
Post-Production Sound Recordist/Mixer:
Brent Burge
Editors: Peter Jackson, Jamie Selkirk
Special Assistants to Producer: Bill Jackson,
Joan Jackson
Consultant Producer:Tony Hiles
Written, Produced, Cinematography,

Makeup Effects and Special Effects by
Peter Jackson
Directed by Peter Jackson
91 mins, 1988 (Wingnut Films/New
Zealand Film Commission)

MEET THE FEEBLES
Cast
Samantha the Cat/the Sheep (voice):
Donna Akersten
Sebastian/Dr. Quack/Daisy
TheCrow/Sandy the Chicken (voice):
Stuart Devenie
Heidi/Robert/Barry the Bulldog
(voice): Mark Hadlow
Sebastian the Fox (voice): Ross Jolly
Wynard the Frog/Trevor the Rat/The
Fly (voice): Brian Sergent
Bletch/Arfur The Worm (voice): Peter
Vere-Jones
Sid the Elephant/The Cockroach/
Louie the Fish (voice): Mark Wright
Heidi the Hippo: Danny Mulheron
Bletch (voice): Doug Wren (uncredited)
Crew
Music: Peter Dasent
Sound Editors: Eric De Beus, Jamie Selkirk
Costume Design: Glenis Foster
Production Design: Mike Kane
First Assistant Director: Chris Short
Editor: Jamie Selkirk
Special Effects: Steve Ingram
Puppet/Designer Maker: Cameron Chittock
Puppet Maker: Richard Taylor
Director of Photography: Murray Milne
Producers: Jim Booth, Peter Jackson
Written by Peter Jackson, Danny
Mulheron, Stephen Sinclair, Frances
Walsh
Directed by Peter Jackson
92 mins, 1990 (Wingnut Films/New
Zealand Film Commission)

BRAINDEAD
Cast
Lionel Cosgrove:Timothy Balme
Paquita Maria Sanchez: Diana Penalver
Mum (Vera Cosgrove): Elizabeth Moody
Uncle Les: Ian Watkin
Nurse McTavish: Brenda Kendall
Father McGruder: Stuart Devenie
Void: Jed Brophy
Zombie McGruder: Stephen Papps
Scroat: Murray Keane
Nora Matheson: Glenis Levesiam
Mr Matheson: Lewis Rowe
Rita: Elizabeth Mulfaxe
Roger: Harry Sinclair
Paquita's Grandmother: Davina Whitehouse
Paquita's Father: Silvio Fumularo
Vet: Brian Sergent
Undertaker: Peter Vere-Jones
Mandy: Tina Regtien
Stewart: Bill Ralston

Winston:Tony Hopkins
Zoo Keeper: Tony Hiles
Drunk: Duncan Smith
Barry: Tich Rowney
Lawrence: George Port
Spike: Stephen Andrews
Spud: Nick Ward
Undertaker's Assistant: Peter Jackson
Lionel's Father: Jim Booth
Young Lionel: Sam Dallimore
Mother at Park: Frances Walsh
Baby Selwyn: Morgan Rowe/Sean Hay
Selwyn Voice: Vicki Walker
Customs Official: Chris Short
Father at Zoo: Jamie Selkirk
Forry: Forrest J. Ackerman
Crew
Costume Design: Chris Elliott
Art Director: Ed Mulholland
Production Designer: Kevin Leonard-Jones
First Assistant Director: Chris Short
Makeup Artist: Debra East
Makeup/Prosthetics: Bob McCarron
Special Effects Coordinator: Steve Ingram
Creature and Gore Effects/Stop Motion
Animator: Richard Taylor
Editor/Associate Producer: Jamie Selkirk
Director of Photography: Murray Milne
Producer: Jim Booth
Written by Stephen Sinclair, Frances
Walsh, Peter Jackson
Directed by Peter Jackson
101 mins, 1992 (Wingnut Films/New
Zealand Film Commission)

VALLEY OF THE STEREOS
Cast
River: Danny Mulheron
Crew
Producers: Jim Booth, Peter Jackson
Written by Costa Botes, George Port
Directed by George Port
15 mins, 1992 (Wingnut Films)

SHIP TO SHORE
Executive Producer: Peter Jackson
children's TV series, 30 mins per
episode, 1993 (ABC TV)

JACK BROWN – GENIUS
Cast
Jack Brown: Timothy Balme
Elmer: Stuart Devenie
Crew
Second Unit Director: Peter Jackson
Producers: Jim Booth, Peter Jackson
Written by Tony Hiles, Peter Jackson,
Frances Walsh
Directed by Tony Hiles
91 mins, 1994 (Wingnut Films/Senator Films)

HEAVENLY CREATURES
Cast
Pauline Yvonne (Parker) Rieper:

Melanie Lynskey
Juliet Hulme: Kate Winslet
Honora Parker Rieper: Sarah Peirse
Hilda Hulme: Diana Kent
Dr. Henry Hulme: Clive Merrison
Herbert Rieper: Simon O'Connor
John ('Nicholas'): Jed Brophy
Bill Perry: Peter Elliott
Dr. Bennett: Gilbert Goldie
Rev. Norris: Geoffrey Heath
Wendy: Kirsti Ferry
Jonathan Hulme: Ben Skjellerup
Miss Stewart: Darien Takle
Miss Waller: Elizabeth Moody
Mrs. Collins: Liz Mullane
Mrs. Stevens: Moreen Eason
Mrs. Zwartz: Pearl Carpenter
Grandma Parker: Lou Dobson
Laurie: Jesse Griffin
Steve: Glen Drake
Orson Welles: Jean Guerin
Mario Lanza: Stephen Reilly
Diello: Andrea Sanders
Charles: Ben Fransham
Pauline Rieper, at five years: Jessica Bradley
Juliet Hulme, at five years: Alex Shirtcliffe-Scott
Vagrant Outside Cinema: Peter Jackson (uncredited)
Crew
Casting (New Zealand): Liz Mullane
Casting (UK): John and Ros Hubbard
First Assistant Director: Carolynne Cunningham
Sound Editors: Greg Bell, Mike Hopkins
Original Music: Peter Dasent
Non-Original Music: 'Donkey Serenade' by Rudolf Friml; extracts from *La Bohème*, *Madame Butterfly* and *Tosca* by Giacomo Puccini; 'When You Walk Through a Storm' performed by Mario Lanza.
Makeup Supervisor: Marjory Hamlin
Costume Designer: Ngila Dickson
Art Director: Jill Cormack
Production Designer: Grant Major
Special Effects and Prosthetics: Richard Taylor
Editor: Jamie Selkirk
Director of Photography: Alun Bollinger
Line Producer: Bridget Bourke
Executive Producer: Hanno Huth
Producers: Jim Booth, Peter Jackson
Written by Frances Walsh and Peter Jackson
Directed by Peter Jackson
98 mins, 1994 (Wingnut Films/Fontana Film Productions GmbH/New Zealand Film Commission/Mirmax Films)

FORGOTTEN SILVER
Cast
Peter Jackson: Himself
Jonathan Morris - Film Archivist: Himself
Costa Botes – Film Maker: Himself
Harvey Weinstein – Miramax Films: Himself

Leonard Maltin – Film Historian: Himself
Sam Neill – Actor/Director: Himself
Colin McKenzie: Thomas Robins
Hannah McKenzie: Beatrice Ashton
Stan the Man: Peter Corrigan
May Belle (research assistant): Sarah McLeod
Davina Whitehouse: Herself
Brooke McKenzie: Richard Shirtcliffe (uncredited)
Narrator: Jeffrey Thomas (uncredited)
Script Supervisor: Frances Walsh
First Assistant Director: Marty Walsh
Sound: Ken Saville
Music: Duncan Davidson, Steve Roche, Janet Roddick
Production Designer: John Girdlestone
Digital Effects: Matt Aitken
Editors: Eric De Beus, Michael Horton
Additional Photography: Nancy Schreiber
Directors of Photography: Alun Bollinger, Gerry Vesbenter
Executive Producers: Peter Jackson, Jamie Selkirk
Producer: Sue Rogers
Written and Directed by Costa Botes and Peter Jackson
55 minutes, 1995 (Wingnut Films/TVNZ)

THE FRIGHTENERS
Frank Bannister: Michael J. Fox
Dr. Lucy Lynskey: Trini Alvarado
Ray Lynskey: Peter Dobson
The Judge: John Astin
Milton Dammers: Jeffrey Combs
Patricia Ann Bradley: Dee Wallace-Stone
Johnny Charles Bartlett: Jake Busey
Cyrus: Chi McBride
Stuart: Jim Fyfe
Sheriff Walt Perry: Troy Evans
Old Lady Bradley: Julianna McCarthy
Sgt. Hiles: R. Lee Ermey
Magda Rhys-Jones: Elizabeth Hawthorne
Debra Bannister: Angela Bloomfield
Harry Sinclair: Desmond Kelly
Steve Bayliss: Jonathan Blick
Deputy: Melanie Lynskey
Museum Curator: Stuart Devenie
Orderly: George Port
Baby in Bouncer: Billy Jackson
Man with Piercings: Peter Jackson (uncredited)
Crew
Casting: Victoria Burrows, Vivienne Kaplan
First Assistant Director: Chris Short
Supervising Sound Editor: Phil Benson
Music: Danny Elfman
Art Director: Dan Hennah
Production Designer: Grant Major
Special Effects Coordinator: Steve Ingram
Creature and Miniature Effects: Richard Taylor
Special Makeup Effects: Rick Baker
Editor: Jamie Selkirk
Directors of Photography: John Blick,

Alun Bollinger
Associate Producer: Fran Walsh
Executive Producer: Robert Zemeckis
Producers: Peter Jackson, Tim Sanders, Jamie Selkirk
Written by Fran Walsh and Peter Jackson
Directed by Peter Jackson
110 mins, 1996 (Wingnut Films/Universal Pictures)

THE LORD OF THE RINGS: THE FELLOWSHIP OF THE RING
Cast
Frodo Baggins: Elijah Wood
Gandalf the Grey: Ian McKellen
Arwen: Liv Tyler
Aragorn: Viggo Mortensen
Boromir: Sean Bean
Bilbo Baggins: Ian Holm
Samwise 'Sam' Gamgee: Sean Astin
Galadriel: Cate Blanchett
Gimli: John Rhys-Davies
Saruman the White: Christopher Lee
Sauron: Sala Baker
Peregrine 'Pippin' Took: Billy Boyd
Meriadoc 'Merry' Brandybuck: Dominic Monaghan
Legolas Greenleaf: Orlando Bloom
Elrond: Hugo Weaving
Gollum: Andy Serkis
Lurtz: Lawrence Makoare
Witch-King: Brent McIntyre
Haldir: Craig Parker
Isildur: Harry Sinclair
Rosie Cotton: Sarah McLeod
The Ring (voice): Alan Howard
Hero Orcs, Goblins, Uruks + Ringwraiths: Victoria Beynon-Cole, Lee Hartley, Sam La Hood, Chris Streeter, Jonathan Jordan, Semi Kuresa, Clinton Ulyatt, Paul Bryson, Lance Fabian Kemp, Jono Manks, Ben Price, Philip Grieve
Cute Hobbit Children: Billy Jackson, Katie Jackson
Albert Dreary: Peter Jackson (uncredited)
Crew
Casting (USA): Victoria Burrows
Casting (New Zealand): Sian Clement, Cynthia Morahan, Liz Mullane
Casting (UK): John Hubbard, Amy Maclean
Casting (Australia): Ann Robinson
Casting (extras): Tina Cleary, Miranda Rivers
First Assistant Director: Carolynne Cunningham
Sound Recordist: Ken Saville
Sound Effects Editors: Brent Burge, John McKay, Tim Nielsen
Dialogue Editor: Jason Canovas
Music Editors: Nancy Allen, Suzana Peric
Music: Howard Shore
'Flaming Red Hair' by David Donaldson/David Long/Stephen Roche/Janet Roddick

Songs: 'Aniron (Theme for Aragorn and Arwen)' and 'May It Be': composed and performed by Enya; 'In Dreams': lyric by Fran Walsh/music by Howard Shore.
Hair and Makeup Designers: Peter King, Peter Owen
Prosthetics Supervisor: Marjory Hamlin
Costume Designers: Ngila Dickson, Richard Taylor
Set Decoration: Alan Lee (uncredited)
Art Directors: 'Peter' Joe Bleakley, Phil Ivey, Rob Outterside, Mark Robins
Conceptual Designers: John Howe, Alan Lee
Sculptor: Virginia Lee
Production Designer: Grant Major
Sculptor/Designer: Mike Asquith
Special Effects Designers/Sculptors: Jamie Beswarick, Shaun Bolton, Daniel Falconer, Sacha Lees, Warren Mahy, Ben Wootten
Special Effects: Weta Workshop
Visual Effects Supervisors: Steen Bech, Geoff Dixon, Mark O. Forker, Dean Lyon, Jim Rygiel
Visual Effects: Weta Digital, Digital Domain, Oktober, Animal Logic, The Post House AG
Special Makeup, Creatures, Armour and Miniatures Supervisor: Richard Taylor
Editor: John Gilbert
Director of Photography (Miniature Unit): David Hardberger
Director of Photography: Andrew Lesnie
Associate Producer: Ellen M. Somers
Executive Producers: Bob Weinstein, Harvey Weinstein
Executive Producers, New Line Cinema: Michael Lynne, Mark Ordesky, Robert Shaye
Co-Producers, Wingnut Films: Rick Porras, Jamie Selkirk
Producers: Peter Jackson, Barrie M. Osborne, Tim Sanders, Fran Walsh
Screenplay by Fran Walsh, Philippa Boyens, Peter Jackson
Adapted from the novel by J. R. R. Tolkien
Directed by Peter Jackson
178 mins, 2001 (Wingnut Films/New Line Cinema)

THE LORD OF THE RINGS: THE TWO TOWERS
Cast
Frodo Baggins: Elijah Wood
Gandalf the White: Ian McKellen
Arwen: Liv Tyler
Aragorn: Viggo Mortensen
Samwise 'Sam' Gamgee: Sean Astin
Galadriel: Cate Blanchett
Gimli/Voice of Treebeard: John Rhys-Davies
Theoden: Bernard Hill
Saruman the White: Christopher Lee
Peregrine 'Pippin' Took: Billy Boyd
Meriadoc 'Merry' Brandybuck:

Dominic Monaghan
Legolas Greenleaf: Orlando Bloom
Elrond: Hugo Weaving
Eowyn: Miranda Otto
Faramir: David Wenham
Grima Wormtongue: Brad Dourif
Gollum: Andy Serkis
Eomer: Karl Urban
Haldir: Craig Parker
Aldor: Bruce Allpress
Madril: John Bach
Man Flesh Uruk: Sala Baker
Sharku/Snaga: Jed Brophy
Eothain: Sam Comery
Haleth, Son of Hamas: Calum Gittins
Gamling: Bruce Hopkins
Theodred, Prince of Rohan: Paris Howe Strewe
Ugluk: Nathaniel Lees
Hama: John Lees
Mauhur: Robbie Magasiva
Grishnakh: Stephen Ure
Cute Rohan Refugee Children: Billy Jackson, Katie Jackson
Man of Rohan: Alan Lee (uncredited)
Crew
Casting: Victoria Burrows, Liz Mullane, John Hubbard, Amy Maclean, Ann Robinson
First Assistant Director: Carolynne Cunningham
Supervising Sound Editors: Mike Hopkins, Ethan Der Ryn
Sound Effects Editors: Brent Burge, Hayden Collow, Kyrsten Mate Comoglio, John McKay, Fabien Sanjurjo, Craig Tomlinson, Dave Whitehead
Dialogue Editor: Jason Canovas
Music: Howard Shore
'Gollum's Song': lyric by Fran Walsh/music by Howard Shore
Hair and Makeup Designers: Peter King, Peter Owen
Costume Designers: Ngila Dickson, Richard Taylor
Art Directors: 'Peter' Joe Bleakley, Dan Hennah, Philip Ivey, Rob Outterside, Christian Rivers, Mark Robins
Set Decoration: Dan Hennah, Alan Lee
Conceptual Designers: John Howe, Alan Lee
Production Designer: Grant Major
Special Effects Designer/Sculptor: Mike Asquith
Creature Effects Supervisor/Designer: Randall William Cook
Special Effects: Weta Workshop
Weta Workshop Supervisor: Richard Taylor
Visual Effects Supervisors: Jim Berney, Joe Letteri, Dean Lyon, John P. Nugent, Jim Rygiel
Visual Effects: Weta Digital, SPI, HATCH, Imageworks, Oktober
Editors: Michael Horton, Jabez Olssen, Loren Squires

Director of Photography (Miniature Unit): Alex Funke
Director of Photography: Andrew Lesnie
Executive Producers: Bob Weinstein, Harvey Weinstein
Executive Producers, New Line Cinema: Michael Lynne, Mark Ordesky, Robert Shaye
Co-Producers, Wingnut Films: Rick Porras, Jamie Selkirk
Producers: Peter Jackson, Barrie M. Osborne, Frances Walsh
Screenplay by Fran Walsh, Philippa Boyens, Stephen Sinclair, Peter Jackson
Adapted from the novel by J. R. R. Tolkien
Directed by Peter Jackson
179 mins, 2002 (Wingnut Films/New Line Cinema)

THE LORD OF THE RINGS: THE RETURN OF THE KING
Cast
Frodo Baggins: Elijah Wood
Gandalf the White: Ian McKellen
Arwen: Liv Tyler
Aragorn: Viggo Mortensen
Samwise 'Sam' Gamgee: Sean Astin
Galadriel: Cate Blanchett
Gimli: John Rhys-Davies
Theoden: Bernard Hill
Bilbo Baggins: Ian Holm
Peregrine 'Pippin' Took: Billy Boyd
Meriadoc 'Merry' Brandybuck: Dominic Monaghan
Legolas Greenleaf: Orlando Bloom
Elrond: Hugo Weaving
Eowyn: Miranda Otto
Faramir: David Wenham
Gollum: Andy Serkis
Eomer: Karl Urban
Denethor: John Noble
King of the Dead: Paul Norell
Grimbold: Bruce Phillips
Deagol: Thomas Robins
Madril: John Bach
Gamling: Bruce Hopkins
Irolas: Ian Hughes
Witch-King/Gothmog: Lawrence Makoare
Rosie Cotton: Sarah McLeod
Isildur: Harry Sinclair
Shagrat: Peter Tait
Orc Lietenant 1: Joel Tobeck
Gorbag: Stephen Ure
The Ring (Voice): Alan Howard
Orc/Sauron: Sala Baker
Children: Billy Jackson, Katie Jackson
Mercenary On Boat: Peter Jackson uncredited)
Saruman the White: (extended DVD edition only): Christopher Lee
Grima Wormtongue: (extended DVD edition only): Brad Dourif
Crew
Casting: Victoria Burrows, Liz Mullane, John

Hubbard, Amy Maclean, Ann Robinson
First Assistant Director: Carolynne
Cunningham
Supervising Sound Editors: Mike
Hopkins, Ethan Van Der Ryn
Sound Effects Editors: Beau Borders, Brent
Burge, Hayden Collow, Tim Nielsen,
Addison Teague, Craig Tomlinson, Dave
Whitehead
Music: Howard Shore
Songs: 'The Steward of Gondor' – lyric
by Philppa Boyens, performed by Billy
Boyd; 'The Green Dragon' – lyric by
Phillipa Boyens, music by David Donaldson,
David Long, Stephen Roche and Janet
Roddick; 'Aragorn's Coronation' – lyric
by J. R. R. Tolkien; 'Into the West' –
lyric by Fran Walsh, performed by Annie
Lennox. All music by Howard Shore
unless otherwise stated.
Makeup Designers: Peter King, Peter Owen
Costume Designers: Ngila Dickson,
Richard Taylor
Art Directors: Joe Bleakley, Simon Bright,
Dan Hennah, Philip Ivey, Christian
Rivers, Mark Robins
Set Decoration: Dan Hennah, Alan Lee
Conceptual Designers: John Howe, Alan Lee
Production Designer: Grant Major
Special Effects Designer/Sculptor:
Mike Asquith
Special Effects Art Director: John Harding
Special Effects: Weta Workshop
Weta Workshop Supervisor: Richard Taylor
Visual Effects: Randall William Cook,
Shane Cooper, Geoff Hadfield, Wayne
Howe, Jake Lee, Evans Mark, Emi
Tahira, Jensen Toms, Sandra Warren
Visual Effects Animators: Shane Acker,
Alex Burt, Richard Dexter, Sophie
Lodge, Robyn Luckham, Jon Tuburfield
Visual Effects Supervisors: Tim Crosbie,
Joe Letteri, Dean Lyon, John P. Nugent,
Jim Rygiel
Editors: Annie Collins, Jamie Selkirk
Director of Photography (Miniature Unit):
Alex Funke
Director of Photography: Andrew Lesnie
Executive Producers: Bob Weinstein,
Harvey Weinstein
Executive Producers, New Line Cinema:
Michael Lynne, Mark Ordesky, Robert
Shaye
Co-Producers, Wingnut Films: Rick Porras,
Jamie Selkirk
Producers: Peter Jackson, Barrie M.
Osborne, Fran Walsh
Screenplay by Fran Walsh, Philippa Boyens,
Peter Jackson
Adapted from the novel by J. R. R. Tolkien
Directed by Peter Jackson
200 mins, 2003 (Wingnut Films/New
Line Cinema)

THE LONG AND SHORT OF IT
Cast
Grizzled Painter: Andrew Lesnie
Woman: Praphaphorn 'Fon' Chansantor
Tall Man: Paul Randall
Bus Driver: Peter Jackson
Crew
First Assistant Director: Elijah Wood
Executive Producer: Peter Jackson
Story by Sean Astin and Dominic
Monaghan
Produced, Written and Directed by
Sean Astin
6 mins, 2003 (Wingnut Films)

KING KONG
Cast
Ann Darrow: Naomi Watts
Carl Denham: Jack Black
Jack Driscoll: Adrien Brody
King Kong/Lumpy the Cook: Andy Serkis
Jimmy: Jamie Bell
Bruce Baxter: Kyle Chandler
Choy: Lobo Chan
Captain Englehorn: Thomas Kretschmann
Hayes: Evan Parke
Preston: Colin Hanks
Herb: John Sumner
Crew
Casting: Victoria Burrows, Daniel
Hubbard, Liz Mullane
First Assistant Director: Carolynne
Cunningham
Music: Howard Shore
Costume Designer: Terry Ryan
Art Directors: Simon Bright, Dan Hennah
Set Decoration: Dan Hennah
Conceptual Designer: Alan Lee
Production Designer: Grant Major
Special Effects Makeup: Kevin McTurk
Special Effects Art Director: John Harding
Visual Effects: Weta Digital
Weta Workshop Supervisor: Richard Taylor
Editor: Jamie Selkirk
Director of Photography: Andrew Lesnie
Producers: Jan Blenkin, Carolynne
Cunningham, Peter Jackson, Fran Walsh
Screenplay by Peter Jackson, Fran Walsh,
Philippa Boyens
Based upon the original story by Merian
C. Cooper and Edgar Wallace/the origi-
nal screenplay by James Creelman and
Ruth Rose
Directed by Peter Jackson
2005 (Wingnut Films/Universal Pictures)

THE LOVELY BONES
Producers: Peter Jackson, Aimee Peyronnet,
Fran Walsh, James Wilson
Screenplay by Peter Jackson, Fran Walsh,
Philippa Boyens
Adapted from the novel by Alice Sebold
Directed by Peter Jackson
2007 (Wingnut Films/FilmFour)

ACKNOWLEDGEMENTS

We would like to thank Lawrence French, Michael Helms and Ian Pryor, whose enthusiasm and assistance has proved invaluable to this anthology.

The following articles appear by courtesy of their respective copyright holders: 'Introduction' by Paul A. Woods, copyright © 2005 by Plexus Publishing Limited. 'Talent Force' by Jeremy Clarke, from *Films & Filming*, September 1989. Copyright © 1989 by Jeremy Clarke. 'This Has Buggered your Plans for Conquering the Universe: The Making of *Bad Taste*' by Ken Hammon, from *The Bastards Have Landed* website. Copyright © 2001 by Ken Hammon. Reprinted by permission of the author. *Bad Taste* review by Kim Newman, from *Monthly Film Bulletin*, September 1989. Copyright © 1989 by Kim Newman. Reprinted by permission of the author. 'Peter Jackson, Master of *Bad Taste*' by Philip Nutman and Giuseppe Salza, from *Gorezone*, January 1989. Copyright © 1989 by Philip Nutman and Giuseppe Salza. Reprinted by permission of the authors. 'Meet your Creature Feature: Foam-Rubber Depravity in *Meet the Feebles*' by Ian Pryor, from *Illusions*, March 1990. Copyright © 1990 by Ian Pryor/*Illusions*. Reprinted by permission. *Meet the Feebles* review by Philip Kemp, from *Sight and Sound*, May 1992. Reprinted by permission of the publisher. *Meet the Feebles* review by Spencer Hickman, from *Psychotic Reaction* issue 2, 1990. Copyright © 1990 by Spencer Hickman. 'I Walked as a Zombie' by Michael Helms, from *Fatal Visions* issue 13, November/December 1992. Copyright © 1992 by Michael Helms. Reprinted by permission of the author. *Braindead* review by Karl Quinn, from *Cinema Papers*, May 1993. Copyright © 1993 by Karl Quinn. Reprinted by permission of the author. 'Antipodal Splattermeister' by Ken Miller, from *Film Extremes* issue 2, 1992. Copyright © 1992 by Ken Miller. 'A Critique of the Judgement of *Bad Taste* or Beyond *Braindead* Criticism: The Films of Peter Jackson' by Lawrence McDonald, from *Illusions*, winter 1993. Copyright © 1993 by Lawrence McDonald/*Illusions*. Reprinted by permission. '*Dead Alive* (aka *Braindead*)' A Retrospective by Guillermo Del Toro, from *Fangoria*, July 2004. Copyright © 2004 by Guillermo Del Toro. Reprinted by permission of the author. '*Heavenly Creatures*' by Steve Braunias, from *Shivers*, February 1994. Copyright © 1994 by Steve Braunias. Reprinted by permission of the author. *Heavenly Creatures* review by Bill Gosden, from the 1994 Wellington Film Festival programme. Copyright © 1994 by Bill Gosden. Reprinted by permission of the author. *Heavenly Creatures* review by Stella Bruzzi, from *Sight and Sound*, February 1995. Copyright © 1995 by Stella Bruzzi. Reprinted by permission of the author. 'Making a Film Out of the Horror of Mother Murder' by Bernard Weinraub, from *The New York Times*, 23 November 1994. Copyright © 1994 by *The New York Times*. Reprinted by permission of the publisher. 'It's All Frightfully Romantic! *Heavenly Creatures* and the Horrors of Adolescence' by Peter N. Chumo II, from *Creative Screenwriting*, September/October 1998. Copyright © 1998 by Peter N. Chumo II. Reprinted by permission of the author. 'Earthy Creatures' by Michael Atkinson, from *Film Comment*, May/June 1995. Copyright © 1995 by Michael Atkinson. Reprinted by permission of the author. 'Heavenly Features' by Denis Welch, from *The New Zealand Listener*, 28 October 1995. Copyright © 1995 by *The New Zealand Listener*. Reprinted by permission of the publisher. 'Gone Not Forgotten' by Geoff Chapple, from *The New Zealand Listener*, 25 November 1995. Copyright © 1995 by *The New Zealand Listener*. Reprinted by permission of the publisher. '*Forgotten Silver*: Interview with Peter Jackson' by Pauline Adamek, from the author's website. Copyright © 1996 by Pauline Adamek. Reprinted by permission of the author. 'Silver Magic' by Jane Roscoe and Craig Hight, from *Illusions*, winter 1996. Copyright © 1996 by Jane Roscoe and Craig Hight/*Illusions*. Reprinted by permission. *Forgotten Silver* review by David Stratton, from *Variety*, 2 May 1996. Copyright © 1996 by *Variety*. Reprinted by permission of the publisher. '*The Frighteners*: Peter Jackson Interviewed by Michael Helms' – Copyright © 1996 by Michael Helms. Reprinted by permission of the author. '*The Frighteners*: The Thrill of the Haunt' by Mark Cotta Vaz, from *Cinefex* 67, 1996. Copyright © 1996 by Mark Cotta Vaz/*Cinefex*. Reprinted by permission. *The Frighteners* review by Todd McCarthy, from *Variety*, 15 July 1996. Copyright © 1996 by *Variety*. Reprinted by permission of the publisher. *The Frighteners* review by Stella Bruzzi, from *Sight and Sound*, February 1997. Copyright © 1997 by Stella Bruzzi. Reprinted by permission of the author. 'Rings Bearer' by Michael Helms, from *Fangoria*, January 2002. Copyright © 2002 by Michael Helms. Reprinted by permission of the author. 'One Ring' by Harry Knowles, from *Total Film*, January 2002. Copyright © 2002 by Harry Knowles. Reprinted by permission of the author. *The Fellowship of the Ring* review by Andrew O'Hehir, from *Sight and Sound*, January 2002. Reprinted by permission of the publisher. 'It is a Dark Time for the Rebellion . . .' by Ian Nathan, from *Empire*, January 2003. Copyright © 2003 by *Empire*. Reprinted by permission of the publisher. 'Creature Effects for *The Two Towers*: Ray Harryhausen Visits Middle-Earth' by Lawrence French. Copyright © 2002 by Lawrence French. Reprinted by permission of the author. *The Two Towers* review by Kim Newman, from *Sight and Sound*, January 2003. Copyright © 2003 by Kim Newman. Reprinted by permission of the author. 'All Hail *The King*' by Lawrence French. Copyright © 2003 by Lawrence French. Reprinted by permission of the author. *The Return of the King* review by Kim Newman, from *Sight and Sound*, January 2004. Copyright © 2004 by Kim Newman. Reprinted by permission of the author. 'Kingdom Come' by Graham Fuller, from *Film Comment*, January/February 2004. Copyright © 2004 by Graham Fuller. Reprinted by permission of the author. 'The Lord of the Oscars' by Russell Baillie, from *The New Zealand Herald*, 2 March 2004. Copyright © 2004 by *The New Zealand Herald*. Reprinted by permission of the publisher. 'Peter Jackson Directs *King Kong*' by Lawrence French. Copyright © 2005 by Lawrence French. Published by permission of the author. '*Kong* Cometh!' by Paul A. Woods, copyright © 2005 by Plexus Publishing Limited.

It has not been possible in all cases to trace the copyright sources, and the publishers would be glad to hear from any such unacknowledged copyright holders.

We would like to thank the following film companies, picture agencies and individuals for providing photographs: Wingnut Films; the New Zealand Film Commission; New Line Cinema; Imagenet; Alex Agran at Arrow Films; Carl Daft at Blue Underground, Miramax and Universal Pictures.